SOCIALIST ECONOMIC REVIEW 1982

SOCIALIST ECONOMIC REVIEW 1982

EDITED BY
DAVID CURRIE
and
MALCOLM SAWYER

THE MERLIN PRESS
LONDON

First published in 1982
by The Merlin Press Ltd
3 Manchester Road
LONDON E14

cover design by Peter Hammarling

British Library Cataloguing in Publication Data

Socialist economic review — 1982
    1. Economics—Periodicals
    2. Socialism—Periodicals
    330'.05   HB1

ISBN 0850362857

Printed by Whitstable Litho Ltd
Whitstable
Kent

Typesetting by Heather Hems
The Malt House
Chilmark Wilts

CONTENTS

INTRODUCTION

The papers in this second volume of the *Socialist Economic Review* were presented and discussed at a conference held at Birkbeck College, University of London in September 1981. The papers have been revised in light of the discussion at the conference and the comments of the working group. The comments of the discussants of the papers, which are included in this volume, generally relate to the versions of the papers presented at the conference.

The economic background to the conference was one of continuing, if not deepening, recession with registered unemployment approaching three million, and a further one million unregistered unemployed, and both widely forecasted to continue rising in the short term. The first paper in this volume by Michael Bleaney describes the depth of the recession, and compares the current recession with that of 1929–31. He examines four key questions arising from the experience of the 1979–81 recession. These are the question of why the exchange rate rose so high and then fell, the explanation of the pattern of wage increases, why the government's policy has been so deflationary and the state of the Medium Term Financial Strategy. On this last question, he concludes that the government's strategy has been in shreds since March 1981.

It has become widely accepted on the left that UK withdrawal from the EEC is necessary for implementation of an Alternative Economic Strategy (AES). In his paper, John Palmer challenges many of the assumptions about the nature of the EEC and the constraints placed by membership on UK domestic policy. He disputes whether many Labour Party proposals (such as increased public ownership) would be challenged by the European Commission. He does, however, see problems emerging from attempts to introduce import controls and increases in industrial subsidies. He argues that the left should take a position on the EEC which is quite different from those of the Euro-Federalists and the nationalists.

The *Socialist Economic Review* 1981 contained much discussion of the AES. In this volume, that discussion is continued and expanded in a number of directions.

The next three papers arose from a session devoted to a socialist feminist perspective on an AES. Most, if not all, discussion of an AES has, by concentrating on issues such as reflation, industrial democracy, avoided mention of any feminist perspective. Jean Gardiner and Sheila Smith focus on the three areas of access to jobs, working hours and equalising pay as those where feminists should press for substantial advances within an AES. They argue for positive action policies in these areas and for the expansion of jobs to concentrate on part-time jobs with flexible hours. Jill Rubery and Roger Tarling examine in some detail the effects of the recession on the position of women in and out of the labour market. They find that there is only limited support for the view that women are affected proportionately more than men by upswings and downswings in the economy. They argue on the basis of their findings that whilst it would be wrong to categorise all women as forming a secondary labour force, it cannot be deduced that women do not form the secondary labour force in sectors which fail to show cyclical vulnerability of female employment. They document the ways in which the reductions in labour market flows (between jobs, etc.) have particularly severe effects on women's access to jobs. Finally, they investigate the deterioration in the conditions of employment for women which have occurred in the last few years.

The paper by Sonja Ruehl argues that feminism must insist that attention be given to gender divisions, despite the pressures to overlook those divisions in response to Thatcherite policies and the urgency of 'getting the economy right'. She argues that there is a strong tendency on the left to discuss women's issues under the heading of social policy even where the issues relate to economic matters. The discussion of social security is used to provide an illustration of this point. She concludes that feminist demands for greater economic equality make it clear that social policy changes cannot be neatly segregated from the economy.

Comments from Irene Bruegel, Veronica Beechey, and Barbara MacLennan conclude the discussion of these important issues, which it is intended to take further in future issues of the *Socialist Economic Review.*

The next two papers present critiques of an AES, one written from a political position to the right of that of most proponents of an AES and the other from a position to the left. The paper by David Lipsey argues, from a position on the centre/right of the Labour Party, that substantial reflation with import controls and an incomes policy will be adequate for a revival of the British economy, without encountering resistance from capitalists. He focuses his attention on two areas of the AES for particular criticism, arguing that the discussion of national planning and of the control of inflation have been inadequate. John Harrison, from a left perspective, argues that an AES is dangerous in that its implementation would meet capitalist resistance on a scale for which it would be quite unprepared. A left government would then be forced either to back down or to proceed further than proposed. He advocates the use of nationalisation, particularly through take-over of factories by the workers in the companies concerned, as a weapon to overcome resistance. Tony

Millwood seeks to rebut these criticisms and to restate the case for the AES.

It has often been argued that the AES has not come to terms with the control of inflation. Brian Burkitt examines the possible role of an incomes policy within an AES. He argues that inflation arises from conflict over income shares between workers and capitalists, and that previous incomes policies have served to reduce the growth of real wages. He argues that price stability and full employment can only be reconciled through a prices and incomes policy, but wage controls operate against the interests of the working class. He suggests more extensive communal ownership of the means of production allied to some form of economic democracy is a basic requirement to avoid a prices and incomes policy operating to reduce real wages. Owen Jones takes a critical look at the way in which working people are referred to in discussions of an AES. He argues that the weaknesses in the role attributed to working people threaten to undermine the chances of an AES achieving its objectives. David Purdy discusses these two papers, and in doing so argues the case for the left to take seriously the planning of wages not only in the future under a future left government but also under less sympathetic governments, and to formulate precisely its demands for institutional changes to accompany this.

The paper by Lesley Day and Chris Pond focus on another area often neglected in discussion of an AES—the appropriate form of taxation. They begin with a brief discussion of the political economy of taxation, and outline the post-war trends in taxation in the UK including the rise in taxation since 1979. Their main taxation proposals are the use of a comprehensive income tax which would broaden the tax base by removing most tax exemptions, and to include capital gains and fringe benefits as part of income, and a wealth tax.

The next two papers are broadly on the theme of industrial policy, and both challenge well-established views on the left. Henry Neuburger argues the role of the manufacturing sector has been over-emphasised in comparison with the rest of the economy. He challenges many of the arguments which have been used to favour manufacturing over non-manufacturing, and argues that there is little to be said for manufacturing relative to non-manufacturing. He advocates that an overall expansion of the economy should be undertaken without placing any special emphasis on manufacturing. Keith Cowling argues for a tough anti-merger policy and the divestiture of large companies in appropriate cases. The rise in industrial concentration in UK is seen as leading to an increase in monopoly power which operates to the detriment of workers and efficiency. The aim of policy is the effective control of major monopolies, with the anti-merger and divestiture backed up with parliamentary committees for monitoring major corporations. Alan Hughes takes issue with both papers, arguing specifically in relation to Cowling's paper that growing concentration in the UK has not meant increased monopoly power.

The paper by Jerry Coakley and Laurence Harris examines the role and nature of financial markets, and challenges the individualistic perspective of these markets used by the Wilson Committee. They employ the criterion of how far the financial sector strengthens monopoly capital for the discussion of whether financial institutions should be controlled or nationalised. A major problem facing any incoming left government is likely to be a flight from sterling. David Currie examines four main questions. The first three are: what should be the left's response to the volatility of the sterling exchange rate; the type of exchange rate policy envisaged within an AES; whether there is an appropriate level of sterling; and finally, what mechanisms of control are available to enforce whatever policies are adopted. He discusses the relative merits of the range of possible control mechanisms, and suggests that, given the difficulties of control in this area, combinations of measures are called for. Grahame Thompson in his discussion points to some of the difficulties that such measures will encounter.

The Cambridge Economic Policy Group have been notable for their identification of the balance of payments as a major constraint on expansion of the economy, and advocacy of import controls as a means of lifting that constraint. (See, for example, Terry Ward's paper in the first issue of the *Socialist Economic Review*.) The final paper by Andrew Glyn argues that the analysis by the CEPG contains an ambiguous and contradictory attitude to the question of profitability.

One of the main purposes of the *Socialist Economic Review* is the promotion of discussion on economic policy on the left, and the challenging of well-ingrained beliefs. Thus there is no attempt to establish any particular line. Authors write under their own responsibility, and positions adopted here do not necessarily correspond with views of organisation and individuals with whom the authors are associated or affiliated, nor with the view of other authors. The working group who are responsible for drawing up the contents of the *Socialist Economic Review* welcome the submission of papers or, ideas for papers. Anyone thinking of offering a paper should send the paper or a synopsis to the editors, c/o Merlin Press. The working group for this year's Review was David Cobham, Keith Cowling, Owen Jones, Chris Pond, David Purdy, Kerry Schott, Adam Sharples, and Sheila Smith, with David Currie and Malcolm Sawyer taking editorial responsibility.

Contributors

Veronica Beechey is Lecturer in Sociology, University of Warwick, on secondment at the Open University.

Michael Bleaney is Lecturer in Economics, University of Nottingham.

Irene Bruegel was Lecturer in Economics at North East London Polytechnic, and is now doing full-time research.

Brian Burkitt is Senior Lecturer in Economics, University of Bradford.

Jerry Coakley is Research Fellow in Economics, The Open University.

Keith Cowling is Professor of Economics, University of Warwick.

David Currie is Professor of Economics, Queen Mary College, University of London.

Lesley Day is Lecturer in Sociology, West London Institute of Higher Education.

Jean Gardiner is Lecturer in the Adult Education Department, University of Leeds.

Andrew Glyn is Fellow of Corpus Christi College, Oxford.

Laurence Harris is Professor of Economics, The Open University.

John Harrison is Senior Lecturer in Economics, Thames Polytechnic.

Alan Hughes is a Fellow of Sidney Sussex College, University of Cambridge.

Owen Jones works in a trade union research department.

David Lipsey writes for the *Sunday Times.*

Barbara MacLennan is Lecturer in Economics, University of Manchester.

Tony Millwood is Lecturer in Economics, Bedford College, University of London.

Henry Neuburger is Economics Adviser to the Leader of the Opposition.

John Palmer is European Editor of the *Guardian,* and based in Brussels.

Chris Pond is Director of the Low Pay Unit.

David Purdy is Lecturer in Economics, University of Manchester.

Sonja Ruehl is a Lecturer at The Open University.

Jill Rubery is Research Officer, Department of Applied Economics, University of Cambridge.

Malcolm Sawyer is Reader in Economics, University of York.

Kerry Schott is Lecturer in Economics, University College, University of London.

Sheila Smith is Lecturer in Economics, University of Sussex.

Roger Tarling is Senior Research Officer, Department of Applied Economics, University of Cambridge.

Grahame Thompson is Lecturer in Economics, The Open University.

THE UK ECONOMY–AN OVERVIEW

Michael Bleaney

'This is a land still alive with energy and enterprise–but energy suppressed, enterprise stifled.'[1]

The Conservative Project

This paper follows on from that presented by Smith and Currie to the last Socialist Economic Review Conference (Smith & Currie 1981). It surveys developments and looks in more detail at the economic strategy of the present government.

As will be argued below, the somewhat messianic approach of the Conservative government to economic policy derives from deeply held convictions about the source of Britain's economic difficulties and the measures required to deal with them. This adds a poignant twist to the apparent deep failure of those policies to date: pragmatic adjustments of policy stance are pregnant with the spectre of a U-turn. Let us start by referring back to the stated principles of the Conservative economic programme. In a speech late in 1978 Mrs Thatcher spelt out the 'essential economic requirements for the recovery of Britain' as follows:

1. Strict control by the government of the money supply.
2. Firm management of government expenditure, to reduce the burden on the economy and leave more in the pockets of the people.
3. Lower taxes on earnings, on capital and on savings.
4. The removal of needless and frustrating restrictions on business expansion, so that new firms are encouraged to grow, to provide new work, new jobs.[1]

By the time of the general election item 2. had crystallised into a commitment to reduce public spending as a proportion of national income, together with cuts in income tax. The Conservatives also committed themselves to a steady reduction in the Public Sector Borrowing Requirement as a proportion of national income. This programme is based on two hypotheses:

1. The familiar monetarist view that monetary discipline (i.e. control of the money supply) is both a necessary and a sufficient condition for the elimination of inflation;

2. The idea that the economy would accomplish a dramatic revival if private enterprise were to be released from excessive burdens of taxation and official regulation and interference.

The empirical support for this second notion is thin to the point of non-existence (Sawyer 1981). Empirical evidence for monetarist propositions in the UK is also weak (Currie 1981; see also the Memorandum by

Professor David Hendry in House of Commons 1981 Vol. III). Thus, despite the affinity of these twin ideas with those which motivate the economic policies of President Reagan and also with the writings of academic monetarists, they could be argued to have little basis in practical experience.

Nevertheless one might argue that this programme contains a deeper point as an attempt to break out of the long-standing difficulties of British capitalism by inflicting an all-round defeat on the working class. A sustained ideological campaign in favour of free enterprise and against state interference and involvement in economic life, in conjunction with legislative attacks on trade unions and in an atmosphere of economic crisis, does stand some chance of weakening the long-established traditions of collective solidarity and defensive militancy of the British workforce. If it succeeded, there could be permanent gains for employers, in the form of a more pliable and flexible labour force, and a less militant one. It is possible that such a breakthrough to higher productivity and profitability could be just what is needed to escape from the vicious circle of low growth, low investment and slow technical advance which has dogged the British economy for decades. Viewed in this light, the Conservative project emerges as a rather ambitious one, which cannot simply be dismissed by refuting certain of the empirical propositions on which it appears to be based.[2]

The Recession
1980 saw a massive recession unequalled since 1931 (in 1981 it is becoming clear that the current recession is beginning to rival that of 1929–31). From 1976 to 1979 the broad pattern was one of slow growth in non-manufacturing employment with employment in manufacturing remaining steady. Since late 1979 there has been a catastrophic decline in manufacturing employment (15 per cent below the 1979 level in the first half of 1981) supplemented by a significant drop in non-manufacturing employment. In addition, short-time working has become widespread. For six months from October 1980 over 10 per cent of all manufacturing operatives were on short time and in July 1981 the proportion was still over 5 per cent. This compares with an average of under 1 per cent for 1977–79. Registered unemployment in the UK (excluding school-leavers) rose by 999,400 from May 1980 to May 1981. The output measure of gross domestic product (GDP) was 5¾ per cent below the 1979 average in the first quarter of 1981 (though other measures showed a less sharp decline). Real GDP only fell 5½ per cent between 1929 and 1931.

Within manufacturing, it is metal manufacture, textiles and clothing and engineering industries which have suffered the sharpest declines in employment. Not surprisingly, it is the areas of the country which depend most on these traditional industries which have been worst hit. In the

West Midlands, the unemployment rate climbed from 6.2 to 12.4 per cent in the twelve months to May 1981 (all figures in this paragraph refer to the seasonally adjusted measure, excluding school-leavers). In descending order of absolute increase in unemployment rate there followed Northern Ireland, the Northwest, Wales, Yorkshire and Humberside and the North. All the four regions with below average unemployment rates in May 1981 also experienced increases in unemployment below the national average (South East, East Anglia, South West, East Midlands). Thus the recession has tended somewhat to exacerbate regional differences, as measured by the absolute spread of unemployment rates (standard deviation = 2.65 in May 1981, compared with 2.19 in May 1980). The one exception to this trend was Scotland, which overall experienced a markedly smaller than average increase in unemployment, although the manufacturing areas suffered as badly as elsewhere. The recession has also exacerbated the problem of youth unemployment (Knight 1981), and has been marked by a sharp increase in female unemployment (Rubery and Tarling, in this volume).

The recession has taken place against a background of a high exchange rate, high interest rates, a persistently and increasingly deflationary fiscal policy, and a general trend towards increased unemployment throughout the advanced capitalist world. But it has been significantly more severe in the UK than elsewhere. Other countries have experienced declining growth rates but not strongly negative ones as in the UK. A critical factor has been the dramatic rise of sterling on the foreign exchange markets. UK trade competitiveness declined by somewhere between 30 and 40 per cent in the two years from the last quarter of 1978 to the last quarter of 1980, and at the time of writing (October 1981) only a certain amount of this has been regained. In addition to the effects on exporting and import-competing industries, the rise in sterling has had important distributional effects, contributing significantly to the considerable rise in real wages which has occurred since the end of 1977, and squeezing profits by keeping down the prices of both imported goods and competing home products. However, for reasons that will be discussed below, this rise in real wages has been quite sharply reversed in 1981.

There have been attempts on the right to dismiss the severity of the recession as the result of sudden de-stocking, an explanation which would seem to imply a fairly rapid recovery once stocks reached the desired level. It is indeed true that the turnround in stockbuilding is sufficient to account for the whole of the fall in the expenditure measure of GDP between 1979 and 1980, but this fact has limited significance. First, stock-building was exceptionally high in 1979, as manufacturers and whole-salers failed to anticipate the fall-off in demand. And second, the rational reaction to the high interest rates and exceptionally low profitability of 1980 would be to run down stocks as much as possible. To regard movements in stockbuilding as an independent cause of the recession is clearly a nonsense.

The most buoyant sources of demand in the current recession have been personal and public consumption. Despite successive rounds of cuts in expenditure plans the government's own consumption of goods and services continued to advance modestly in 1980, whilst personal consumption was also up, despite a high savings ratio, as public sector workers gained through the comparability principle pay increases which most of their private sector counterparts had won in 1979. This permitted the gain in real wages of 1978 and 1979 to be consolidated despite a falling trend in wage settlements towards the end of the year. Investment in fixed capital declined greatly from its late 1979 peak, but investment intentions worsened sharply, suggesting a marked fall-off in fixed investment in 1981. Export volume declined during 1980 in response to depressed world trade and a rising pound, but import volume fell back even more (still only partially reversing the great surge forward in 1979, however). In conjunction with sharply improved terms of trade, this produced an unexpected balance of payments surplus.

The remarkable and alarming feature of the current situation is that the most severe post-war recession has brought forth a crop of intensely pessimistic economic forecasts. Forecasting organisations using 'Keynesian' models can see no obvious source of stimulus under present policies. The government's expenditure plans include some fairly sharp reductions before 1983/4. Real disposable incomes are falling at the moment, partly as a result of heavier taxation, although the impact of this on personal consumption will probably be mitigated by a fall in the savings ratio. Fixed capital formation looks set to fall in 1981 and the National Institute forecasts that it will stagnate in 1982. Trade flows should start to reflect the high level of sterling (the Treasury was forecasting a 5½ per cent drop in export volume in 1981 at the time of the budget). Since all the destocking of 1980 did not succeed in reducing the stock-output ratio, stock reductions will almost certainly prove to have continued into 1981.

This evidence must be set against government attempts to argue that the recession has touched bottom. There is no doubt that the rate of descent has been much slower in 1981, but there is still no tangible sign of recovery. Unemployment, albeit a lagging indicator, continued to rise through the summer at a rate which, in any previous recession, would have characterised only the worst period of decline. The crux of the problem is the stance of government policy. It is unprecedented in any post-war recession, let alone one of the present scale, to have a plan of macroeconomic policy foreseeing increasing restriction in both fiscal and monetary dimensions for several years ahead.

In discussing the experience of the last two years, it is perhaps useful to pinpoint certain key questions.

1. Why has the exchange rate risen so high, and then fallen?
2. What is the current state of the Medium Term Financial Strategy?
3. Why has government policy been so deflationary? (I shall discuss this in conjunction with 2.)
4. How can we explain the pattern of wage increases?

The Exchange Rate

With the exception of a few months in the second half of 1979, the effective exchange rate for sterling rose continuously from the beginning of 1979 until January 1981. The total appreciation over this period was more than 20 per cent. The loss of competitiveness was greater since production costs in domestic prices rose faster in the UK than abroad during this period. From January to July 1981 the exchange rate fell about 9 per cent, and then a further 6 per cent by the end of September. Since the disparity between UK and overseas inflation was reduced or even eliminated, at the time of writing (October 1981) part of this lost competitiveness has been regained.

The rise in the exchange rate in 1979 and 1980 is usually explained in terms of three factors: interest rates, North Sea oil and intensely deflationary government policy. Interest rates were higher in the UK than abroad as a consequence of the attempt to hit monetary targets. North Sea oil production increased rapidly, particularly in 1979, and the UK became self-sufficient in oil in 1980. Probably more important, however, from the point of the exchange rate, was the generally unanticipated massive rise in the world price of oil in 1979/80 following the interruption of Iranian exports. This made sterling more attractive by worsening the current account balances of the other major countries.

Nevertheless these factors alone do not explain why sterling reached such a crippling level in 1980. The Treasury, the Bank of England and the National Institute did not anticipate the extent of the appreciation and could not have done so on the basis of their econometric models (i.e. even if they had forecast all explanatory variables correctly). A common explanation is that North Sea oil has gone to the collective heads of the financial markets. It seems more likely that they have been seduced by monetarism. Financial markets have been impressed by Conservative willingness to impose successive doses of deflation on the economy, even in the face of unprecedented rises in unemployment, in pursuit of the Medium Term Financial Strategy (MTFS). This appears to them as a genuine reordering of priorities, with the return to full employment being made firmly conditional on a defeat of inflation. In other words, the political character of Mrs Thatcher's regime, and in particular the indifference to traditional liberal and working-class concerns, has inspired confidence in the future strength of sterling. The fact that the record on money supply control has been rather tawdry is a relatively minor blemish, so long as Mrs Thatcher seems prepared to stick to her guns.

If this explanation is correct, then the exchange rate experience of 1979 and 1980 represents the operation of 'monetarism in one country'. With the advent of President Reagan, monetarism has become international and the dollar has shot up. By October 1981 the pound has depreciated by some 15 per cent in nine months. There were two distinct phases to the depreciation. Until the beginning of July, it was mainly a matter of the rise of the dollar, with virtually no depreciation against other European currencies. Then, from July to September the pound fell by nearly 10 per cent against those currencies, and relatively little against the dollar. This depreciation is significant (being greater than the 1967 devaluation) but still insufficient. Since the first phase, up to July, can largely be explained by the export of monetarism to the United States, it is the second phase which represents a real reversal of trend. My own impression is that it reflects growing doubts about the future course of UK policy, as a result of suspicions that the money supply may once again outrun its target in 1981/2 combined with widespread rumours over the summer that the cabinet would not accept any more deflation now that a general election is only two years away.

The Medium Term Financial Strategy

The MTFS was published at the time of the 1980 Budget and envisaged a rate of growth of the money supply (sterling M3) falling from between 7 and 11 per cent in 1980/1 to between 4 and 8 per cent in 1983/4. The purpose of extending announced monetary targets for several years ahead was to bolster expectations of declining inflation and to convince the private sector that the government would not waver from its chosen course of a steady fall in monetary growth. But sterling M3 very quickly moved above its target range and shot up with the ending of the supplementary special deposits scheme (the corset) in July 1980. The government did not take the measures necessary to rein it back, and by February 1981 sterling M3 was 20 per cent above February 1980 (of which only 4 per cent is estimated to have been due to distortions associated with the removal of the corset). Other, wider or narrower, measures of the money supply did not grow quite so fast, and the government has argued on the basis of this and other evidence that monetary conditions have remained tight. Whether or not this is true, it is beside the point: the significant fact is that the MTFS has fallen at the first hurdle.

This experience does not prove, in my view, that money supply control is an impossibility. It can easily be explained by the government's unwillingness to maintain interest rates at or to raise them to a high enough level to bring sterling M3 back within its target range. High interest rates have proved highly unpopular in business circles and also with the large number of households who have sizeable mortgages. They have dismayed

Tory supporters more than any other aspect of government economic policy. Having discovered this after raising Minimum Lending Rate to a record 17 per cent in November 1979, the government has aimed at a steady but sustained fall to more acceptable levels. Conservative policy became, not just money supply control, but money supply control *without excessive interest rates*. This was a key change, because it explains why, in the face of an appalling recession, fiscal policy has been so deflationary.

This was stated explicitly in the original formulation of the MTFS. 'It is not the intention to achieve this reduction in monetary growth by excessive reliance on interest rates. The government is therefore planning for a substantial reduction over the medium term in the Public Sector Borrowing Requirement (PSBR) as a percentage of Gross Domestic Product.'[3] In truth, a direct empirical relationship between the PSBR and monetary growth is hard to identify (Savage 1979). Nevertheless, with given interest rates and banking regulations, the PSBR is the one weapon which the government has available to achieve its monetary targets. Even if the volume of bank lending to the private sector may be unpredictable, the government is still reducing its own contribution to money creation when it cuts the PSBR. Moreover, the announced PSBR forecast may have a significant impact on interest rate expectations and thus influence monetary growth through its impact on the demand for government securities outside the banking system.

The 1980 budget was framed in a context of a Treasury forecast of a fall in GDP on unchanged policies, and rising unemployment. Nevertheless the budget was somewhat deflationary, with public expenditure plans for 1980/1 being reduced and the tax changes being broadly neutral in their impact on aggregate demand. The PSBR for 1980/1 was forecast to be £8½ billion, or 3¾ per cent of GDP at market prices, compared with 4¾ per cent in 1979/80. This decision to cut the budget deficit seems to have reflected two factors:

1. A desire to leave a sufficient margin of safety against any upward pressure on interest rates;

2. A curious theory of unemployment. The present government seems unwilling to recognise that the unemployment figures are heavily influenced by the level of demand in the economy; it prefers to believe that in some deeper sense they register its state of health. This induces extreme optimism about future unemployment: the government appears to believe that its economic programme will ultimately provoke a strong economic revival, even if in the short run it is deflationary.[4] Reflation is dismissed as a capitulation to the misguided theories of its predecessors.[5] Academic monetarism must bear the responsibility for lending to these attitudes a veneer of intellectual respectability.

By the autumn of 1980 the severity of the recession and the disarray of monetary policy were readily apparent. Unemployment was moving upwards at a rate touching 100,000 a month. Some nationalised industries were making much bigger losses than forecast and the PSBR was now expected to reach £11½ billion for 1980/1. The CBI was pressing hard for a reduction in interest rates. The November mini-budget continued the theme of deflation in the cause of reducing interest rates and maintaining the MTFS. Minimum Lending Rate was reduced to 14 per cent, and a whole package of measures was announced aimed at reducing the PSBR for 1981/2. Employees' National Insurance contributions were to be increased from 6¾ per cent to 7¾ per cent from April 1981. A supplementary oil tax would be introduced. Local authority spending was to be reduced in 1981/2 by 3 per cent. And to offset additional expenditure on employment measures, unemployment benefit and nationalised industries, all central government programmes other than health and defence would be cut by 2 per cent (defence escaped with a smaller cut after a vigorous political fight). These measures highlighted the destabilising character of the PSBR as a target variable.

In early 1981 the government seemed to have decided on a strategy of promoting recovery by lowering interest rates, which it was hoped would reduce the exchange rate as well as offering direct relief to beleaguered firms. Thus on 5 January, the banks' Reserve Assets ratio was reduced from 12½ per cent to 10 per cent, to counteract any upward pressure on interest rates during the company tax payment season. In the run-up to the budget, the decision to cut MLR was heavily leaked and the effective exchange rate fell by 3 per cent between January and April. Meanwhile, sterling M3 was running a long way outside its target range. The PSBR forecast for 1980/1 was now even greater than in November and the government was facing very serious problems in formulating the 1981 budget. The PSBR for 1981/2 was threatening to be much larger than indicated in the MFTS, despite the November measures. A choice had to be made between yet more deflation in order to keep to the MTFS, and a tacit abandonment of previous economic strategy in order to engineer some sort of recovery.

The government chose the former course. It cut MLR by 2 per cent, but in order to keep monetary growth within the previously published target range of 6–10 per cent, it took steps to reduce the forecast PSBR for 1981/2 to £10½ billion or 4¼ per cent of GDP. These measures included heavy increases in excise duties (almost double what was necessary for maintaining their real value) and the non-adjustment of income tax allowances, as well as a special windfall tax on bank profits. The National Institute of Economic and Social Review (NIESR) estimated the impact of these measures on the PSBR to be over £4 billion in both 1981 and 1982,[6] and this is a measure of the size of the deflationary shock contained in the budget. This is in addition to the changes already announced in November 1980.

Since the budget, the monetary situation has been confused by the effects of industrial action in the civil service. The trend of world interest rates has been upwards, and in September the government, worried about the speed of decline of the exchange rate, engineered a rise in UK short-term interest rates. The money supply has grown faster than would be consistent with monetary targets, but it is not clear how much of this is simply the effect of tax revenue being delayed by industrial action.

Wages, Prices and Profitability

The Conservative government has not so far operated a formal incomes policy, although it is perhaps moving in that direction. As already explained, it relied initially on the market discipline, to be imposed through monetary policy, to restrain wages. This demonstrably failed as wage settlements in 1979/80 rapidly increased with the removal of the incomes policy constraint. Around the summer of 1980 a new phase began in the labour market, although this is somewhat obscured in the statistics by the staging of some public sector pay awards and the delays associated with the Comparability Commission. This new phase was characterised by much lower pay increases, often less than 10 per cent, as the flood of redundancies excited widespread fear over job security. In the public sector, the government set a target of 6 per cent, and was able to impose something close to this on the weaker unions, but did not risk confrontation with the stronger ones (miners, electricity, gas, water workers) who consequently gained increases in the region of 10 to 13 per cent. The rate of increase of average earnings during 1981 has been about 10 per cent at an annual rate.

The government's problem is that this is not yet low enough from its point of view. With the stabilisation and even slight fall in the exchange rate, the deceleration of inflation looks to have been halted at an annual rate of around 11 per cent. To push the inflation rate down further requires lower wage increases. If the recent deceleration of wage increases had been caused by a reliable 'Phillips Curve' effect, there would be room for official optimism, since unemployment is likely to go on rising. It seems more probable, however, that the wage negotiations of 1980/1 reflected exceptional financial pressures on companies and *very rapidly rising* unemployment. It was not the competition from outside the factory gates so much as the fear of the firm going bust which induced the moderation. If this is correct, then there can be no guarantee of further deceleration of wages as the decline in manufacturing employment is stemmed. Indeed the fall in real disposable income caused by recent tax and social security contribution increases could create significant upward pressures on wage claims (the Tax and Price Index in July stood 14.9 per cent above a year earlier).

Profits have been squeezed very hard by falling demand and a rising exchange rate. The real pre-tax rate of return on fixed assets of industrial and commercial companies (excluding North Sea oil operations) is estimated to have fallen below 3 per cent, compared with over 6 per cent in 1978 and over 5 per cent at the bottom of the last recession in 1975. The downward slide may be halted in 1981 but is unlikely to be significantly reversed.

Unlike in previous recessions, manufacturing productivity (output per man-hour) has scarcely fallen at all. There are two possible explanations for this. One is that the recession has enabled employers to overcome opposition to more efficient and more flexible work practices and so laid the foundations for a permanent increase in labour productivity; the other is that pessimism about future orders and current financial pressures have made companies much less willing to hoard labour. So far there is little evidence in favour of one as opposed to the other, but I tend to favour the latter.

Assessment

Since the budget of March 1981, the government's economic strategy has been in shreds. Not only has the impact on the economy been horrific; but it has failed to carry through any of the changes which it claimed were a necessary ingredient of economic revival. The money supply has not been controlled as promised; indeed by basing the current 6 to 10 per cent target on the actual money supply at the end of 1980/1 rather than on the upper end of the target range, the credibility of the MTFS has been very seriously weakened. This decision amounts to a signal that, as well as allowing sterling M3 to outrun its target if it can only be prevented from doing so by raising interest rates to excessive levels, the government will not attempt to claw back the excess in the next year. The MTFS is thus no different from the previous monetary policy: a series of annual targets which may or may not be met in practice. The only new element is the formal commitment to declining monetary growth—but there must now be some doubt about the strength of this commitment.

The ratio of public expenditure to GDP and the burden of taxation have not been reduced. The volume of government spending rose by more than 1 per cent in 1980/1 and is now expected to rise by ½ per cent in 1981/2. All cuts have therefore been postponed to 1982/3 and 1983/4, whereas in the 1980 White Paper on public expenditure (Cmnd 7841) the bulk of the reduction was intended to have occurred by 1981/2. Moreover, because of the fall in GDP, the ratio of public expenditure to GDP has risen significantly over the past two years. This has occurred in part because of the automatic enhancement of expenditure during a recession, which was not fully anticipated, but also because the government has not been prepared to make really stringent cuts in major areas of expenditure.

The burden of income tax on all except the highest incomes is now as high as when the Conservatives came to power (Day and Pond, in this volume). The incomplete indexation of allowances in 1980 and the absence of indexation in 1981 have more than offset the effects of the 1979 reduction in the standard rate from 33 to 30 per cent. Meanwhile the burden of indirect taxation has risen, mainly because of the increase in the rate of VAT to 15 per cent. Thus there has been no 'restoration of incentives' as compared with 1979 for the bulk of the population.

The inevitable conclusion is therefore that, whether or not the Conservative election programme was misguided, it has not been implemented. Nevertheless Britain has experienced a massive recession of the sort which many non-monetarists predicted would happen if a government committed to monetarism came to power. This has occurred because the government has pursued a consistently restrictive monetary policy and an intensely deflationary budgetary policy, whilst the favourable impression on the foreign exchange markets has pushed sterling to absurdly high levels. Additional factors here have been the drift of the world economy towards recession and very large oil price rises in 1979 and 1980.

The prospects for the future must be gloomy. If the government continues to cling on to its MTFS then it is simply not possible to identify any source of impetus towards recovery. Macroeconomic policy will remain restrictive and the pound will remain a strong currency. Investment will remain depressed by low levels of capacity utilisation and, since workers have not yet been cowed into a permanent state of submission, a significant rise in the profitability of new investment projects is not to be anticipated. At the same time, Mrs Thatcher herself is so strongly committed to the present policy that a U-turn cannot be accomplished without a major political upheaval.

A programme of revival must, in the first instance, include a substantial and sustained dose of reflation. This cannot be just a fiscal expansion; to bring about the devaluation required by manufacturing industry requires the abandonment or at least relaxation of monetary targets. Such a programme of reflation cannot by itself solve the whole range of problems besetting the British economy. But it is a necessary ingredient. Without it there can only be slow strangulation.

NOTES

1. Address of Margaret Thatcher to Paddington Conservative Association 18 January 1978.
2. This argument is developed at greater length in Bleaney (1982).
3. *Financial Statement & Budget Report*, 1980–1, p. 16.
4. Ibid., p. 4.

5. For instance at the Ottawa economic summit in July 1981 Mrs Thatcher is reported to have stated that 'reflation is not a way of reducing unemployment' (*Times*, 22 July 1981). In the wake of the loss of approximately 1,400,000 jobs through deflation, this is a fantastic statement.
6. *National Institute Economic Review*, May 1981.

REFERENCES

Bleaney, M. F., 1982, 'Conservative Economic Strategy', in S. Hall & M. Jacques (eds.), *The Politics of Thatcherism*, Lawrence & Wishart.

Currie, D., 1981, 'What's Left of Monetarism?', *Socialist Economic Review 1981*, Merlin Press.

House of Commons, 1981, *Monetary Policy*, (third report from the Treasury and Civil Service Committee), 3 vols., HC (1980–81) 163 I–III.

Knight, K.G., 1981, 'The Composition of Unemployment', *Socialist Economic Review, 1981*, Merlin Press.

Savage, D., 1979, 'Monetary Targets and the Control of the Money Supply', *National Institute Economic Review*, August.

Sawyer, M., 1981, 'Incentives, Taxation, Social Security and the State of the British Economy', *Socialist Economic Review 1981*, Merlin Press.

Smith, R.P. & Currie, D., 1981, 'Economic Trends and Crisis in the UK Economy', *Socialist Economic Review 1981*, Merlin Press.

THE EEC—AN OVERVIEW

John Palmer

The publication of the Labour Party's plans for withdrawing Britain from the Common Market has, once again, put the EEC and European strategy on the political agenda of the left.[1] It seems certain that the years to the next election will be increasingly dominated by a campaign to commit the next Labour government to taking Britain out of the EEC. Within the left the argument is already being heard that a 'precondition' for the implementation of socialist policies—notably a socialist economic strategy to tackle the crisis—is British withdrawal from the European Community.

At the same time the EEC itself is in a state of considerable crisis. Years of inflation, declining (now mostly nil) economic growth, persistently high and growing unemployment and a widening gap between the performances of the more and the less productive and competitive economies has called into question the very ability of the EEC to survive. It is now accepted that it cannot survive—let alone meet a political commitment to accept Portugal and Spain as members—in anything like its present form.

The past year has seen the steady erosion of all those governments committed to Keynesian or neo-Keynesian policies and the objectives of cautious economic growth. The one exception is France where the election of a socialist President and a socialist-communist government has been accompanied by an attempt to reflate out of stagflation and mass unemployment.

Elsewhere the political pendulum has favoured right of centre opposition parties who increasingly espouse national variations on the monetarist themes so far largely pioneered by Mrs Thatcher and the British Conservatives. At the same time the recession has weakened—though not as yet fatally undermined—the strength of organised labour. As the recent report of the European Trade Union Confederation makes clear, workers in most EEC countries are experiencing pressure on their real wages and living standards. Attempts to advance the frontiers of welfare reformism have given way to a dogged defensive struggle against the counter-reforms of most European governments, of whatever political complexion.

The debate about the future of the EEC has inevitably focused on the reform of the European Community budget and the spending priorities it enshrines. It has become accepted orthodoxy in both Brussels and the national capitals of most EEC countries that without some drastic reform of the Common Agricultural Policy, the budget is doomed to something

13

close to bankruptcy as expenditure (notably on the CAP) exceeds the fixed sources of EEC budget revenue.

Less attention is paid to the institutional crisis of the Common Market. Contrary to what is frequently thought in Britain the past decade has seen the steady erosion of the supra-national powers and character of the European Commission. The Council of Ministers—the major legislative body of the EEC—is little more than a cockpit for the competing and conflicting interests of the ten member states. The European Parliament is a political joke, lacking even the semblance of the role and powers of national parliaments and without a substantial European 'executive' with which to contest control of Europe's affairs.

But at the heart of the dilemma of the European Community is the search for capitalist solutions to the economic crisis which have condemned the bulk of Western Europe's traditional heavy industries—its major sources of employment—to wholesale contraction and the threat of extinction. Even with a boom—if and when that should occur—there seems no future for the greater part of these traditional industries in the face of competition from the new highly competitive producers in Japan and the newly industrialised Third World countries. The history of European integration shows beyond doubt that economic boom has been the principle motor for the evolution of the European Community. Purely ideological and political issues—such as 'Franco-German reconciliation' and post-war enthusiasm for a federal Europe played their part. But it was sustained economic growth and the prospect of being able to exploit an ever larger European market that led to the creation of the European Coal and Steel Community, the precursor of the founding of the European Community in 1958.

The Treaty of Rome is deeply imbued with the conviction that West European capitalism can sustain self-perpetuating economic growth only on condition that it permits the more or less untrammelled operation of free market competition and that, at the appropriate moment, obsolescent national political and economic structures are not allowed to impede continued economic integration but give way to the evolution of supra-national 'European' institutions, leading to eventual full European union. The gospel of free market laissez-faire was never as universal in application—even in the early years of the EEC—as theory indicated. The separate ECSC Treaty of Paris envisaged a considerable degree of 'interventionism' in the steel industry as well as accompanying social policies to assist steel workers affected by rationalisation and closure which were in advance of national policies in several member states. Agriculture was the other glaring exception to the free trade rule. Originally conceived as an inducement to the French ruling class to accept the greater benefit German industry could be expected to draw from increasing European trade integration, the CAP has, in practice been of greater benefit to the farmers of West Germany, the Benelux countries and Denmark than it has to French farmers. Conversely French industry has been better able to exploit the opening of an integrated European market, notably in the high technology industries, than expected—partly due to the economic reforms prepared under the Fourth Republic but implemented under De Gaulle.

The CAP is of course protectionist and *dirigiste* to a point. It has encouraged massive and high costs of production of many basic foodstuffs and has evolved a system of market price support and subsidies for both stockpiling and export dumping of excess production which has brought the EEC budget close to collapse. The beneficiaries have not been the so-called peasant or small farmers held up in pro-CAP propaganda as the social justification for its policies.[2] Thousands of these farmers have disappeared in the past 15 years and the high, guaranteed prices set to give an inadequate return to the remaining 'uneconomic producers' actually give super profits to the highly capitalised factory farmers which now dominate European agriculture.

Even during the years of economic boom—until the late 1960s—it became clear that there was no automatic link between economic integration and political union. By the time of the crisis in relations between De Gaulle and the EEC Commission in the early 1960s the boom had produced a whole generation of European trans-national corporations. These companies had a vested interest in ever greater integration and the emergence of a strong sponsoring 'state' at a European level able to champion their interests in the struggles to come with the United States and Japan. The confrontation between De Gaulle and the Commission was, at heart, all about the assumption that the Commission, having successfully piloted the EEC through its initial phase of integration, should move on to the next steps to European union during which it would necessarily acquire greater supra-national powers. De Gaulle's triumph marked the beginning of the decline of the Commission and the effective abandonment of its hopes of becoming the 'embryo-government' of the EEC.

Even at the height of the boom the discrepancy between the competitiveness of the different European capitals was a source of concern to national governments. The initial success of the Six in maintaining some momentum towards integration was based on the fact that those differences of economic performance were not intolerably great. They were to become much greater when, more or less simultaneously, the Six became the Nine—with the entry of Britain, Denmark and Ireland—and the already faltering economic boom gave way underneath the 1973 OPEC oil price increase.

The years since 1973 have seen a slow but accelerating retreat from the goals of full economic and political integration and an equally striking retreat from pure free market policies. The past eight years have seen a further loss of power and prestige by the Commission. Its capacity to generate new impulsions towards integration has been seriously—perhaps fatally—undermined. The decline of the Commission began under the Presidency of M. François—Xavier Ortoli but gathered pace under the four year tenure of Mr Roy Jenkins, which ended in 1980. The only initiative Jenkins got accepted was the introduction of the European Monetary System (by eight of the then nine member states) but it seems unlikely to act as a bridge towards monetary union of the type traditionally favoured by the Commission.

The slow-down in intra-cyclical growth rates in virtually all the EEC economies and the remarkable growth in unemployment has led to a multiplication of the internal stresses and strains within the EEC. The crisis has made governments much more 'cost conscious' about the net balance of their payments and receipts from the EEC budget and this concern about the impact of EEC expenditure on national budgets deficits has made all governments much less keen on schemes to increase spending at an EEC level—even in areas which meet their general approval such as energy research or the encouragement of the high technologies. The stagnation in EEC policy-making has meant that the pattern of EEC expenditure has been frozen in a mould which is bad for those countries which draw little benefit from the operation of the Common Agricultural Policy. It has been this inability to expand alternative policies which would be more interesting to countries like the UK which accounts for much of the massive British net budget contribution which became so much a political issue in the closing months of the Callaghan Labour government.

Mrs Thatcher has made much political capital out of this lopsidedness in the EEC. The monetarist, right wing of the Tory Party has always had its doubts whether the Heath wing of the party, and subsequently in the 1975 renegotiation of EEC terms, the Labour Party, really got a good deal for Britain. The alliance of the monetarists and a section of the more strident 'Little Englanders' in the Tory Party has proved one of the few electoral assets of the Thatcher government. It suited Thatcher's book to exploit as much as she could from the prospect that Britain— under existing EEC policies and the budget system—stood to contribute ever larger sums of money to a patently wasteful system of EEC expenditure. The Thatcher strategy of summit brinksmanship and undiluted 'Euro-bashing' paid off in large measure in the temporary settlement of the UK budget issue in the May agreement negotiated in 1980. That ensured that Britain would—by one means or another—be returned about two-thirds of its gross contribution—but only for a temporary period. But at the time of writing (July 1981) the future of the agreement limiting Britain's budget contributions has been well and truly linked to the future of the EEC budget as a whole.

In effect the British (and the West Germans, the current 'pay masters' of the EEC) are being told by the other member states that if there is to be a ceiling on their financial liability, London and Bonn will have to lift their veto on new budget revenue for the budget. The British and Germans have been keen to keep the lid on budget revenue (which is limited by agricultural levies, EEC customs duties and up to one per cent of VAT transfers) in order to put the maximum pressure on the other EEC governments to bring spending on the CAP (a little under 70 per cent of the total budget) under control. But in the whole argument the British Tories (and the right wing of the Labour Party) have exaggerated the significance of the budget issue as such. While Britain's (uncorrected) net budget payments are running at present at about £1,000 million a year—this is less than the cost of the British government operation in Northern Ireland and a fraction of total government spending.

More to the point the net budget contribution is, itself, less than the total transfer of resources from the (mainly wage earning) consumer to continental farmers due to the fact that under CAP rules the consumer is bound to put food at (higher) EEC prices than at (lower) world market prices.[3] However this could change in the years ahead if, as some CAP strategists assume, higher world population and the generic inability of the Stalinist agricultural systems in both Russia and China result in a rising world demand for Europe's surplus products. According to this scenario rising world demand will steadily erode the premium European food prices enjoy over world prices. That in turn will reduce the price gap which needs to be bridged (out of the EEC budget) when the farm surplus is dumped on world export markets. Against this 'optimistic' fact is the trend of agricultural productivity to rise in Europe, the US and some other major food producing regions, thus risking an increase in global surpluses. Such an increase would quickly plunge the budget—which still only totals about £13 billions or less than 10 per cent of UK government spending—into total chaos.

Whatever happens to agricultural spending, the CAP resource transfer between the EEC and Britain is itself overshadowed by the total foreign trade deficit between Britain and the EEC. Although there is evidence that the relative trade deficit with the EEC has been coming down faster than with other countries in recent years, much of this seems due to the UK domestic slump. The simple fact is that EEC membership plus free trade has been a disaster for British industry and British employment which no amount of EEC propaganda can cover up.[4] The original pro-market slogan: 'To ensure jobs for all the boys—join the Common Market', has now turned into a parody. Britain is being drained of resources both by its structural inability to meet the competition of the other EEC countries—most obviously in manufactured goods—and by the adverse movement of capital out of Britain to the EEC. But this is no more than par for the course in all relations between more or less competitive capitals under conditions of free trade. Trade is a mechanism for the transfer of resources from Britain not just within the EEC but the advanced industrial capitalist world as a whole. It is also a mechanism for intra-regional resources transfers within the UK.

It is hardly surprising then that successive British governments (whatever the intensity of their 'European faith') have been in the vanguard of those states within the EEC trying to halt and reverse the process of economic integration. The Tories, as much as Labour before them, have fought in the Council of Ministers to diminish the supra-national authority of the Commission in sensitive areas covering economic and competition policy. The British have also swallowed a lot of words about the unqualified merits of free trade. In areas such as steel and textiles the UK has pressed hard for tough protectionist policies to keep out low cost imports from the newly industrialised countries and others. Where the Commission has been unwilling or unable to negotiate protection agreements with other countries—as for instance cars—the British government has insisted on making its own bilateral import restraint arrangements.

Other governments have not been slow in following the lead of the British (and even more the French). Indeed the debate in Brussels now is between those who believe in a highly modified form of free trade (with the dangers of national governments acting on their own trade accord where the pressure of competition is too great) and those who believe in 'managed foreign trade' or a 'fortress Europe' approach. The options were discussed in a recent report by European Research Associates[5] which warned that insistence in maintaining the formal pretence of a commitment to free trade might encourage the 'Balkanisation' of Europe, with each member state acting as it saw fit in the light of increasing world competition.

The drift to protectionism of one kind or another has brought the EEC into increasing trade conflict with its rivals/allies in the Western Alliance as well as with the increasingly significant newly industrialised countries in Asia and parts of Latin America. The Reagan Administration in the US and the Japanese government do not disguise their alarm at the new European commerical 'isolationism'. Within the EEC there is now growing support for the 'fortress Europe' approach particularly among members of the European Parliament now that the trade war drums are being beaten about the Common Market. The advocates of comprehensive EEC wide import controls argue that unless the Common Market moves in this direction it will inevitably 'Balkanise' under the pressure of world trade conflict. They point to the mosaic of national import restrictions on Japanese cars introduced by nearly all the governments in the EEC during the past year directly because of the failure to agree on a 'Community' approach.

But it is most unlikely that the Ten will be able to agree on an across-the-board policy of trade protection. Too much European industry is controlled by extra-European trans-national companies which stand to lose more than they would gain in any tit-for-tat struggle to keep out imports. It may be therefore that protectionism is restricted to industries such as textiles (where protection is sanctioned under the Multi-Fibres Arrangement), steel, shipbuilding and some other traditional industries. In practice the kind of controls on imports referred to obliquely in the Labour Party's NEC document would—protestations to the contrary not withstanding— hit hardest at developing countries and especially the NICs (newly industrialised countries).

In the meantime how are the EEC countries to encourage the expansion and increased competitiveness of the newer, high technology industries such as telematics? At one level the Ten recognise the need for action on an EEC basis with an integrated Community market encouraging the most efficient producers to develop on a European basis.[6] But it is doubtful whether national governments will go that far with a policy which might require them to back out of any national attempt to develop their own high technology industries.

The fact is that the crisis exercises a contradictory pressure on the European Community. It simultaneously pulls the member states apart from each other and forces them together for better mutual protection. That is why, at different times, the EEC can seem either hopelessly divided and at other times as the most cohesive trade and commercial negotiating bloc in the capitalist world. It is this contradictory pressure—and the need to find a new and less rigid balance between areas of national and European competence—which renders the present institutional set up in Europe so obsolescent.

All of these internal pressures are bound to be further exacerbated by the proposed enlargement to include Portugal and Spain. The EEC is here on the horns of an ideological dilemma which no longer corresponds to its purely economic interest. The EEC is going to find it difficult enough reforming the present pattern of spending and keeping its overall budget under control without having to help finance the integration of two more poor European countries. The gap in wealth and productivity between the strongest and the weakest will widen massively[7] with the enlargement to twelve. As a result the economic sinews of mutual interest holding the Common Market together are bound to weaken further, faster.

It is against this background that the British left finds itself, once again, caught up in the argument about British membership of the EEC. It is difficult to recognise in the conventional case for withdrawal much that relates to the present realities of the EEC. The picture presented by both the Labour Party and Communist Party advocates of withdrawal seems based on an out-of-date picture of an increasingly integrated, semi-federalist Community possessing powerful supra-national institutions. The traditional case for British withdrawal rests on two distinct and questionably related premises. The first is that the EEC is an organisation dedicated to the maintenance of capitalism in Europe and hence necessarily hostile to the socialist aspirations of a Labour—particularly a left Labour—government. The second is that membership of the EEC is an affront to Britain's parliamentary system of government and—more vaguely—to British national sovereignty.

Orthodox anti-marketeers on the left insist that there is little in common between their opposition and that of the outright British nationalists such as Enoch Powell. But this is simply not true. The central emphasis of orthodox Labour (and Communist Party) opposition to the market rests on the usurpation by the EEC Commission, the Council and the other bodies of the functions and powers of British government bodies. But this is the constant theme running through Powellite opposition to EEC membership.

The left has also not really evolved a distinct position from the right over the two most conventional British objections to the EEC, the Common Agricultural Policy and the Brussels budget. The general line of criticism against the EEC is that it is bad for British consumers and harmful to the interests of 'efficient' British farmers. At no point is there any class analysis of European agriculture and precious little attempt to pose a specifically socialist alternative to either the traditional EEC policy of a high price and highly protected farm policy or to the UK Tory policy aimed at driving small farmers off the land in the interests of the larger capitalist farmers. The Labour left is also deeply ambivalent in its attitude to the general questions raised by the EEC budget and the present pattern of spending. Labour anti-marketeers have never really made it clear whether or not they are in favour of the modest increases in non-agricultural spending—particularly on regional and social development—favoured by the Commission. Increased EEC spending on the unemployed would fit in with Labour's overall social and political priorities but would represent a mild accretion in the role and influence of the EEC vis-a-vis national government.

The net result is that the Thatcher government is indirectly given aid and comfort in its campaign to hold down EEC spending for doctrinaire monetarist reasons. Even within a reformist perspective Labour should be pushing for every conceivable penny it can get from the Brussels budget and insisting (in the face of Tory government opposition) that the money must be *added* to national state expenditure and not used (as at present) as a substitute for government spending, in other words as a disguised reduction of the Public Sector Borrowing Requirement.

There is no doubt of the capitalist nature of the EEC, its institutions and of the Treaty of Rome. However it should be noticed that within this context the EEC Commission tends to be marginally to the social democratic left of national governments. It has been the Commission which has urged greater public spending, less reliance on purely monetarist policies to contain inflation and has pressed mildly reformist legislation for instance on work sharing and forcing the trans-national companies to disclose information.

Nor is it clear quite what policies the Labour Party at present advocates would be prevented from being introduced by the EEC. Certainly there is no reason to think that the minimal extension of nationalisation proposed by Labour would evoke a Brussels veto when the Mitterrand government is going ahead unchallenged with far greater acts of state ownership. None of Labour plans for taxing the rich or increasing welfare benefits could be expected to lead to problems since countries like Denmark and Holland are already further down this road than Labour even proposes to go.

Equally there is no evidence that a Labour renunciation of US cruise missiles, abandonment of Trident or even withdrawal from NATO would be inconsistent with EEC membership. The Dutch have announced their intention to abandon Cruise, the Danes permit no nuclear weapons on their soil and the Irish are not even in NATO. Nor is it the case that Labour's plans to extend worker's rights to be consulted and even have a say in industrial decision making would bring the wrath of the Brussels bureaucracy on its head since several EEC countries already operate or propose to operate similar schemes.

There are, of course, problems. They essentially touch on two related questions: import controls and subsidies and other state aids to help ailing British industry. Many of these would conflict with EEC competition rules. There is no evidence that the kind of import controls envisaged by Labour form part of a socialist strategy to transform the ownership and control of British industry. Even a 100 per cent Tory government which sought to impose controls on imports from other EEC countries or protect UK industries to the disadvantage of other EEC countries could well find itself in trouble with the Commission and the Treaty of Rome. Even a moderately protectionist government in Britain is likely to come up against the EEC Commission and the principles of the Treaty of Rome. However when Italy imposed sweeping import deposits in the spring of 1981 while disapproving noises were made in Brussels, the Council of Ministers agreed to give Italy a 'derogation' from its free trade doctrines.

It is also true that the Davignon steel regime does envisage the eventual elimination of state subsidies to the steel industry. But it should be noted that, in practice, the Davignon system of production quotas and guide-line prices has been biased against the more competitive steel producers (notably in West Germany) and is much more favourable to the UK and other less competitive steel-making countries who would have faced even worse problems of capacity cutbacks in a free-for-all situation. It should be recalled, however, that the EEC is already moving in a protectionist direction over a growing range of imports from outside the EEC. The time is almost certainly coming when the EEC is going to have to amend its own rules to permit some regulation of intra-EEC trade. What any British government outside the EEC would quickly discover is that selective import controls will anyway run foul of British membership of GATT (the General Agreement on Tariffs and Trade) and would actually be more exposed to retaliation outside the EEC than inside.

It is instructive in this context to look at what the Labour Party NEC document on withdrawal actually says. Once out of the EEC Britain would 'work within the OECD [Organisation of Economic Co-operation and Development] . . . for a reflation of spending and trade, on a planned basis'. Yet the OECD is, as an organisation, far more consistently opposed to trade protection than the EEC. A Labour government which waited on the approval of the OECD or the GATT for its 'trade planning' might have to wait for a very long time indeed. Yet a Britain outside the EEC, but still honouring its full free trading pledges could expect—at best—only the most marginal gains from its new freedom to buy food in cheaper world markets and its relief from the net EEC budget contribution. The NEC document also stresses the importance of restoring trade links to the 'Scandinavian countries whom we left when we dropped EFTA [European Free Trade Association] for the EEC'. But there is virtually full free trade now between EFTA and the EEC so that closer links with EFTA would only duplicate Britain's vulnerability to increased imports from the EEC.

The Labour Party also has illusions about the possibility of recreating the pre-EEC accession trade links with the Commonwealth. Many of these countries are now associated with the EEC through the Lomé Convention and many of those who are not, would like to be.[8] Australia and New Zealand have radically changed the pattern of their agricultural trade and may be less keen to go back to traditional cheap food supplying arrangements with the UK. Britain may well find that it is easier to take unilateral action inside the EEC (which is anyway moving to forms of trade protection on its own, collective account) than outside where it would face the full wrath of the GATT and the OECD more or less alone.

What is less clear is just how Britain could be expelled from the EEC if it did pursue policies which were condemned by the Commission or the other member states? The so-called Luxembourg 'compromise'—installed after the confrontation between De Gaulle and the EEC—gives national governments a veto over all important decisions of the Council. Nor is it the case that all countries always respond fully and rapidly to adverse decisions of EEC institutions—such as the European Court. There have been many cases where individual countries have ignored this or that ruling—at least until such time as they forced a reconsideration and a compromise on more acceptable terms to them. A recent case in point was the French government's defiance of a ruling of the European Court forbidding a French ban on British lamb imports. This ban maintained until the French secured—after much acrimony—a more favourable EEC 'lamb regime'. Much the same thing happened over the refusal of Belgium, France and West Germany to pay their full share of a special 1980 EEC supplementary budget. after many months of confusion and recrimination, a compromise was devised when some unexpected surplus funds were 'discovered' in the EEC farm budget.

Interestingly the NEC document takes an ultra 'Communitaire' line in rejecting the notion that the Treaty of Rome and its obligations could be ignored when it suited, saying, 'We do not see this as a proper basis for cooperation.' But why would cooperation be any easier if Britain, outside the EEC, was imposing wholesale restriction on the exports of other EEC countries? Nor would a campaign for withdrawal which essentially would be based on national claims to 'sovereignty' and the restoration of 'national independence' be likely to appeal to the labour and socialist movements in the rest of the Common Market. This would hardly be the basis for a wider European socialist 'cooperation'.

None of this adds up to the belief that the European Community can be reformed by a series of negotiations into some kind of socialist united states of Europe. It is highly doubtful whether the EEC can even be radically reformed within the system given the vested interests of so many EEC governments in the status quo. Certainly the CAP is a long way from being destroyed and the overall balance between agricultural and non-agricultural spending will change only very slowly. It might be that the strains of attempting even a modest reform at the same time as integrating Portugal and Spain will prove too much and the EEC will have to break up and reform as some looser EFTA type association of European states with particular groups of countries within the wider association proceeding at their own speed with selective economic and industrial integration.

The prospect of a 'multi-tier Europe' clearly has attractions for Labour leaders like Michael Foot and Peter Shore (as well as the ex-pro-market enthusiast Denis Healey) who are all worried at the disruption which might be caused to their general links with their Western allies by a too peremptory withdrawal from the EEC. It could even have attractions for the Thatcherite Tories (such as the group led by Teddy Taylor) who see a tightly knit EEC as a threat to Britain's independence and to its traditionally strong ties to the United States. Indeed a fervent—if sometimes concealed 'Atlanticism'—also runs throughout much of the anti-EEC arguments of Labour centre-right figures such as Peter Shore. This, as much as Shore's support for Israel, explains his bitter opposition in the House of Commons to efforts by EEC foreign ministers to find the basis of a wider peace process in the Middle East which also met with opposition in Washington.

It is impossible to separate a political judgment about a possible Labour withdrawal from the EEC from the political content of Labour's overall programme for government. The class character of the latter is bound to shape the class character of the former. Labour's general programme is a species of reformism somewhat to the right of what was promised by the Labour government before the elections of 1950 and 1951 (with the important exception of Labour's stand on nuclear weapons which, at the time of writing remained unclear). If withdrawal was part and parcel of a strategy for transforming British society; for openly challenging the bourgeois state and military machine and for assisting the extension of workers' power in all spheres, it would make more sense than it does in the light of Labour's very cautious and—in part—reactionary social and economic programme. At best the Labour Party's overall policy reflects the undetermined outcome of the internal policy struggle between left and right.

The struggle of the left inside the party to focus attention on the basic options facing the movement in a period of intensifying crisis can only be diverted by launching what is bound to be an electorally popular (because fundamentally nationalist) campaign on the EEC. For too many in the Labour leadership the EEC is precisely an issue which substitutes for policies which challenge the basis of British capitalist power. The position can be summed up as follows: withdrawal from the EEC should bring some tangible but modest financial benefits (around £750 million a year in current prices) from savings on the net UK budget contribution. This would be largely offset by the exchequer costs of moving to a system of deficiency payments in agriculture. There should be some real resource savings for the consumer but less today than 15 years ago because of the changed trade patterns of the cheaper Australasian food producers. The closer world and EEC agricultural prices move into alignment the smaller will be the resource saving generated by being able to 'shop around' in the cheapest international food markets.

As against this (as the Labour NEC document admits) the government would incur additional spending costs by having to finance and support British farming. It would also have to make good the (admittedly highly marginal) loss of revenue from the regional and social funds of the EEC. There would be the acquisition of a freedom to control trade and capital movements (but as we have seen these would remain subject to Britain's wider commitments to bodies such as the GATT, OECD and—in the case of capital movements—the IMF).

There is also substance in the Labour case against the undemocratic character of the EEC institutions. The Council of Ministers is one of the very few legislative bodies in the capitalist world which meets and deliberates behind closed doors. The British House of Commons exercise a grotesquely inadequate surveillance of the Council while the European

Parliament can have no meaningful role in this area while nation states maintain a veto over decisions in the Council. The Labour NEC document is also right to assert that 'membership of the Community has also made it more difficult for MPs to bring Ministers properly to account for their actions over EEC matters'. But what is to stop parliament taking the necessary powers to bring ministers to heel or even taking powers (as the Danish Folketing has done) to actually mandate ministers *before* they attend meetings of the Council and verify after that they acted according to that mandate?

Given the Labour Party's reformist position on imports, investment, agriculture and employment—and given its desire to retain the closest links with other 'Western' institutions such as NATO, the OECD, GATT and the IMF—it is difficult to see what can be better reformed outside rather than inside the EEC. Indeed to the extent that the reformists in the Labour Party have little clue about the changes in the pattern of EFTA and Commonwealth trade in the past decade and underestimate the problems of survival in the increasingly hostile internationalist capitalist world, they may be creating more obstacles to their desired goals by retreating into what in practice would be a 'little England' stance.

On the other hand the hopes of the 'European' right wing (particularly the coterie around Roy Jenkins and the SDP) are almost certainly doomed to failure. Reforms of the EEC there can and probably will be. But such reform is unlikely to keep pace with the pace and scope of the crisis within the EEC. The sheer differences of economic interest and performance between the different EEC economies and the prospective exhaustion of the economic and political resources to make a further enlargement to twelve nations work—could mean that the EEC will relapse into a body rather more similar to EFTA; that is to say a customs union with a machinery for coordination of foreign and certain other policies.

The socialist left can and should take a position quite different to both the discredited Euro-federalists and the nationalists. In practice this means trying to give a European dimension to the articulation of left policies for British Labour. If 'trade planning' is part of that strategy, what would it actually mean for those EEC countries with whom Britain trades? These are actually issued which should be raised now at a European level by the left in Britain. The same holds true for more immediate issues such as campaigning about jobs, racism and the threat of nuclear war. A start has been made in the last area with the creation of the Campaign for European Nuclear Disarmament. Why is there not a 'European' right to work campaign. Why not set up a European campaign to fight racism and fascism, particularly given the evidence of effective European coordination by the extreme Right? The European trade-union movement has been extremely interested by the implications for their own struggles against factory closures and mass unemployment of the

Lucas Aerospace shop stewards' initiative on 'alternative socially useful production'.

Even a cursory examination of the real world suggests that any attempt to build 'socialism in one country' today is even more surely doomed to failure than 50 years ago. Nor is it the case that the Labour NEC document embodies any clear strategy for even attempting a national socialist construction. Rather the document embodies elements of a left reformist programme, elements of a corporatist state capitalism and elements of an old fashioned attempt to make the British economy a more competitive component of world capitalism. Such an amalgam of policies may, however, bring a future Labour government into collision with the EEC and its constituent governments. But such collisions are much more likely to be over Britain's 'right' to enforce its own health safeguards over poultry imports or to defend doorstep milk deliveries than over any radical programmes of nationalisation. In these circumstances a campaign for EEC withdrawal could, paradoxically, become a diversion for facing up to the real constraints which the EEC could represent for a government elected on a mandate for sweeping social change. Any government in any EEC member state attempting to introduce socialist change can expect to end up in head-on conflict with the EEC and its institutions.

But British Labour also has natural class and political allies in Europe. In such a conflict these allies could and should be appealed to. This is all the more elementary since the crisis facing organised labour is so similar throughout western Europe. In that sense socialist opposition to the EEC does imply the counter demand for the 'socialist united states of Europe'— even as an ultimate goal. The truth is that most British anti-marketeers on the left talk the language of national sovereignty rather than the language of international socialism. But such language disguises a real commitment on behalf of Labour leaders to the British capitalist state, which commitment will prove a fatal flaw in any of the various 'alternative' strategies being urged on Labour from the left.

NOTES

1. *Withdrawl from the EEC*, published by the Labour Party National Executive Committee, June 27, 1981.
2. *The Great Milk Robbery*, published by Agenor of Brussels, March 1981.
3. The Institute for Fiscal Studies has calculated the total resource transfer from Britain as a result of the fact that EEC food prices are higher, on average, than world prices up to £2500 million a year. Clearly this figure will fluctuate depending on the variable gap between European and world market prices.
4. In the year before EEC entry Britain was in overall trade balance with the EEC. Last year the UK's annual deficit in manufactures was running at £5000 million and will be substantial again this year. The Bank of England now admits that far from entry having led to a big net inflow of capital to service the UK market, there has been a big net outflow of capital. Although EEC membership involves

an eventual obligation to permit free movement of capital, few member states have abandoned all exchange controls and the British government's decision to do so was entirely on its own responsibility.

5. 'EEC Protectionism: Present Practice and Future Trends', *European Research Associates* (39, Bd. Elovis, Brussels 1040), July, 1981.

6. *Telematics—Urgent Need for Concerted Action,* Report by the EEC Commission, Brussels, September 1980.

7. Advice of the Commission on the implications of the application by Portugal and Spain to join the EEC, Brussels, September 1978.

8. Phil Leeson writing in the Communist Party pamphlet, *The Common Market— Let's Get Out,* admits that many developing countries not associated with the EEC in the Lomé Convention would like the terms of raw material export price stabilisation offered by the Stabex arrangement in Lomé. Leeson goes so far as to quote—approvingly—Commissioner Cheysson's description of the Lomé Convention as 'an incomprable instrument, unique in the world and in history'. The relationship between the EEC and its Lomé associates is one of economic domination but more complex than is suggested in the description 'neo colonial'.

SOCIALIST FEMINISM AND ECONOMIC STRATEGY

Jean Gardiner and Sheila Smith

Introduction

Many discussions in socialist politics presume a fundamental unity of interests among members of the working class. This view is often accompanied by the notion that reference to divisions within the working class, along sexual, racial or other grounds, are divisive, and prevent the building of a political movement of the working class united around a socialist strategy. Socialist feminism has provided a powerful critique of this view, yet the implications of the socialist feminist critique have not been fully worked out in all areas of socialist political practice and strategy. The papers in this section are a contribution to the development of this critique in the area of socialist economic analysis and policy. The economic situation of women, especially married women and women with children, generally differs fundamentally from that of men. Hence two tasks confront us: first, these differences need to be investigated and analysed in detail; second, the formulation of socialist economic strategies needs to be changed to take these differences into account.

The reconstitution of socialist economic strategy to take account of differences in the economic situation of men and women, and of feminist demands, is a complex task. There is frequently a token attempt to take account of women's demands, which simply takes the form of adding extra items on to a pre-existing agenda. This token acknowledgement is, however, totally inadequate, for it fails to confront several political issues raised by feminism. In the sphere of economic policy, there may be a conflict of interests between men-in-general and women-in-general, in which case the constitution of the agenda itself is an issue of dispute. This may arise, for example, over working hours, job-sharing, wage differentials, the access of women to higher paid jobs, the distribution of wage labour and domestic labour between men and women, etc. The breaking down of the relative economic privileges which men have achieved and protected and the relative improvement in women's economic position will only begin to take place if the socialist economic agenda is reconstructed. Furthermore it may be necessary to reconsider even the concepts involved in the definition of socialist economic objectives. For example, what does 'full employment' mean for women with children? Hitherto 'full employment' has meant full employment in wage work for men; but women's relation to wage work and domestic labour is so different from men's, that a concept which relies on a male wage-worker as a norm has little relevance to large numbers of women.

These are some of the issues raised by the papers in this section, which hopefully will give rise to a long and constructive debate.

FEMINISM AND THE ALTERNATIVE ECONOMIC STRATEGY

Jean Gardiner and Sheila Smith

Despite a growing recognition of the failure of the AES in its different formulations to have anything specific to offer women, hardly any discussion has yet taken place on how this major weakness can be rectified. The main reason for this is that amongst socialists it has been easier to focus on the mechanisms for securing a shift in the balance of power from capital to labour than to confront problems associated with the distribution of resources and relations which the working population. Here we attempt to raise some of the most difficult issues in this area with the intention of encouraging a wider discussion out of which hopefully some answers will begin to emerge.

In a period of recession and mass unemployment the problem of divisions emerging between employed and unemployed, women and men, black and white people, becomes considerably more acute and apparent than in a period of boom. Inability or unwillingness on the part of the left and the labour movement to confront and tackle divisions as they arise is one of the main reasons why such periods of capitalist crisis do not automatically lead to a leftward shift in political mass consciousness. It is, therefore, crucial that a government that came to power committed to implementing the AES in a context of severe economic and social problems was as prepared to tackle potential conflicts and divisions amongst the mass of the population as it was to deal with, for example, economic sabotage on the part of the multinationals. A left government that failed to develop mass support amongst women and men for its policies would stand little chance of withstanding political opposition from its major enemies. This is a complex issue, however, since there are senses in which the interests of men and women may be fundamentally antagonistic. This antagonism provides an important reason for the attempt to discuss whether feminist demands are compatible with the AES.

Most versions of the AES involve a more or less detailed set of policy proposals for expanding the economy, increasing democratic control and planning, increasing the social wage, reshaping the welfare system and increasing control over international trade. These are all vital elements of an economic strategy which can begin both to provide genuine benefits for the mass of women and men and to raise political consciousness around a socialist alternative. However, such policies only begin to change the economic context in which some of the specific problems faced by women can be tackled. Let us remind ourselves of the major economic

31

problems women face: low pay at work; unequal access to jobs and training; hidden unemployment; financial dependence on men; excessive share of unpaid work. All these problems require a twofold attack. On the one hand, social policies are required that expand and transform employment opportunities and social, educational and health services. On the other hand, men have to accept a loss in the relative economic privileges they have enjoyed. For example, if women's pay is to improve relative to men's, men's pay will, inevitably be less in relation to women's. It is the left's unwillingness to face up to the implications for men of women's demands that so often reduces these to a meaningless shopping list tacked on to the end of a policy statement. A feminist approach to the AES must instead concern itself with the question of how to achieve a more equitable way of sharing between men and women, society's resources on the one hand and its paid and unpaid work on the other.

This paper will focus on three areas which must be tackled if the AES is to become a meaningful strategy for women. These are access to jobs, working hours and equalising pay. Many other important issues are left out or only referred to briefly because they cannot all be satisfactorily discussed in the space of one paper. We have chosen to focus on how to tackle the unequal relationships of men and women in the world of work and how to make the world of work more responsive to people's domestic lives because this must be the starting point for challenging the sexual division of labour in the home and women's financial dependence on men.

It may be useful to begin with a brief summary of some of the changes that have taken place in recent years in the relative position of men and women in the economy. These changes mean that traditional assumptions about a clear-cut division in family responsibilities between men and women in the workforce (i.e. men working to support a family, women temporarily working to support themselves or for 'pin-money') are increasingly untenable. The big rise in the proportion of the labour force who are women (40 per cent by the end of the 1970s) has been accompanied by major changes in the family responsibilities of women at work.

Because of the contraction in family size and childbearing period, the proportion of married couples with dependent children has declined. Only 58 per cent of married men under 65 now have dependent children. Within the male labour force as a whole, including the single men, only about 40 per cent now have dependent children. Within the female labour force about 33 per cent are now married women with children. Another 5 per cent roughly are non-married mothers with dependent children. Thus almost the same proportion of women (38 per cent) as men (40 per cent) in the labour force now have responsibility for dependent children. Because of the rise in the proportion of mothers in paid work a declining proportion of male workers are sole family breadwinners. Only about 18 per cent of all men in the labour force now provide sole financial support for a wife and dependent child or children.[1]

Yet much of men's relative economic privilege, despite all the talk of equal pay and equal opportunity, continues to rest on assumptions such as the notion that men as a group are entitled to a family wage, because of their financial responsibilities. If fewer than one in five male workers now conform to the traditional stereotype and growing numbers of women make a crucial contribution to family support, a complete reappraisal of the way in which jobs and income are allocated between men and women is needed, on grounds of family needs as well as equal opportunities.[2]

Access to Jobs

Whilst different discussions of the AES have put forward varying estimates of the level of registered unemployment that would be acceptable as a first round full employment target (varying from 300,000 to 700,000), all accept that returning to full employment should be a first priority of the strategy. However, the problems that a left government would incur in carrying out that commitment, given the mass unemployment and industrial decline it would inherit are increasingly being recognised. As every month goes by with its toll not just of lost jobs but also of depleted productive capacity, the prospect of a left government securing a return of registered unemployment below the one million mark with a relatively smooth five-year term of office appears harder and harder to achieve. Even if a government committed to the AES were elected tomorrow, it would be faced with an unemployment level of approaching four million (including unregistered unemployed but excluding another half-million on temporary government employment creation schemes or on short-time working) as well as the prospect of a further expansion in the labour force over the next five years of about 0.8 million.

It has been estimated that about 2.2 million new jobs could be created in five years under the AES, assuming that policies could secure a 3 per cent annum average growth rate for the economy.[3] Given the time it would take to rebuild the seriously depleted productive capacity of British industry, it is unlikely that growth rates above this figure could be achieved. It is not difficult, therefore, to see the scale of the problem that returning to full employment implies.

Whilst it is important to recognise the advance that policies designed to create over two million new jobs in a five-year period would represent over policies pursued by British governments throughout the last decade, it is also crucial to tackle the genuine fears that women have that full employment for them will be postponed for a much longer period and that employment for women will continue to be in low-paid and boring jobs. After a steady rise in the labour force participation rates of women for some thirty years, there has been an abrupt reversal recently. About half a million women appear to have dropped out of the labour force between 1977 and 1980, discouraged by the lack of job opportunities available.[4] The impact of unemployment on women is considerably less visible than its impact on men, not only because more women than men are discouraged from seeking work by the lack of job opportunities but also because many more women who are seeking work do not register as unemployed because they are not entitled to benefit. Moreover, women are more vulnerable to unemployment than men because of their concentration in relatively unskilled and part-time jobs and their more frequent movement into and out of the labour force.[5] This greater vulnerability is reinforced by the revival of divisive attitudes about women's jobs being of secondary importance, which a recession such as the present one encourages. The vigour with which such attitudes have re-emerged demonstrate how fragile and superficial a concept equal opportunity remains in terms of mass consciousness.

If women's aspirations are to be met, the AES must embody a strategy not only for increasing employment, but also for beginning to tackle the acute job segregation that works so much to women's disadvantage at present. The current development of positive action policies within the TUC is therefore very much to be welcomed. Such policies must have a crucial role to play within the AES from its inception.

Positive Action

The growing recognition within the trade-union movement of the need for positive action stems from an acknowledgement of the limits of what has been achieved by existing equal rights legislation. Positive action is concerned primarily with opening up employment opportunities for women in areas from which they have traditionally been largely excluded and with getting employers, unions, and bodies responsible for education and training to take necessary action to facilitate this: e.g. the adoption by each employer of an equal opportunity programme based on a review of patterns of discrimination and job segregation in the existing workforce and incorporating negotiated targets and timetables for eliminating discrimination at all levels of job grading.[6]

Despite growing support for positive action in unions at a national level, there is still widespread uncertainty and considerable opposition to the idea in the trade-union movement as a whole. This is partly due to a lack of understanding of the meaning of positive action and an unjustified fear that men will now be the victims of discrimination. However, opposition is also based on the recognition that positive action confronts existing male privilege more directly and effectively than previous approaches to equalising opportunity have done. Thus, while positive action merely aims to provide women with the positive support and encouragement that will enable them to have equal access with men to

employment and training, it does mean a challenge to preferential treatment for men. One of the problems in winning acceptance of these changes
is that because of the subtle and often indirect ways in which sex discrimination has operated in the past, many men do not yet recognise
the relative advantages they have enjoyed. The priority that has been
given to men's access to jobs and to men's pay has been seen as natural
rather than preferential. There is a deep-seated belief that women are
by nature less able to perform the jobs from which they have been excluded
in the past. Mass acceptance of positive action will therefore be hard to
achieve and will depend on a major ideological campaign to raise men's
awareness. High levels of unemployment also make these changes in
attitudes that much harder to bring about. It is therefore crucial that
these problems are explicitly recognised and discussed.

Discussions of positive action programmes have also emphasised the
need to incorporate within them special provision for employees with
parental responsibility. Such provision should include the provision of
nursery and school holiday child-care facilities, an extended period of
parental leave following the birth of a child, part of which could be taken
by the father or the mother, paid time off work to look after sick children,
greater flexibility in working hours, part-time jobs at all levels of pay and
seniority, including traditionally male jobs, and equal employment rights
for part-time workers.

If such policies are not adopted and fought for, the relative position of
women in terms of access to jobs could continue to deteriorate even under
an expansionary AES. Without major changes in the present systems of
education and training, women would be unable to take advantage of the
requirements for skilled labour in high technology industry or the need
for engineers, designers and planners stimulated by economic reconstruction. Given the scale of the unemployment problem, women's right
to work could still be treated as secondary and they could continue to be
segregated into whatever low-paid jobs remained.

Since positive action will only be effective in the long term if attitudes
towards the role of men and women in the economy change, the trade-
union movement must play a central role in its implementation. However,
government policies would also be needed to supplement what could be
achieved through collective bargaining. This could involve positive action
policies being required of all public sector employers, and all private
sector employers engaged on government contracts or involved in planning
agreements with the government. Some changes in legislation would also
be required. The Sex Discrimination Act and Equal Pay Act should be
strengthened and amalgamated and the Employment Act amended. A
comprehensive policy to tackle sex stereotyping and discrimination in
education and training will also be required.[7] Finally a major drive to
expand nursery and school holiday provision should be given the highest

possible priority within the expanded social spending programme.

Working Hours
Given the importance attached by many women with children to short and flexible working hours and the recent growth of support within the trade-union movement for reducing working hours in order to expand employment opportunities, it is worth giving particular attention to this issue.

If it is the case that reducing working hours would create additional jobs, then it would appear to be a policy with a dual benefit for women. On the one hand, it would have the effect of reducing unemployment more rapidly than the expansionary policies of the AES could otherwise achieve, thus improving overall employment opportunities, including those for women. On the other hand, it might open up more specific areas of work to women with domestic commitments from which previously excessive hours excluded them. Moreover, it could also increase the availability of men to take a greater share of domestic labour.

It is, therefore, important to examine the implications of changing working hours and explore some of the problems raised. First, let us examine the conditions under which a reduction in working hours would create more jobs, by looking at the example of cutting overtime. Excessive overtime is the major factor pushing up the average full-time weekly hours worked in Britain to a figure considerably in excess of those worked in the other major industrial countries. Britain is the only West European country apart from Portugal with no legal restrictions on the amount of overtime worked. The main reason why attempts to reduce overtime in the past have failed is its close association with low pay. 'Overtime is worked in Britain largely as a method of ensuring adequate earnings for many groups of male manual workers whose current basic rates are too low to ensure reasonable living standards.'[8] These workers are concentrated in the public sector (e.g. railways and postal services) and in a range of private industries (e.g. baking and textiles).

The elimination of overtime would therefore require substantial increase in the basic pay of most workers for whom it has represented a major component of earnings in the past. It would also incidentally benefit those women whose pay is at present adversely affected by the fact that they work in industries where men supplement their earnings by means of overtime. Women are less likely to be able or willing to work overtime and therefore have their earnings depressed by the lowness of basic rates.

To what extent would the elimination of overtime also increase the number of jobs? If it led to an increase in output per hour worked and no increase in labour costs, there would be no need to hire additional workers and so no new jobs would be created. If on the other hand, productivity did not rise in this way or the nature of the job was such that total hours worked could not be reduced without damage to the service provided (e.g. public transport), then the number of jobs would increase but so would labour costs.

The financial implications of creating jobs through the elimination of overtime must therefore be recognised. It is true that a large part of the increased labour costs would arise in the public sector where they would be partially offset by the reduction in the cost of maintaining people unemployed. However, some extra finance would have to be found. In the private sector, the financing of increased labour costs arising from shorter working hours would have to be tackled in the context of the government's economic strategy for those industries affected. Otherwise private firms might respond by putting up prices or cutting investment and the original boost to employment provided by reduced working hours would be negated.

Reducing working hours could therefore lead to the creation of additional jobs, although the extent to which this would occur would be limited by the financial constraints within which the AES would be operating and the productivity gains resulting from shorter working hours. Eliminating overtime would, however, have other benefits for women in terms both of improving the pay of women working in the industries affected and increasing the time available for men to spend with their families. These other benefits should be taken into account to a greater extent than is generally the case at present with trade unions.

However, it is likely that the process of reducing working hours would have to go well beyond the elimination of overtime to a working week of thirty hours or less for many jobs to become attractive to women with children or for men to take a considerably greater share of domestic responsibilities.

Since it is unrealistic to assume, given the problems of economic reconstruction, that working hours could be reduced under the AES to a point where the division between full-time and part-time work (officially thirty hours or less) was eliminated, it is important to consider both ways of making full-time hours more flexible and responsive to the domestic commitments of workers, and also ways of extending and enhancing the status of part-time employment.

Systems of flexible working hours which began to appear in the UK in the 1970s, particularly amongst non-manual workers, could be adopted more widely in many more jobs. Flexible working hours (FWH) is an arrangement whereby, within set limits, employees may begin and end work at times of their own choice, provided that they are all present at certain 'core-time' periods of the day and that within a specified time—usually a week or a month—they work the total number of hours agreed. If the 'core-time' period coincided with school hours, and the maximum possible flexibility was built into the system, FWH would open up many more jobs to working mothers and would enable many more fathers to take more responsibility for childcare. It is crucial, however, that unions and workplace representatives, *including women*, are involved in the formulation of such systems, which has not always been the case in the past.

Because it is possible to gear FWH to the daily timetable of domestic commitments, it is probably a more attractive working arrangement for most mothers than the compressed work sheet which is the other major recent innovation in working arrangements. Here the working week is compressed into four, or four-and-a-half days instead of five. The problem with this arrangement is that, in the absence of any significant reduction in hours, the four full days worked consist of very long hours to offset the extra day or half-day of 'leisure'.

Considerably more thought, therefore, needs to be given to the question of how working hours should be made more flexible, in the context of specific industries and occupations, if this is to provide genuine benefits for parents in general and mothers in particular. Thought should also be given to the possibilities of job-sharing.

Trade unions, socialists and feminists have all expressed reservations about part-time employment for a number of different reasons. However, part-time employment is likely to have an important role to play long after the inception of the AES, both in terms of increasing the number of job opportunities available and in terms of improving access to jobs for those with major domestic commitments. It is important also for the Left to recognise that many women at present opt for part-time work as a positive choice, despite all the disadvantages at present attached to it in terms of lower pay and fewer rights. It is true that some women work part-time at present because adequate childcare facilities to enable them to work full time do not exist and so much of the burden of housework falls upon them. However, others value the time they spend on activities which working full-time would preclude, e.g. time spent with children and time involved on a voluntary basis in the community. We must, therefore, recognise that unless and until full-time hours worked can be substantially reduced, part-time work will continue to be favoured by many employees even if there is a massive expansion of childcare provision and a major increase in men's share of domestic labour.

Once we recognise that part-time jobs are a necessary and positive feature of the economy, a number of steps need to be taken both to make part-time workers a fully integrated section of the labour force and trade-union movement and to extend part-time employment opportunities to men. Part-time employment should be available at all levels of pay and should be covered by the same promotion opportunities and employment rights as full-time work and comparable social security entitlements. Specifically, all parents could be entitled to temporary periods of part-time employment while their children were young with a guaranteed option of returning to full-time employment at a subsequent stage.

These changes would depend on trade unions extending the unionisation of part-time workers and incorporating these policies into the collective bargaining process. There would also be a need for the government to give backing to the collective bargaining process through legislation and other means such as those described above in the section on positive action.

If these changes were carried out and if some of the steps, discussed elsewhere in this paper, were taken to raise women's pay, to eradicate men's low pay and to increase state support for the cost of children, the conditions would be created for increasing numbers of men, especially fathers, to recognise the advantages for them in trading money for hours by means of part-time employment. This would represent a major contribution towards a more equitable sharing of paid and unpaid work between men and women.

Equalising Pay

As far as jobs and pay are concerned, women remain trapped in a vicious circle that can only be broken by a major and comprehensive set of initiatives on the part of a government committed to ending women's financial dependence on men. As long as women's pay remains so much lower than men's, men's jobs will continue to be treated as of primary importance. And because men's jobs are treated as primary, women continue to be expected to accept low pay. Raising women's pay relative to men's must be an essential part of a strategy to end the sexual division of labour and establish a partnership between men and women in which each takes responsibility for their own financial support and that of their dependents, and each takes an equal share in domestic labour. As long as men's wages remain a lot higher than women's, it is impractical to assume that many men will opt for part-time employment or full-time childcare to enable wives to work full time. The large gap in earnings between men and women perpetuates the traditional assumption that a man's major contribution to a family is financial whilst a woman is primarily expected to perform the unpaid work.

In 1980 women's hourly earnings were on average only 73.5 per cent of men's.[9] And this figure somewhat overstates women's actual relative pay since it excludes both overtime payments, which accrue to many more men than women, and part-time workers, mostly women, whose hourly earnings are less than full-time workers. Between 1970 and 1977 there was an improvement in women's pay relative to men's from 63.1 per cent to 75.5 per cent. Since 1977, however, this improvement has begun to be eroded. Most of the limited progress that took place up to 1977 can be attributed to the implementation of the Equal Pay Act. Neither collective bargaining nor government pay policies as they have operated have provided a systematic means of raising women's relative pay.

The Limits of Collective Bargaining

In the 80 years between 1888 when the first TUC resolution calling for equal pay was passed and the late 1960s when the recent movement for equal pay developed among women trade unionists, there had been no overall improvement in the relative earnings of women workers. It is not difficult to identify some of the reasons why collective bargaining had failed to achieve any progress. Women had remained a minority, albeit a growing one, within union membership. Even in unions representing largely female memberships, e.g. some textile unions, women were rarely involved in the organisation and leading positions. Trade unionists generally acquiesced in the dominant view of society that men should be paid more than women because they were the family breadwinner and were, therefore, entitled to a family wage.

Even if attitudes were different, there are limits to what could be achieved through collective bargaining because part of the problem of women's low pay has always been their concentration in low paid and poorly organised industries where collective bargaining has not achieved much for men either (e.g. retail distribution). The other party to collective bargaining, the employers, have always been committed to unequal pay for women because of the growing number of industries which have depended on cheap female labour.

Moreover, collective bargaining is primarily concerned with improving the overall level of wages and conditions and defending the rate for the job. Reducing differentials between groups of workers has not been a consistent goal of the trade-union movement as a whole. Within particular unions, wages strategy has varied in accordance with the balance of power between different occupational groups amongst the membership which, in turn, has been affected by changing labour market conditions. Pressure for greater egalitarianism at certain times in certain industries has been balanced at other times and elsewhere by pressure for restoration of relativities and differentials. The overall effect of these pressures is a remarkable stability in the distribution of wages amongst male workers as well as between men and women. In 1886 the lowest paid 10 per cent of male manual workers earned 68 per cent of average earnings. This differential was exactly the same in 1980.[10]

Incomes Policy and Equal Pay

The improvement in women's relative pay between 1970 and 1977 was the direct result of the 1970 Equal Pay Act and not of government incomes policies, despite the inclusion in those policies of flat rate elements which were supposed to favour the low paid. The years when a flat rate incomes policy was operating, e.g. the £6 limit for all workers earning less than £8,500 in 1975-76, were not years in which particularly rapid progress in women's pay took place. The biggest increase in women's relative pay occurred in 1974-75, the first year of the 'Social Contract' when a percentage rather than flat rate policy was in operation. This was the last year for employers to bring women's pay in line with the Equal Pay Act which would account for a bunching of equal pay settlements at that time.

Government incomes policies in the 1970s were an attempt to redistribute income from wages to profits. No serious onslaught on pay inequalities was ever intended although flat rate elements were introduced to make the policies appear fairer to those in greatest need. In practice many lower paid workers, including many women, did not receive the increases to which they were entitled under specific incomes policies e.g. the £6 limit.[11] Overall flat rate policies appear to have done nothing to improve the relative pay of the low paid.[12] This may have been because steadily rising unemployment was already affecting job opportunities available, particularly for the lowest paid workers, women, young people and the unskilled. Higher paid workers were probably better placed, not only to secure their flat rate entitlement but also even larger wage increases by means of promotion and job changes. Pay policies of this kind are therefore not a method to adopt in order to bring about improvements in women's relative pay overall. The limited improvements that have taken place have resulted from government intervention aimed specifically at women's pay in the form of equal pay legislation.

Since the scope for improvement under this legislation has been exhausted, the most important factors now perpetuating unequal pay have become increasingly apparent. These are the way in which women are segregated into 'women only' jobs and the way in which jobs done by women are systematically undervalued. Inequality in pay is, therefore, closely linked to the question of access to jobs. To a great extent, women's low pay is the result of their concentration in a narrow range of low-paid jobs. There is also evidence that this segregation has intensified since the Equal Pay Act came into force as a means of reducing the scope for comparability between men's and women's work. '. . . employers have reacted to the legislation by setting up "women-only" grades and. . . have not been adequately challenged by the trade-union movement.'[13]

Thus the allocation of jobs between men and women has in turn been influenced by the deepseated assumption amongst both employers and employees that men's relatively high pay must be maintained. This assumption continues to be perpetuated by the view that men as a group are entitled to a wage that enables them to support a wife and family. Yet, as we have seen, the concept of male breadwinner and family wage is quite inapplicable today to the existing labour force and patterns of family financial support. Even in the past, it is unlikely that many working-class families were able to survive permanently and exclusively on a father's wage. Certainly, today there are relatively few families that can manage adequately for long periods on the basis of one male wage alone. All the notion of a family wage serves to do is to maintain the low pay of women workers and to make it harder for women to contribute towards a decent standard of living for their families.[14]

The downgrading of women's status in the labour force which such attitudes foster is expressed in the method used to evaluate predominantly female jobs. For example, job evaluation schemes sometimes reinforce the differential between men's and women's pay by giving 'male' elements such as strength a higher value than 'female' elements such as dexterity. However, it is also important to point out that skill is not a purely technical issue and it is, therefore, very difficult to measure it in an objective way. Low pay is generally associated with a lack of bargaining power among groups of workers and an inability to project their skill and the value of their jobs. Because women have been less well organised than men and concentrated in jobs with lower bargaining power, women's skills have been systematically undervalued.

Much more progress on women's pay could therefore be achieved in particular workplaces and sectors of the economy if the trade-union movement at all levels took up the ideas associated with positive action and were supported in this by stronger equal opportunities legislation. What is needed is a campaign both to open up women's access to training and jobs from which they are largely excluded and to eradicate sexual bias in the methods by which work is evaluated and pay is calculated. Such a campaign will only succeed if it is backed by a concerted effort to challenge the traditional deep-seated attitudes which perpetuate women's low pay and to strengthen the bargaining power of women inside union structures.[15]

However, positive action by specific employers and unions can only deal with part of the problem of job segregation and unequal pay because of the way in which women are also concentrated in low-paid sectors of the economy. This is one reason why women's low pay represents such an intractable problem in a capitalist economy and cannot be tackled by collective bargaining alone. On the one hand low pay may be associated with industrial decline and low productivity and profitability as in some manufacturing industries like textiles and clothing. On the other hand it is often the result of a poorly organised workforce or one that is lacking in bargaining power. This tends to be the case amongst the many women working in service industries. Profits may be high but the small scale and isolated nature of the workforce, low levels of unionisation and the excess supply of workers available to the employer keep pay levels depressed. Service workers in the public sector e.g. nurses are more often unionised but lack effective means of industrial action and therefore have very little bargaining power.

A substantial narrowing in the differential between men's and women's pay will only be achieved therefore if policies are adopted by government and trade unions which begin to tackle some of these fundamental causes of low pay. In the context of the AES we have to consider what steps could be taken to make it possible for the earnings of workers in low-paid sectors to rise faster than those in relatively high-paid sectors.

In the case of declining manufacturing industries low pay should be tackled as part of the strategy for industrial regeneration. Import controls and employment subsidies, combined with expansionary policies for the economy as a whole, would not only be a means of maintaining and expanding production and employment, raising profitability and generating finance for investment. They should also be seen as a means of improving the relative pay and conditions of the workforce.

Where women's low pay is associated with low levels of unionisation much will depend on intensified efforts on the part of the unions themselves to tackle the problems. Such efforts would be greatly assisted by involving more women with direct work experience in the relevant areas, in full-time official and leadership positions. As far as the government is concerned minimum wage legislation might be the most effective means of supporting union efforts to improve women's pay in low-paid service industries. In the public sector the government would be in much more powerful a position to improve the relative pay of the lowest paid service workers. This in time would have beneficial effects for private sector workers in comparable jobs by setting new pay standards.

It is crucial however not to underestimate the problems the AES would face in tackling low pay and to be aware of the limits of what could be achieved in the short run. Pay will go on being closely linked to the bargaining power of groups of workers, both because of the anarchic and unplanned way in which a still primarily capitalist economy will be operating and also because of the collective bargaining traditions the trade union movement has evolved. By encouraging debate on these issues now however we can be hopeful that the AES will begin to challenge some of the limits imposed by capitalist economics and to open up space for socialist and feminist ideas and greater egalitarianism to flourish. This would mean major changes in the nature and scope of collective bargaining. On the one hand the benefits of collective bargaining need to be extended to many more women and low paid workers. On the other hand the bargaining power of those men whose organisational strength has enabled them to enjoy relative economic advantages vis-a-vis other workers will need to be channelled in more political directions from which working people who lack industrial strength will also benefit. Isolated incidents in the past such as the action taken by miners in support of striking nurses several years back indicate what could be achieved in this respect.

There is a vital final element in a strategy for tackling unequal pay. That is reform of the system of state financial support for children via the tax and social security system. In recent years the state has made a very small and declining contribution to the financial costs of bearing and raising children. Because maternity and child benefits represent only a small fraction of these costs women's financial dependence on men is reinforced. The notion of men as family breadwinners remains central to the existing tax and social security system and will only be effectively challenged when maternity and child benefits are raised to levels that more closely correspond with the actual cost of having children. A first step towards this would be to use tax revenue saved by the abolition of the married man's allowance, worth £4.44 a week to all married men regardless of whether or not they have dependent children, to raise child benefit. It has been estimated that, if this policy was adopted, child benefit could rise by £3 and £1¼ billion would still be left for other purposes.[16]

Conclusion

Under present government economic policies and with the continuation of the present recession, the vicious economic circle in which women are trapped is likely not only to be maintained but to become even more oppressive. The AES on the other hand could begin to create the conditions for that vicious circle to be broken, and could therefore be developed into a strategy with mass appeal for women.

But can the AES tackle the major problems that a commitment to genuine economic equality for women would involve? Can it take on board the major ideological task of getting men to accept that an end to discrimination against women means a loss of relative advantages for them? Will it be able to increase employment opportunities sufficiently rapidly to prevent divisive attitudes from taking over? Will it incorporate a commitment towards improving the relative position of the low-paid in general and women in particular? Will it be able to assert the kind of control over the capitalist sector which will begin to make this possible?

The answers to these questions will only emerge out of a much wider discussion on the left and in the labour movement. What is certain is that unless this discussion begins to take place now the chances of the AES fulfilling the potential it has for women are very slim.

NOTES

1. Figures are derived from the *General Household Survey 1978* and *Social Trends 1981*.

2. For more discussion, see J. Coussins and A. Coote, *The Family in the Firing Line*, NCCL/CPAG 1981 and H. Land, 'The Family Wage', *Feminist Review*,

No. 6, 1980.

3. S. Aaronovitch, *The Road from Thatcherism,* Lawrence and Wishart, 1981.
4. *Cambridge Economic Policy Review,* April, 1981, p. 41.
5. See J. Gardiner, 'Women and the Recession', *Marxism Today,* March 1981.
6. For further details and discussion, see 1981 TUC *Women's Conference Report,* and S. Robarts with A. Coote and E. Ball, *Positive Action for Women,* NCCL, 1981.
7. For more detailed recommendations, see TUC *Women's Conference Report,* 1981 and S. Robarts, 1981.
8. *Labour Research,* May 1981.
9. *Department of Employment Gazette,* October 1980.
10. *Ibid.*
11. See C. Pond, *Low Pay Paper,* No. 15, May 1977, 'For Whom the Pips Squeak'.
12. See A.J.H. Dean, 'Income Policies and Differentials', *National Institute Economic Review,* August 1978, No. 85.
13. TUC *Women's Conference Report,* 1981. See also M.W. Snell, P. Glucklich and M. Povall, 'Equal Pay and Opportunities', *Department of Employment Research Paper,* No. 20, 1981.
14. See J. Coussins, 1981.
15. For more detailed discussion, see TUC *Women's Conference Report,* 1981, and S. Robarts, 1981.
16. J. Coussins, 1981.

WOMEN IN THE RECESSION

Jill Rubery and Roger Tarling

1. Introduction

This paper is concerned with the impact of the recession on women's employment prospects. In the milder recessionary conditions of the early and mid-1970s prospects appeared good. Far from women losing their recently achieved gains in employment opportunities, their employment continued to rise as did their participation rates. Moreover it was in this period, from 1973 to 1976, that women secured their only major improvement in relative wage levels. Women's earnings rose from that seemingly rigid level of 60 per cent of male earnings[1] to stabilise at around 70 per cent; a remarkably rapid restructuring of earnings in the post war period when there were few sustained relative changes in industry or occupation average earnings of such a magnitude (Godley, 1977; Tarling and Wilkinson 1977). It appeared that far from women providing a vulnerable 'reserve army of labour', they were becoming an integrated and relatively protected part of the labour force.

In the early 1980s fears have re-emerged that deepening economic recession will have a disporportionately severe effect on women's employment. These fears stem from the rapid reduction in female employment since 1979, and the rapid rise in the unemployment rate for women since 1976, an increase of 150 per cent compared to 75 per cent for men, and the actual decrease in the participation rate since 1977 mainly attributable to the inability of married women to re-enter the labour force after having children (Cambridge Economic Policy Group (CEPG) 1981). Such fears are bolstered by both moral and more direct pressures (such as public expenditure cuts on nursery education) to persuade women to remain at home.

Our main concern in this paper is to examine the available evidence on women's employment position in the recession, including women's job opportunities, their access to wage employment and the terms and conditions on which they are employed. We will be less concerned with breakdowns in occupational segregation and access to higher paid jobs: it is the expansion of job opportunities, the moderation of the impact of family commitments on access to wage employment (through for example the expansion of part-time work) and improved minimum terms and conditions of employment that have been of greatest importance to most working-class women in the post-war period, and all these gains are now under threat. First, however, we need to consider the nature of women's position

47

in the labour market and its implications for women's employment prospects.

2. Women's Employment Position in Recession: Theoretical Standpoints

There is general agreement that women form a distinct labour market group occupying a special position or positions in the labour process. As recession is unlikely to have an even impact on all labour market groups, there are strong reasons for expecting the impact on female employment to differ from that of male employment. However there is much less general agreement on the nature of women's special position in the labour market, and therefore no consensus view on the consequences of recession for women.

Bruegel (1979) identified three main standpoints and provided a useful synthesis. The simple view that women provide a reserve army of labour that can be attracted into or repelled from the labour market according to aggregate labour demand cannot be substantiated (Beechey 1978). The experience of the 1970s when women's employment continued to rise when men were experiencing net job loss contradicts this model and provides support for Milkman's view (1976) that female labour is used in completely different parts of the labour process from male labour, and cannot therefore provide men with a buffer against unemployment. For Milkman the boundaries between male and female jobs are determined by ideological, social and cultural factors and are independent of the level of aggregate demand: men will not occupy women's jobs whatever the level of male unemployment. Bruegel accepts that there will be no direct substitution of male for female workers at least in the short term but argues that Milkman has omitted to recognise the importance of economic factors in determining the structure of occupational segregation by sex. One of the factors that will determine which jobs become feminised will be the stability of employment prospects: 'a job is "women's work" partly *because* it doesn't offer stable and continuous employment' (p. 15).

In these circumstances women are likely to be more vulnerable to redundancy than men within the same firm or industry, even though this impact on employment opportunities is being counter-balanced by an expansion of female dominated industries and sectors (as was the case in the 1970s with the growth of employment in private services and the public sector). The protection offered for women's employment from structural changes in the industrial and employment system, in which we include both the trend increase in the share of female labour and the expansion of female dominated sectors, cannot be expected to continue in the long term. In any case women as individuals will not be protected from economic fluctuations unless they are employed in relatively stable jobs within each employment sector. It may also be the case that even if the majority of women are in relatively stable employment, the majority of unstable jobs are still filled by women, thereby protecting men from unemployment. Aggregate employment trends are thus not a satisfactory test of the reserve army hypothesis.

In Bruegel's analysis the 'reserve army' and the 'occupational segregation' explanations of women's employment position can be considered complementary and not contradictory standpoints. Women do not provide direct substitutes for male labour but do act as indirect 'buffers' by filling the more unstable jobs. Women's vulnerability to job loss derives both from the nature of their jobs and from their labour supply characteristics. Women in employment are more likely to be laid off, even those with job specific skills, because they have limited alternative job opportunities and firms can expect to be able to re-employ the same workers in the upturn, and also because they are likely to have been more recently recruited than men, on the last in, first out principle. Women are also vulnerable to employment loss in a recession because they are more likely to have withdrawn temporarily from the labour market and cannot re-enter unless there are vacancies.

The third standpoint in the debate on women's position in the recession is that the increase in economic pressures on firms will encourage them to use women as a cheap labour substitute for male employees (Gardiner 1976). In these circumstances there could even be an expansion of women's employment based on the exploitation of women's disadvantaged position in the labour market. Employment on these terms not only denies women the right to reasonable reward for labour but also threatens the terms and conditions on which organised labour, both male and female, are employed. However Bruegel finds no evidence of this effect in recessionary conditions and argues plausibly that substitution of female for male labour is more likely to take place in a period of restructuring when new technologies are introduced and new jobs created through the emergence of new firms or the relocation of existing ones. This process of restructuring requires capital expenditure and is therefore more likely to take place in a period of expansion.

In our view Bruegel's scepticism of the likelihood of substitution was probably correct for periods of relatively mild recession and mainly short-term cyclical fluctuations in activity. In the current severe economic recession the case that women may be used as a cheap labour substitute becomes altogether more plausible. The collapse of aggregate demand is destroying jobs on a permanent and not just a cyclical basis as firms are forced out of business and industrial plants closed down and sold off. Restructuring is therefore being forced on industry through closure, and through the high levels of unemployment forcing redundant managers and skilled workers into becoming self-employed and small entrepreneurs. In addition the recession has coincided with a period of rapid technical change that will force at least some firms into adopting new techniques if they are to stand any chance of survival. In these conditions new jobs are still likely to be relatively scarce, but evidence suggests that most of them will nevertheless be found in small firms and in new firms, mainly located away from the principal industrial areas where trade-union protection of wages and conditions is most strongly established. These firms both serve new markets, and thus help to moderate the recession, and compete with existing firms, in this case often destroying existing jobs at the same time as creating new ones (Fothergill and Gudgin, 1982; Birch 1979). The main reasons behind the restructuring of industry on these lines may not be the exploitation of low-paid labour, although the likelihood of exploitation increases in circumstances of high unemployment and no traditional trade-union organisation.

We would, therefore, go further than Bruegel in synthesising these three approaches to women's employment position in the recession. In the downturn the impact on women's employment will be primarily determined by the rate of job loss in female employment areas, but as the recession continues there will be some job creation, some of which will provide direct substitutes for existing jobs with inferior terms and conditions of employment. However this substitution effect will only expand women's employment opportunities in the aggregate if it is men's jobs that are being replaced. New firms may be more likely to break down traditional sex segregation barriers and therefore there will be some direct effect on men's employment. However, the more dominant effect of employing women on poor terms and conditions is likely to be on other women workers. In the short term the number of women employed may remain similar or even expand but on worse terms and conditions; in the long term vulnerability to job loss will increase if the new jobs offer less secure employment conditions than those destroyed in the more organised sectors.

We do not therefore expect to find a simple relationship between economic decline and women's employment position. The impact on employment levels will depend on changes in sector shares and on labour turnover rates, as well as on the nature of the jobs in which women are employed, and on the implementation of redundancy policies. Most importantly our discussion of the likely effects on the employment structure suggests that most of the statistical indices on women's employment are likely to be pulled in both directions; recessionary conditions will bring about the destruction of low-paid and insecure jobs but also create conditions favourable to the establishment of those types of jobs. These problems mean that a satisfactory analysis of the forces bringing about changes in women's employment position can only be achieved through case study analysis. This paper is mainly concerned with the consideration of available aggregate data on trends in women's employment but in interpreting these trends we will use our knowledge of the factors influencing women's employment at the level of the firm which we have acquired from extensive survey work of industries characterised by low-paid and usually female employment.[2]

3. Employment Levels and Employment Change

Bruegel demonstrated the cyclical vulnerability of women's employment in manufacturing industry by graphing the annual percentage changes in female employment and the annual percentage changes in male employment from 1950 to 1978. Women's employment both rose at a faster rate than men's in all upturns and fell at a significantly faster rate in all downturns. We have adopted a similar approach to study the nature of cyclical employment change for women by regressing the percentage change in female employment on the percentage change in total employment.[3] If the rate of change in female employment is more cyclically volatile than that for total employment then the beta coefficient should be significantly different from one and greater than one.

This method confirms Bruegel's findings of amplified cyclical employment changes for women in manufacturing[4] in the UK over the period 1960 to 1980, but the same analysis applied to other employment sectors in the UK (Table I) failed to reveal any other areas in which women's employment change was significantly different from men's.[5] Total female employment showed the same cyclical vulnerability as female manufacturing employment but this result probably reflects the influence of manufacturing.

Although we are here primarily concerned with the effect of recession on women in the UK, the proposition that women tend to occupy cyclically unstable positions in the labour market could be expected to have general applicability to advanced industrialised countries. Table II shows the results of applying a similar regression analysis to employment change by broad sector in the US, Belgium, Sweden, Japan and West Germany. Only two countries revealed any tendency for women's employment to be more cyclically volatile, the US[6] and Belgium, and although the changes in total female employment were significantly greater than those for total employment only the manufacturing and the finance sectors showed significant beta coefficients. Moreover the significant coefficients in finance are more likely to result from an increased rate of feminisation in the periods of rapid expansion than from vulnerability to job loss as employment in the finance sector rose consistently throughout the period.

These results provide only limited support for the view that women are affected more than proportionately by upswings and downswings in the economy; this behaviour is confined primarily to manufacturing and not common to all countries. However these results must be treated with caution. We have been attempting to discover if women are employed in the cyclically sensitive employment areas, but women are also employed

Table I

The relationship between percentage changes in female employment and total employment by broad sector in the UK, 1960–1980

equation: $\%f = \alpha + \beta \%t$

Sector	α	β	Standard error of estimate	Significance test: 5% level $H_0 : \beta = 1$, $H_1 : \beta \neq 1$
Transport and communication	1.90 (0.36)	1.460 (0.294)	1.4	
Manufacturing	-0.00 (0.21)	1.375 (0.091)	0.8	*
Finance etc.	0.46 (0.52)	1.071 (0.148)	1.1	
Community, social and personal services	0.56 (0.29)	1.069 (0.112)	0.7	
Agriculture	1.45 (1.59)	1.054 (0.374)	4.2	
Wholesale, retail trade and hotels	0.35 (0.11)	1.040 (0.056)	0.5	
Construction	2.29 (0.60)	0.810 (0.160)	2.6	
Mining	0.94 (1.46)	0.478 (0.269)	4.3	
Electricity, gas, water	2.71 (0.59)	0.364 (0.228)	2.6	* (–)
All Industries and Services	0.24 (0.12)	1.230 (0.093)	0.4	

Note: in Tables I–III, the figures in brackets are standard errors.

Table II

The relationship between percentage changes in female employment and total employment in manufacturing, finance and all industries in selected countries

equation: $\%f = \alpha + \beta \% t$

Country	Period	α	β	Standard error of estimate	Significance test: 5% level $H_0 : \beta_1 = 1, H_1 : \beta \neq 1$
Manufacturing					
Sweden	1970–78	0.62 (0.74)	1.447 (0.244)	2.1	
United Kingdom	1960–80	-0.00 (0.21)	1.375 (0.091)	0.8	*
Belgium	1960–78	0.03 (0.27)	1.353 (0.097)	1.1	*
United States	1971–78	0.99 (0.20)	1.350 (0.047)	0.5	*
Germany	1962–78	-0.09 (0.35)	1.291 (0.143)	1.4	
Japan	1960–78	-0.04 (0.68)	1.103 (0.197)	2.4	
Finance					
United States	1971–78	0.33 (0.66)	1.264 (0.123)	0.8	*
Belgium	1960–78	0.38 (0.70)	1.219 (0.037)	2.7	*
United Kingdom	1960–80	0.46 (0.52)	1.071 (0.148)	1.1	
Germany	1962–78	-0.42 (0.66)	1.066 (0.174)	2.0	
Sweden	1970–78	0.13 (1.11)	0.837 (0.228)	2.2	
Japan	1960–78	2.33 (0.94)	0.616 (0.154)	2.8	* (–)
All Industries and Services					
United States	1971–78	-0.02 (0.48)	1.362 (0.158)	0.5	*
Japan	1960–78	-0.53 (0.74)	1.294 (0.239)	1.3	
Belgium	1960–78	-0.19 (0.19)	1.256 (0.087)	0.4	*
United Kingdom	1960–80	0.24 (0.12)	1.230 (0.093)	0.4	*
Sweden	1970–78	-0.09 (0.28)	1.159 (0.112)	0.3	
Germany	1962–78	-0.03 (0.17)	1.041 (0.111)	0.6	

in relatively stable areas, for example clerical work. Moreover in employment sectors where women predominate they must necessarily form the
core labour force even if. they also provide the labour force for the variable
or secondary jobs. Our analysis is too aggregated to capture the effects of
women performing different functions within the industry's labour process;
our results show that it would be wrong to categorise all women as forming a secondary labour force, where in this context we define secondary to
mean vulnerable to employment loss. But equally we cannot deduce from
this analysis that women do not provide the secondary labour force in
those sectors which fail to show a vulnerability to cyclical factors for
total female employment.

The importance of occupational distribution in influencing the overall
cyclical sensitivity of women's employment can be implied from the
results of similar regressions for industry order levels for UK manufacturing (Table III). Five out of fourteen industry order levels have beta
coefficients that are significantly different from and greater than one; all
are industries where women form a substantial proportion of the main
manufacturing labour force but which could not be classified as female
dominated industries. Of the remaining nine—two, clothing and textiles—
are predominantly female industries and women will form both the core
and the secondary labour force.

In six of the industries women are probably mainly employed in
relatively stable occupations, in white collar jobs, or in ancillary manual
jobs. This occupational distribution is implied by high shares of non-
manual workers in total female employment and by low shares of female
manual workers in the total manual labour force.[7] Instrument engineering
is the exception to this pattern as it has a relatively high proportion of
women in the manual labour force (37 per cent) but a beta coefficient of
only one. Apart from this exception, it seems that although men are
employed in secondary type jobs in specific industries, in particular those
where women for historical, social or technological reasons have been
excluded, women usually provide the labour force for these types of jobs
wherever they have a substantial presence in the overall labour force.

The vulnerability of women to cyclical fluctuations in the 1970s must
be set against the continuing expansion in female employment over the
same time period. Although in manufacturing, women's employment
actually fell in both absolute and relative terms in the UK during the
1970s, it is probable that many of those displaced from manufacturing
found alternative employment in the expanding public and service sectors.
The very narrow range of earnings levels for the majority of female occupations, and the limited promotion opportunities and rewards for long
service or for specific skills for female employees mean that the financial
impact of job loss is relatively low, provided another job can be found.
Many women even in the period of job expansion were undoubtedly

Table III

The relationship between percentage changes in female employment and total employment in manufacturing industries in the UK, 1960–1980

equation: $\%f = \alpha + \beta \% t$

Industry	α		β		Standard error of estimate	Significance test: 5% level $H_0: \beta = 1, H_1: \beta \neq 1$
Electrical Engineering	-0.07	(0.41)	1.681	(0.138)	1.8	*
Food, drink, tobacco	0.02	(0.25)	1.385	(0.141)	1.0	*
Metal goods	-1.10	(0.31)	1.339	(0.103)	1.4	*
Other Manufacturing	-0.69	(0.33)	1.307	(0.095)	1.5	*
Paper, printing, publishing	-0.16	(0.22)	1.298	(0.096)	1.0	*
Vehicles	-0.22	(0.48)	1.276	(0.210)	1.8	
Chemicals and allied	-0.38	(0.35)	1.206	(0.169)	1.6	
Mechanical engineering	-0.15	(0.28)	1.173	(0.089)	1.2	
Timber and allied	0.02	(0.39)	1.051	(0.113)	1.7	
Clothing	0.24	(0.14)	1.032	(0.043)	0.5	
Instrument engineering	-0.33	(0.53)	1.000	(0.179)	2.3	
Textiles	-1.01	(0.32)	0.973	(0.068)	1.0	
Bricks, pottery and cement	-0.06	(0.64)	0.949	(0.206)	2.6	
Metal manufacture	-0.10	(0.46)	0.931	(0.106)	1.8	

Note: The list of industries excludes Coal and Petroleum, Leather and allied, and Shipbuilding, where the level of female employment does not warrant this analysis.

forced to withdraw from the labour market when laid off because of the limited *local* job opportunities but others could move relatively freely into other female employment areas. But in aggregate there are few sectors where employment opportunities are now expanding.

Table IV shows that non-public employment is falling rapidly and that although public expenditure cuts have not yet resulted in reductions in employment, employment levels have stabilised and there is no scope for absorbing the displaced women from the private sector. As a consequence the unemployment rate for women has risen 260 per cent since June 1975 compared to a 130 per cent increase for men (Table V). In March

Table IV
Changes in female employment in the UK, June 1971–March 1981
(thousands)

	June 1971–1975	June 1975–1978	March 1978–1981
All industries and services:			
Total	+748	+184	−435
full-time	− 46	+ 56	−343
part-time	+794	+128	− 92
Manufacturing:			
Total	−169	− 86	−376
full-time	−222	− 43	−265
part-time	+ 53	− 44	−111
Other industry and private services:			
Total	+427	+207	− 94
full-time	− 20	+ 69	− 91
part-time	+447	+140	− 3
Public services: [1]			
Total	+490	+ 63	+ 35
full-time	+196	+ 30	+ 13
part-time	+294	+ 32	+ 22

1. Public administration, health and education.

SOURCE: *Department of Employment Gazettes*

1981 the aggregate unemployment rate was still lower at 6.6 per cent, compared to 11.8 per cent for men, but excludes the ever increasing number of 'discouraged' women workers (CEPG 1981). Moreover the aggregate rate of job loss between March 1980 and March 1981 was approaching that of men's (−4.9 per cent compared to −5.7 per cent), a very sharp turnround from the almost consistent upward trend in women's employment since 1959 and the equally consistent and almost as steep

Table V

Participation, employment and unemployment in the UK, 1961–81

	June 1961–71	1971–75	1975–77	1977–79	1979–81[1]
Males					
Participation rates (annual percentage point change)	−0.5	−0.2	−0.4	−0.6	
Employment (annual rate of change)	−0.6	−0.3	−0.6	+0.1	−4.3
Unemployment[2] (average rate in period)	2.5	4.2	6.5	6.8	9.2
(end period rate)	4.4	5.1	6.8	6.2	11.8
Inflow to unemployment (annual average in period, as per cent of employment)	21.4[3]	20.2	20.0	17.4	19.4
Females					
Participation rates (annual percentage point change)	+0.5	+0.8	+0.8	−0.2	..
Employment (annual rate of change)	+0.8	+2.2	+0.4	+1.4	−3.7
Unemployment[2] (average rate in period)	1.1	1.3	3.0	3.8	4.8
(end period rate)	1.3	1.8	3.4	3.7	6.6
Inflow to unemployment (annual average in period, as per cent of employment)	12.1[3]	10.8	11.8	11.7	13.9

1. June 1979–March 1981.
2. Excluding school leavers.
3. 1967–1971 only.

SOURCE: Department of Employment Gazette
1951–71 Census of Population
1973–79 EEC Labour Force Survey.

downward trend in aggregate male employment since 1966. Actual falls in public employment are to be expected in the future, and the public expenditure cuts are likely to have most impact on traditional female employment areas such as nursery education and the school meal service. Private and business services have also reached the end of their expansionary period with the first proposed redundancies in banking,[8] the most secure and consistently expanding employment sector in the 1970s. Even the relatively stable clerical areas of employment are now under threat. Previously considered as an irreducible overhead, clerical work is now subject to the same threats of rationalisation through the introduction of new technology and cuts in customer services as manual labour. The impact of the recession is therefore felt not only by those in secondary-type employment but also by those in the more primary and stable sectors where changes in economic and technological conditions are undermining their security of employment.

4. Access to Employment

So far we have considered the impact of the recession on the cross section of women workers currently in employment. The maintenance of employment opportunities for women requires not only the right to remain in employment but also the right to ready access to employment after temporary withdrawals from the wage labour market. Women's more frequent withdrawals from the labour market are probably primarily for family reasons and not because of a weak orientation to work; these family reasons range from the obvious ones of leaving to raise children or because of husband's geographical mobility to withdrawals because of the absence of available work in a suitable locality or between suitable hours to meet family commitments. Withdrawals for this last reason may be wrongly interpreted as indicating only a secondary attachment to work; these women are not withdrawing because they are bored, or because they have sufficient 'pin money' but because of the absence of job opportunities.

Reductions in labour market flows have particularly severe effects on women's access to jobs: both those seeking to return to work, and those who have lost a job and are seeking to replace it with a very similar one, would face reduced employment opportunities. Economic recession reduces labour market flows by decreasing both the number of new jobs, and the number of vacancies to replace workers who have quit because firms use 'natural wastage' to reduce their labour force. Recession also encourages workers to stay in their current jobs because of the lack of alternative job opportunities and because of the greater security afforded by long service where redundancies are determined on a first in last out basis. All these factors tend to exclude those currently out of work from 'competing' for jobs in the labour market; those without recent work experience are always likely to be at a disadvantage when applying for jobs but none more so than when there are no vacancies for which to apply.

The tendency for the number of job openings to reduce in a recession has become much stronger in the second half of the 1970s. The engagement rate[9] for men remained at the relatively low level of around 20 per cent of employment from 1975 to 1978 and since then has declined steeply, to 13 per cent by 1980. There has been an even sharper and fairly continuous decline in the engagement rate for women since 1973. From an average level of around 45 per cent of employment in the 1960s and early '70s the rate had fallen to only 20 per cent by 1980. A similar pattern is found in the discharge rate, which declined to a new low level of around 21 per cent for men from 1976 to 1980, compared to previous discharge rates of between 23 and 25 per cent in downturns. For women the decline was again much more dramatic, falling to between 35 to 29 per cent in the 1976 to 1980 period, while in the prior 15 year period it was almost always well over 40 per cent (figure 1). Even in 1980 when notified redundancies reached record levels the male and female discharge rate was relatively very low at 22 per cent for men and 34 per cent for women. This fall in the rate has occurred because declines in voluntary quits have more than offset the rapid rise in involuntary discharges over the same period.

The increasingly involuntary nature of discharges amongst women can be implied by the rise in the number of women registering as unemployed relative to the total number of discharges. While the discharge rate for females in manufacturing fell from 44 per cent in 1968 to 33 per cent in 1980, the annual flow of women registering as unemployed rose from 12.5 to 14.4 per cent of the employed labour force. Over the same period the discharge rate for men in manufacturing also fell by over a fifth but the flow of unemployment registrants also fell from 21 to 20 per cent of the employed labour force. This slight evidence of convergence in male and female behaviour is probably explained by a reduction in voluntary quits for both groups; women who leave jobs are now less likely to be voluntarily withdrawing from the labour market and hence register as unemployed;[10] men who are dissatisfied with their current employment ensure that they have alternative employment before quitting their job and do not risk a spell on the unemployment register. This change in behaviour for men must have been quite strong because of the undoubted rise in involuntary quits over the same period.

The decrease in the discharge rate suggests that women cannot be categorised as inherently unstable workers as has been implied in some analyses of women's labour market position including some of the labour market segmentation literature (Doeringer and Piore, 1971). Women's turnover rates are clearly mainly attributable to either economic objectives or to withdrawal from the labour market for domestic reasons. When the economic advantages of job mobility decrease, and the economic consequences of temporary withdrawals increase, the turnover rate for women falls. In the process the ability of firms to lower employment levels through natural wastage is reduced, a perverse effect for those firms that employ women because they have a high turnover rate which eases the problem of employment adjustment. Data from *Social Trends* show that women

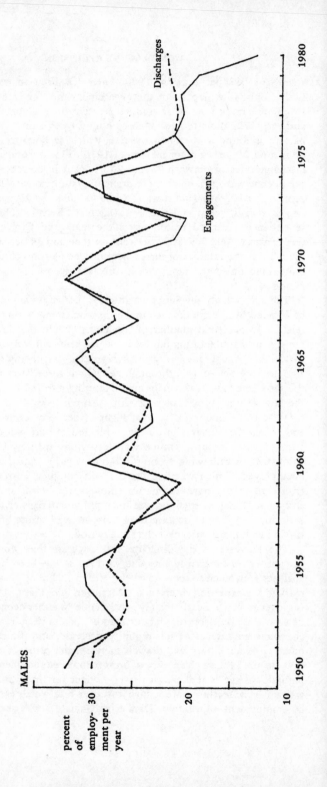

Figure 1. Turnover rates in manufacturing by sex, 1950–1980

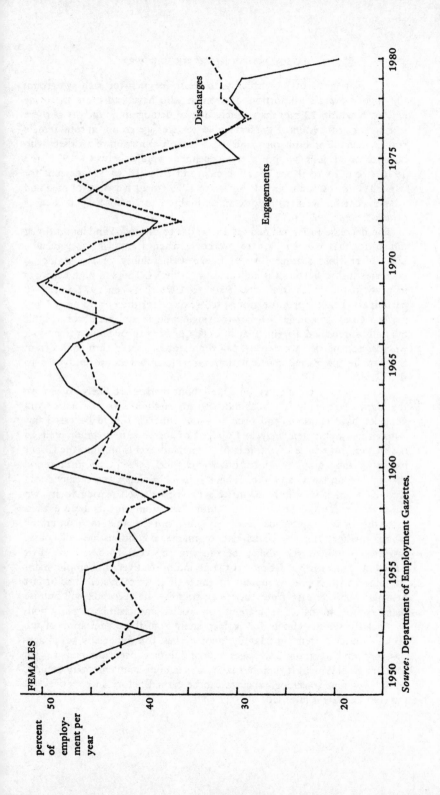

FEMALES

percent of employment per year

Discharges

Engagements

Source: Department of Employment Gazettes.

have similar levels of job mobility to those for men for each age group; the higher overall proportion of women who have had more than one employer within 12 months is solely due to demographic factors as there is a higher proportion of the less stable younger age groups in total female employment. For both men and women the proportion of workers who have changed jobs within a year declined rapidly between 1973 and 1976 (from 14 to 9 per cent for men and from 18 to 12 per cent for women) and rose only slightly again by 1979 (to 11 per cent for men and 13 per cent for women) despite an undoubted rise in forced job changes (*Social Trends* 1981, p. 78).

The decrease in labour market flows adds to the social and institutional difficulties that women have to overcome when attempting to return to work after child rearing. The particular vulnerability of this group to decreases in job openings is indicated by Table VI. This shows the changes in participation rates from the 1950s to 1979. Between 1977 and 1979 participation rates for most groups fell (except for men up to age 24 and single women up to age 24), but for single women and male workers this fall only intensified a trend that has been present throughout the period, whereas for married women the fall represented a sharp turn round from the rapidly increasing participation rates recorded consistently up to that date.

These barriers to re-entry into the labour market are likely to remove the right of individuals and families to make choices over whether and when to have children, and over how the children should be cared for. Women in employment may feel obliged to postpone or abandon plans to have children because of the fear of permanent exclusion from the labour market if they quit their jobs; others may feel forced into motherhood through redundancy and the difficulty in obtaining a replacement job. And all women may have to make a choice between rearing their own children or finding some other child care arrangements before their maternity leave expires because they may not be able to re-enter the labour market after that date. Labour market conditions have of course historically limited the ability of the working class to determine their social and family organisation but the period of relatively full employment combined with the development of the welfare state system had at last provided some release from these constraints. The recession will impose many other forms of constraint on social and family organisation; particularly serious effects for women stem from the organisation of the social security system on a family income basis. It is financially advantageous for women earning low wages or working on a part-time basis to give up their employment if their husbands are claiming supplementary benefit, as only £4 plus travelling expenses can be earned before an effective 100 per cent tax rate is imposed.

Table VI

Changes in activity rates in the post-war period by age, sex and marital status in the UK (percentage points per year)

	1951-61	1961-66	1966-71	1971-73	1973-75	1975-77	1977-79
Males							
aged 15–19/16–19[1]	−0.9	−0.8	−1.9	−1.3	−0.6	+1.0	+0.3
20–24	−0.3	+0.1	−0.5	−0.4	−0.1	0	+0.4
25–44	0	−0.1	−0.1	0	−0.1	0	−0.2
45–64	+0.3	−0.3	−0.1	0	−0.3	−0.6	−0.7
65+	−0.6	−0.3	−0.8	0	−2.0	−1.0	−1.6
Females							
Single, widowed, and divorced							
aged 15–19/16–19[1]	−0.8	−1.0	−1.1	−1.9	−0.8	+1.2	+0.3
20–24	−0.2	−0.5	−1.1	−1.5	−0.6	+0.5	+0.6
25–44	+0.4	−0.1	−0.8	−0.3	−0.3	−0.2	−0.2
45–59	+0.9	+0.5	+0.1	0	−0.1	−0.6	−0.5
60+	+0.1	+0.2	−0.4	−0.4	−0.6	−0.8	−1.0
Married							
aged 16–19	+0.3	+0.5	−0.4	+3.2	+2.0	+1.4	−2.0
20–24	+0.5	+0.4	+0.4	+2.8	+1.5	+2.4	−0.7
25–44	+0.8	+1.7	+0.9	+2.5	+1.8	+2.0	−0.2
45–59	+1.1	+2.7	+3.6	+2.5	+0.6	+1.1	−0.5
60+	+0.3	+1.0	+0.4	−0.2	−0.2	−0.5	−1.2

1. 16–19 after 1971.

SOURCE: *1951–71 Census of Population; 1973–79 EEC Labour force survey; Social Trends* (1981, p. 72).

5. Terms and Conditions of employment

The right to reasonable employment conditions should be as vigorously defended as the right to work. This is so not only to prevent exploitation but also to dispel the idea that a choice may have to be made between jobs and reasonable employment standards. This idea is found in neoclassical theory where employment opportunities are said to be traded against improved employment conditions, and is used by governments and firms to try to persuade workers that the only way to maintain employment is to accept lower wage levels and reductions in employment benefits. Accepting lower wage levels will not, however, increase the level of aggregate employment although the low paying firms may survive at the expense of higher paying firms elsewhere in the economy. It is not simply a question of whether women should be prevented from entering low paid employment through institutional measures to control and maintain minimum employment conditions, in order not to undermine the position of men in the labour market. Indeed it is more likely that low-paid female employment will be used as a substitute for higher paid female employment (for example homeworkers acting as substitutes for directly employed labour), and there would be no net increase even in women's job opportunities.

The main fallacy in neoclassical theory is that there is a market clearing wage which sets a uniform floor to wages, and factors such as legal minimum wages and trade-union organisation serve to raise wages above market price. There is however no evidence of a market determined floor to wages, particularly in a recession; minimum wages are maintained by expected standards of living and by institutional organisation of the labour market (Wilkinson, 1981; Humphries, 1977). Not all employment sectors are equally protected by these institutional arrangements, and women are particularly vulnerable to exceptionally low pay because of their position in the family structure which means that they are often seeking additions to family income, essential for the family's standard of living, but not related to their own consumption requirements, and because they are usually ineligible for social security benefits which only provide a floor for the main breadwinner's wage levels.

Women's supply conditions make them very vulnerable to low pay even in periods of high demand but even more so in periods of recession. Women are more likely to be employed in non-union firms where pay rises may be postponed or abandoned and as job opportunities diminish they may be forced to accept even lower paid and less secure employment, as for instance homeworkers or casual workers. However aggregate earnings data would not necessarily reveal an increased proportion of very low-paid women in a recession. This is partly because current earnings surveys fail to cover large areas of low-paid female employment (for example homeworkers and part-timers not in PAYE) but also because the recession can be expected to have destroyed a disproportionate share

Table VII

Dispersion of gross hourly earnings: Lowest decile as a percentage of the corresponding median (full-time aged 18 and over)

	Manual women	Non-manual women	All women
1970	74.2	62.3	68.0
1971	73.3	63.9	67.9
1972	71.6	62.7	66.6
1973	71.2	64.7	67.7
1974	71.7	65.3	68.7
1975	70.5	67.1	68.5
1976	71.1	64.7	67.1
1977	73.2	68.3	70.1
1978	74.2	69.1	70.5
1979	75.5	69.2	71.2
1980	74.2	68.2	69.6

SOURCE: *New Earnings Survey.*

Table VIII

Percentage of the firms inspected by the Wages Inspectorate paying arrears to workers

1967	1968	1969	1970	1971	1972	1973	1974	1975	1976	1977	1978	1979	1980
18.0	17.2	16.8	15.0	14.9	18.6	21.6	21.9	28.9	35.4	37.4	33.4	32.0	35.1

SOURCES: Winyard (1976)
Department of Employment Gazettes

of low-paid jobs, forcing many into unemployment. In fact the lowest decile of women's earnings, as recorded by the New Earnings Survey, has remained a relatively stable proportion of median earnings[11] over the time period but this would imply that a higher proportion of women have become vulnerable either to low pay or to unemployment over this period (Table VII).

Some direct evidence of an increase in vulnerability to low pay is found in the data on workers' earnings in industries covered by wages councils. The incidence of underpayment of wages council workers has increased dramatically through the 1970s: in 1967 only 18 per cent of establishments inspected were underpaying but by 1973 this proportion had risen to 22 per cent and leapt to 35 per cent in 1976 and has remained at this higher level (see Table VIII). This higher rate of underpayment is no doubt partly the result of the relative improvement in wages council rates during the late 1970s. However these improvements only re-established wages council rates at the same level relative to minimum rates set by voluntary collective agreements as existed in the early 1960s, that is at approximately 90 per cent of voluntary agreement minimum rates (Craig et al 1982). These data show the real problem of maintaining reasonable payment levels in periods of high unemployment in the non-trade union organised sectors.

Our own research into the role of legal minimum wages (Craig et al 1982) in determining pay suggests that wages council industries are not necessarily any more prone to paying low wages than other industries, and it is probable that the non-unionised firms outside the wages council sector will be paying even lower wages. Our evidence indicated that many firms if provided with legal minimum wage levels would observe these, but left to their own devices (or subject only to nationally agreed minimum wage rates with no system of enforcement at establishment level), they would pay only sufficient to attract and keep the labour they required. Under current labour market conditions the level of wages that would satisfy these criteria is even lower than when our survey was conducted between 1977 and 1979. The majority of workers who were underpaid in these sectors were women and there is little doubt that conditions of employment will have remained poor and in some cases deteriorated.

Wage levels are only one aspect of the conditions of employment the security of employment and the opportunity to adjust employment arrangements to fit with women's family commitments are two other aspects of great concern to women and which are often closely inter-related. There are three main types of working arrangements that allow women to undertake wage work at the same time as taking prime responsibility for childcare. These are part-time work, homework and casual work. Firms use these types of employment to serve relatively similar functions but these functions may vary from periods of economic upturn to economic decline. In the upturn the use of all these employment forms is partly explained by labour shortage; firms vary the employment contract to mobilise new sources of labour, and in these conditions the women employed can at least influence their hours of work if not their wage levels. In the downturn these employment forms are used primarily to match the quantity of labour purchased to production requirements, and to benefit from the lower wage levels at which women for these types of jobs are usually available. The initiative for organising this type of work is firmly in the hands of the employer in the recession and although the working arrangements may still be compatible with family commitments in some circumstances, in others the hours fixed for example for part-time work may be very inconvenient.

Because of the different purposes for which these employment forms are used it is difficult to predict the impact of the recession on their incidence. Where used to meet excess demand or to bolster labour supplies they will disappear with the downturn in demand. Where used to avoid fixed employment costs or to lower wages costs, the increased economic pressure and uncertainty will favour their use. Data on the extent of part-time working are compatible with our predictions of considerable job destruction and job creation in part-time work (Table IX). In manufacturing there has been a sharp fall in part-time work. Here part-time work was mainly concentrated in twilight shifts to meet excess demand and increase labour supplies. In services, private and public, part-time work has continued to increase in relative importance and even to show some absolute increases. In sectors such as retail, and catering, the increased share is undoubtedly due to a strategy to concentrate labour employed at periods of peak customer demand, and this means part-time employment.

The sector with the most dramatic rise in part-time employment is other business services, with a net increase of 40,000 jobs from 1978 to 1981 and an increased share from 62 to 87 per cent of total female employment. This rise probably implies a marked rise in the use of agency or casual workers for clerical and other administrative work. Use of casual workers is subject to the same conflicting trends as part-time work: catering contract work and contract cleaning have both expanded throughout the 1970s but catering contract employment, accounting for 55,000 workers in 1971, had fallen back to 66,000 by 1981 from 72,000 in 1978. This change is more likely to be the result of a cut in canteen facilities than a switch back to directly employed canteen services, and these trends can again be expected to be reversed if the cuts in public sector employment lead to further switches towards contract labour as has already happened in the Ministry of Defence. Contract cleaning was estimated to involve no less than 200,000 workers in 1980 (ACAS 1981).

Information on the use of outwork is not available at national level

Table IX

Part-time employment of females in the UK by sector, 1971 and 1981

| | June 1971 | | March 1981 | |
	Thous.	% of female employment in each sector	Thous.	% of female employment in each sector
All Industries and Services	2757	33.5	3587	41.1
Agriculture and index of production industries:	550	21.2	459	23.1
of which: manufacturing	471	20.1	370	21.6
Service industries	2207	39.2	3128	46.4
of which: Transport and Communication	45	17.6	55	20.2
Distribution	591	42.1	722	50.6
of which: retail trade	535	45.8	650	55.4
Insurance, banking etc.	124	25.3	236	36.4
of which: other business services	60	50.6	145	87.3
Professional and scientific services	834	43.0	1177	47.7
of which: education	519	52.7	676	55.6
medical	273	35.0	436	42.1
Miscellaneous services	483	46.8	779	59.3
of which: sport and betting	43	56.2	64	61.8
hotels, restaurants, pubs and clubs	209	54.5	352	72.1
Public administration	130	25.8	158	26.1

SOURCE: *Department of Employment Gazettes.*

but our own research group's survey of the economic, technological and work organisation factors that led firms to use outwork would predict a very variable impact on the use of outwork. Some of the homeworkers were employed in declining industries in firms that were in danger of going bankrupt if demand continued to decline but in others the low labour costs associated with homeworking was a factor enabling the firm to compete. Again in some cases homeworkers were being used as a buffer for periods of high demand and in these firms homework had already contracted, but in others they were performing essential parts of a production process and would continue to be used but provided with a smaller and probably more irregular volume of work (Rubery and Wilkinson 1980, 1981).

These types of employment contract clearly provide opportunities for women to obtain access to employment when constrained by family commitments. The danger is that these types of work will be used as a means for exploiting female labour; all provide a basis on which female labour can be differentiated from the main labour force to form a secondary employment sector. Our own survey of homeworkers and of catering contractors, together with case study evidence on the use of part-time workers show that most firms pay their workers on a different and inferior basis than the main labour force even when lower wage costs were not the prime reason for using this type of labour. For catering contractors, however, the ability to pay low wages and to differentiate catering workers from shop floor workers was the main basis on which they competed with directly run canteens (Craig et al 1980, mimeo). Our survey results showed that workers employed by catering contractors were likely to be lower paid than those directly employed in the private sector or in the highest paid public sector, and moreover over 25 per cent of contract workers included in our survey were paid less than other catering wages council minimum rates (see Table X). Similar or even worse pay conditions were found by ACAS in contract cleaning (ACAS 1981). In these circumstances the changes that are taking place in the public sector are most disturbing. This is the area where most progress has been made in establishing minimum employment standards for all types of workers,[12] but these conditions are now under threat, first because of increased use of contract labour and second by attempts to casualise directly employed labour. In Lincolnshire the county council was only prepared to continue the school meals service if school meals workers were employed only on a termly basis and forewent their paid school holidays (already only provided for at half pay). There is little prospect of improving protection for part-time workers in the private sector if standards in the public sector cannot be maintained.

Increased economic pressure on firms under the impact of declining and destabilised product markets is certain to have repercussions on

Table X
Minimum hourly rates for canteen workers
(pence per hour)

	(Number of observations	Mean	Lower quartile	Median	Upper quartile
Private sector	(357)	124	110	114	136
Public sector	(136)	127	118	125	152
Catering contractors	(144)	116	110	115	125

Minimum hourly rate June 1979: Licensed Residential Establishments Wages Council = 112 pence per hour.

SOURCE: DAE survey of minimum wages in industrial and staff canteens, June to August 1979 (Craig et al 1980, mimeo).

employment conditions unless these are defended through trade-union organisation and through institutional and legal protection of minimum standards. In a period when stronger controls and intervention are required because of the increased threat to these minimum standards the current government's policy is to reduce even those limited employment guarantees that are provided by the legal system. The rationale for this policy is of course that the recovery from recession requires reductions in real wage levels and in labour costs through a return to a competitive labour market. Already through the Employment Act the government has taken action to reduce the degree of institutional protection in the labour market. This action has been portrayed by the government as an attempt to curb the excessive power of trade unions; this view has been accepted by the press, and there has been little attention to the fact that the main effects of these measures will be felt by the lowest paid, least protected and usually non-union labour.

The change in employment legislation on unfair dismissal will have the most widespread impact on female workers. In firms with less than 20 workers, no claims for unfair dismissal can now be made until after two years of continuous employment. Women are the most likely to be affected both because they withdraw more often from the labour force, and because they dominate the small establishment service sectors. Women currently face very great difficulties in re-entering the labour market, but even if they succeed in finding employment they will often remain unprotected by legislation for two years. During this period they may be even more vulnerable to losing their jobs because firms will be able to hire and fire recent recruits without restrictions, and it could be that women could find themselves forming a permanent secondary labour force, never employed in a job for more than two years and therefore never provided with job protection.

The tightening of maternity leave provisions (and their abolition in small firms) also comes at a time when it is more important for women to maintain access to their current jobs as alternative job opportunities are not available.[13] This change in employment legislation clearly has a direct impact on women but other changes introduced in the Employment Act will have a more disguised but equally serious effect on women workers. Two measures are liable to increase the opportunities for non-union firms, and even unionised firms with pockets of non-union labour, to pay lower wages. The abolition of the schedule 11 clause in the Employment Protection Act means that for the first time since 1959 there is no procedure by which firms not actively involved in collective bargaining can be required to meet even minimum standards in pay and conditions unless they are engaged in work for the public sector. This schedule was in practice used primarily to increase wages to the 'going rate' or average rate in an area, and most claims were made on behalf of already unionised labour. It also, however, provided a basis on which national minimum terms and conditions could be imposed upon non-union firms. The government justified the abolition of the schedule on the grounds that the 'going rate' provision has been exploited in periods of incomes policies, but the removal of protection of minimum rates which had in fact previously been provided by the 1959 Terms and Conditions of Employment Act was less well publicised. The changes in legislation on secondary picketing and blacking of firms also restrict the ability of unions to control wages throughout an industry: for example in printing the unions have tried to restrict the growth of non-union printing establishments, not entirely successfully, by blacking any print work that comes from an 'unfair house' but this procedure is no longer considered a 'fair' union practice immune from breach of contract proceedings. It is women workers in print and in other industries who dominate non-union and low-paid employment areas and these changes in employment legislation provide further barriers to the establishment of effective protection in these secondary employment sectors.

6. Conclusions

Women face a double jeopardy in a shrinking labour market. They face the risk of becoming unemployed, or the risk of being used as cheap and disposable labour, outside even the minimum job protection provided by employment legislation and collective bargaining agreements. If women's employment levels are protected in the short term through an expansion of secondary-type employment the net effect in the long term will be to increase the insecurity of women's employment, and to pose a threat to the current level of regulation and protection afforded through institutional control of primary-type employment.

Once the long-term destabilising effects of the expansion of secondary employment are recognised, it becomes clear that far from withdrawing from the campaign to improve women's employment conditions for the sake of maintaining employment opportunities, the two campaigns must be pursued together. Women's right to work must also involve the right not to work for low wages and on a temporary and insecure basis. Probably the most difficult obstacle to overcome in combining these objectives is the tendency for a very high proportion of jobs which are organised to fit with family commitments to fall into the secondary-type employment sectors. This problem will be exacerbated if in sectors where part-time work has been established with primary employment conditions, for example in the public sector, there is a cut back in either the extent of part-time working or a move towards more casual employment conditions. If women requiring more flexible types of work are excluded by employers and by trade unions from primary employment sectors, then they will be forced into accepting casual employment outside with consequent destabilising effects for the employment system.

NOTES

1. See for example Amsden (1980, p. 11): 'It is written in the Bible that the value of a woman shall be assessed at three fifths the value of a man. . . whatever might have happened in the interim, women today still earn approximately 60 per cent of what men earn. No less invariant has been occupation segregation by sex.'

2. This survey work was carried out by the Labour Studies Group at the Department of Applied Economics (DAE) primarily for a research project investigating the effects of abolition of wages councils on pay and employment conditions, sponsored by the Department of Employment. The results of the surveys for three of the six industries considered have been published (Craig et al, 1980 DAE Research Papers 12., 15. and 18. and the overall analysis and conclusions of this project, relating not only to the effect of the abolition of minimum wage regulation but also to the nature of secondary type employment sectors and their implications for wage regulation in Britain are to be published shortly (Craig et al, 1982).

3. The specification of the relationship is:
   $$\% f = \alpha + \beta \% t$$
   where % f = annual percentage change in female employment
   and   % t = annual percentage change in total employment
   A constant share of female in total employment would appear as $\alpha = 0$, $\beta = 1$: a trend increase in the share of female employment would give rise to $\alpha > 0$ and a pro-cyclical variation in the share of female employment would give rise to $\beta > 1$. The data used for industrial economies are taken from OECD and cover wage and salary earners. Data for individual manufacturing industries in the UK are taken from national sources.

4. We obtained a similar result using shift-share analysis to standardise for changes in the structure of manufacturing industry over the period taking 1970 as the base year.

5. Electricity, gas, water indicate that women's employment is more stable than

men's, but women are primarily clerical workers.

6. The time period for the US is relatively short and is dominated by the major downturn in employment in 1974.

7. In 1970, for the six industries concerned, vehicles, chemicals, mechanical engineering, timber, bricks etc. and metal manufacture, the shares of non-manual employment in total female employment were 52 per cent, 48 per cent, 53 per cent, 38 per cent, 31 per cent, and 50 per cent respectively compared to the manufacturing average of 31 per cent; and the shares of female manual workers in total manual workers were 9 per cent, 24 per cent, 12 per cent, 14 per cent, 20 per cent, and 8 per cent compared to the manufacturing average of 28 per cent. Source: New Earnings Survey sample numbers 1970.

8. In 1981 the Midland Bank announced plans to make substantial cuts in head office staff that could not be achieved through natural wastage or redeployment.

9. The engagement rate and the discharge rate are calculated for four separate four-week periods each year, and are the number of engagements and discharges (and other losses) in the period as percentages of the number employed at the beginning of the period. The figures do not include persons engaged during the period who also left before the end of the period. The figures used in the graphs are estimates of annual rates based on the four periods.

10. Some of the increase in the propensity to register as unemployed is no doubt attributable to the phasing out of the option for married women not to pay full national insurance contributions after 1975. It is unlikely, however, that this change would explain all the increase (see Owen, 1976).

11. The lowest decile did rise relative to the median but this effect was probably less than would be expected under the spate of the flat rate income policies in the mid 1970s.

12. It is probable that in fact less progress has been made in providing reasonable employment conditions for female workers in the public sector than has been assumed. Difficulties experienced have been in negotiating bonus schemes for school meals workers because they are already working at such high levels of productivity even though only paid minimum wage rates. These high productivity levels are partly achieved through the non negotiated staffing ratios that local authorities use, and which also lead to changes in staff levels according to demand for school meals on a term by term basis.

13. It is also likely that firms will now be less flexible in applying the maternity leave provisions and any women wishing to return to work will have to be prepared to do so on a full-time basis with no re-arrangements of working conditions to fit their changed family circumstances.

REFERENCES

Advisory, Conciliation and Arbitration Service, 1981, *Report no. 20 The Contract Cleaning Industry.* HMSO, London.

Amsden, A. ed., 1980, *The Economics of Women and Work.* Penguin, London.

Beechey, V., 1978, 'Women and production' in Kuhn, A. and Wolpe, A.M. eds. *Feminism and Materialism.* Routledge and Keegan Paul, London.

Birch, D.L., 1979, The Job Generation Process: MIT Program on Neighbourhood and Regional Change. MIT mimeo. Cambridge, Mass.

Bruegel, I., 1979, 'Women as a reserve army of labour: a note on recent British experience'. *Feminist Review*, pp. 12–23.

Cambridge Economic Policy Group, 1981. *Cambridge Economic Policy Review: Economic Policies in the UK.* Gower, Farnborough, Hampshire.

Craig, C., Rubery, J., Tarling, R., Wilkinson, F.,
  1980, *Abolition and After: the Paper Box Wages Council*. Department of Employment Research Paper no. 12.
  1980, *Abolition and After: the Jute Wages Council*. Department of Employment Research Paper no. 15.
  1980, *Abolition and After: the Cutlery Wages Council*. Department of Employment Research Paper no. 18.
  1980, *Abolition and After: the Industrial and Staff Canteens Wages Council*. DAE, Cambridge, mimeo.
  1982, *Labour Market Structure, Industrial Organisation and Low Pay*. DAE Occasional Paper, Cambridge University Press, Cambridge, forthcoming.
Doeringer, P. and Piore, M., 1971, *Internal Labour Markets and Manpower Analysis*. D.C. Heath, Lexington, Mass.
Fothergill, S. and Gudgin, G., 1982, *Unequal Growth: Urban and Regional Employment Change in the UK*. Heinemann, London.
Gardiner, J., 1976, 'Women and unemployment', *Red Rag* No. 10.
Godley, W., 1977, 'Inflation in the United Kingdom' in Krause L.B. and Salant, W.S. ed. *Worldwide Inflation*. Brookings, Washington D.C.
Humphries, J., 1977, 'Class struggle and the persistence of the working-class family', *Cambridge Journal of Economics*, pp. 241-258.
Milkman, R., 1976, 'Women's work and economic crisis', *Review of Radical Political Economy*, pp. 73-97.
Organisation for Economic Cooperation and Development, 1976, 'The 1974-75 Recession and the Employment of Women' in Amsden, ed., 1980, op. cit.
Owen, S.J., 1976, *Women opted-out of National Insurance*, mimeo, Economic Advisers' Office, Department of Health and Social Security.
Rubery, J. and Wilkinson, F., 1980, Homeworking in ex-wages councils: report to the Department of Employment, DAE, Cambridge, mimeo.
Rubery, J. and Wilkinson, F., 1981, 'Outwork and segmented labour markets' in F. Wilkinson, ed., 1981, *The Dynamics of Labour Market Segmentation*. Academic Press, London.
Tarling, R. and Wilkinson, F., 1977, 'The Social Contract', *Cambridge Journal of Economics*, pp. 395-415.
Winyard, S., 1976, *Policing Low Wages*, Low Pay Pamphlet No. 4, Low Pay Unit, London.
Wilkinson, F., 1981, 'Preface' in F. Wilkinson, ed., 1981, *The Dynamics of Labour Market Segmentation*, Academic Press, London.

FEMINISM AND ECONOMISM

Sonja Ruehl

The actions of the Thatcher government have propelled the economy into such a position that to question the urgency of 'getting the economy right' is impossible; insisting that we should pay attention to gender divisions at the same time can seem like a diversionary heresy and yet this is what feminism must insist on. Thatcherite economic policy and the monetarist ideology that accompanies it has been revealed in left analyses as a thin disguise for a political attack on the power of the labour movement. Although these left analyses challenge the primacy of the 'purely economic' contingencies that right-wing Conservatism would like to present us with, it is a view likely to leave us thinking in terms only of an attack by capital on labour. There is no obvious space for feminist concerns even if the political will is there to include them. Somewhat paradoxically, the reinterpretation of monetarism as a political weapon directed at the unions has been accompanied by an intensification of the need felt on the left to articulate and fight for a coherent, specifically *economic* opposition. Partly, this is a political struggle over economic ideology, but the ways in which feminism can engage with that struggle are not immediately apparent. The struggle is concerned with an area, in particular the formation of economic policy, which is often construed as gender-free, or at least in which gender-specific concerns are not made explicit. One manifestation of this difficulty is the way in which gender divisions are sometimes construed as belonging to the realm of 'social policy'. 'Social policy' in this sense represents a wider social context for the core of oppositional economic policy but it is not essential to it. This clearly raises problems not only about the separation of feminist concerns but also about the conception of 'social policy' and its relation to the economy.

There is evidence on the left of a considerable will to involve feminism, but at the same time there is a perplexity as to what that would mean. There is a perceived separation of 'feminist' and 'socialist' analysis and struggles. Among feminists, there is also anxiety about the possible erosion of support for feminism on the left as the impact of the recession forces more women back into the family. The gains in employment opportunities of the 1960s and 1970s provided a material base for the upsurge of feminism, and these are now being lost.

These are the issues explored in this paper. It begins with a brief discussion of an earlier paper which discussed the problem of integrating socialist and feminist approaches. The second section points out that there is some evidence of a desire for this socialist-feminist integration amongst the British left. The final parts of the paper look at this issue of integration in more depth.

1. Sex and Class

Such an anxiety is expressed in the paper written by the Sex and Class Group for the Conference of Socialist Economists conference this year. The main body of the paper is concerned with looking, in the light of feminism, at specific areas of importance to the CSE in recent years. These include social security, domestic labour, the labour process, trades unions, incomes policy and the Alternative Economic Strategy. However, the introduction to the paper raises more general questions about the integration of feminist and socialist alternatives. It attempts to argue against the 'inclusion' of feminism in the form of the addition of questions of women's oppression which are simply tacked on to socialist alternatives and strategies that are not in themselves thought out in terms of gender. Indeed feminist concerns enter almost as an afterthought. In a way it is an argument that, before feminist concerns can be properly taken into account, a prior conversation needs to be had about what that project means and why it may be difficult.

The introduction to the CSE paper situates these anxieties in terms of a debate with economism. Starting with a note on the tendency for Marxist analysis to focus exclusively on exploitation within the wage relation, it acknowledges the challenges that have been made to such an emphasis. Lenin's argument for a political unity of all 'oppositional strata' is agreed to be 'one model at least for a socialist strategy based on an integration of exploitation and oppression'; but the Leninist model would still leave women's oppression defined as a separate area of struggle. Thus one way the threat of economism appears in the paper is as a 'tyranny of categories'. The boundaries between 'exploitation' and 'oppression' are drawn up in such a way that gender divisions are separated off, either in terms of being ideological rather than economic, or else as being located within the family. Implicitly, the construction of analytical categories is taken to be a constraint on working out an integration of socialist and feminist policy.

As a result, it is argued, policy becomes a subject area of 'economics' where categories are typically set up in such a way that gender divisions seem irrelevant to them. What is more, this is described as far from incidental. It is a reflection, or a reproduction, of the characteristics of capitalism itself. Capitalism creates distinctions between productive and unproductive labour, it separates the workplace from the home, and so on. Capitalism itself divides up the world into categories such as 'wage labour' or 'skilled labour' which seem to be neutral categories as far as gender is concerned. On the other hand, however, the paper argues that gender divisions really ought to be written into these categories, because they are not in fact neutral in gender terms, in the real world. Capitalism has not in fact created a proletariat which is just homogeneous 'wage labour'; it is divided by sex and race. 'Without losing sight of the ways in which capital tries to fit everything into value categories, we should resist the tendency merely to reproduce these categories in our own analysis of capitalism.' Behind this assertion is a worry that while feminism may challenge economics as a subject to take cognisance of gender, the very way its concepts are framed continually resists such a challenge.

The left's tendency to see the categories of economics as gender-free is, the paper argues, reinforced by the effects of radical right-wing policy. If the separation in analytic terms of an 'economic' sphere, in which gender divisions seem extraneous or irrelevant, is the reflection of a real tendency of capitalism to impose the law of value, then this tendency will only be intensified by a government whose policy is directed at clearing space for an extension of the unimpeded operation of market forces. Thatcherism has asserted the primacy of 'the economy' as a terrain with unquestionable imperatives all its own. Monetarist ideology has replaced a multiplicity of economic objectives with one single priority; that of the elimination of the single *bête noire* of inflation. Inevitably, this affects the terms on which socialist alternatives can be fought for. The desire to put forward a coherent core of economic policy alternatives to Thatcherism, which would challenge monetarism on its own ground, is understandable—but nevertheless worrying to feminists.

Partly, this worry is related to what is seen as a traditional economism in the British trade-union movement. If it is true that unions have been too narrow in the pursuit of straightforward economic interests in the past, it is even more obvious that recent government policy has served to narrow their focus even further. Unions have been forced into a defensive concentration on job security. Second, this is construed as worrying to feminists because, with high unemployment and falling output, economic decline will be seen as threatening the working class as a whole and there will be resistance to formulating economic policy to take account of divisions within it. Reinterpreting monetarism, not in terms of purely economic exigencies, but as a political attack on the power of organised labour makes it tempting to see organised labour as 'standing for' the working class as a whole without investigating further the divisions which differentiate the impact of the right-wing onslaught. In this way, the analysis of gender divisions and policy formulated around it can come to seem like a 'luxury'. Gender division within the working class implies the possible conflict of interests, which are not all reducible to those of a homogeneous proletariat.

Economism, then, is construed as a shadow hanging over feminism.

Analytically, because the present crisis fosters an emphasis on economic categories, grounded purely in production, and with no necessary content in terms of gender. Politically, because this separating-off of gender divisions is liable to make women's subordination into a subsidiary 'issue' and a postponable second stage of strategy. Women's subordination is possibly defined out of the 'economic' and into the 'social'; but in any case, feminist concerns are seen as a separable dimension that can be added on later.

The corollary of this is that looking outside economics towards 'feminism' for an analysis of gender divisions, as if this were an extra consideration that could somehow be imported, will not be good enough. Socialist objectives themselves may even have to be rethought in the light of feminism. Looking at the working class as divided by gender is argued to be important from the start, because a unity of class interests between men and women cannot simply be assumed. There may be conflicts of interest within the working class along gender lines, and these conflicts will not go away but will weaken working class unity if not acknowledged. Furthermore women, as a weaker section of the working class, may systematically lose out.

2. Gestures of Goodwill?

It is the intention of the present paper to take up some of the questions raised by the view outlined in the section above. It will not try to substantiate or disprove it as an accurate picture of the state of affairs on the left. However, it is worth pointing out that there *is* evidence of some intention to take feminism seriously, and although not consistent or pervasive enough, this interest is more than a negligible gesture. Feminism has attracted attention, both by its success as a political movement and because of changes in the economy. The increase in waged work for women has especially brought it to the attention of socialists. This increase has in some ways made gender divisions more visible. For instance, the difficulty for married women of negotiating paid work, housework and childcare has been much discussed in the press. Although married women entering the labour force might seem to lessen gender division, when compared with a situation where men are in full-time paid work and women are full-time housewives, the increased employment of women has instead focused attention on gender divisions. Furthermore, that attention has not just evaporated. The fact that women have come into the labour force in increasing numbers means that their subsequent disappearance is documented in studies of unemployment, for instance, and is more likely to be officially recorded. Women *are* discussed as a more vulnerable section of the working class in some analyses. 'Rethinking socialist objectives' is on the agenda—and not only in terms of feminism. Some critiques of the Alternative Economic Strategy point up a disillusionment with state intervention *per se*. Feminism appears as an argument for reconsidering the meaning of socialism in ways that connect directly with the conditions of people's lives and are not only thought about in terms of a mainstream political tradition. Some discussions both of unemployment and of the Alternative Economic Strategy have recognised the importance of groups 'marginal' to the labour force, including married women, and the increasing numbers dependent on state benefits. Addressing the need to involve those people, including women, who are not organised as wage labour is seen as part of the opposition to current policy. Thus in a somewhat fragmentary way, there are spaces in such discussions where feminism can be taken seriously.

3. Economism, Separate Spheres and the 'Social'

Nevertheless, the Sex and Class Group's perspective raises some interesting questions. Though it does not construct a well-defined target labelled 'economism', it addresses certain economistic tendencies. Gender is consigned to the realm of 'ideology' and is not part of the economic base, nor of the real struggle. Alternatively gender is consigned to the separate space of the family, leaving production to be analysed outside the system of production and reproduction. Or sometimes gender is subsumed under the apparent unity of the working class represented by the trade unions and struggles at the point of production. At the same time there is a sense in which the explanation offered in the introduction to the paper to explain the separation of questions of gender, is itself economistic. The analytic categories of economics are argued to be gender-neutral because the boundaries or distinctions between them 'reflect' or 'reproduce' the way capitalism divides up the world. That is, they are rather to be 'read off' from a logic of capitalism. Extending the sphere of operation of market forces is argued to exacerbate this tendency for the analysis of capitalism simply to 'reflect' divisions created by capitalism. Political analyses which, as it were demystify monetarist ideology as a class offensive are seen as easier to make than feminist political analyses. This is because political analysts are working within a framework based purely around production. This line of argument is then the basis of a certain pessimism about the possible impact of feminism in the current economic situation; and it is a pessimism which seems to have an inevitability about it.

However, much of the analysis in the main body of the CSE paper goes on to show, through looking at more specific instances, that the way capitalism has divided up the world is not really neutral as between men and women. The proletariat is not in fact homogeneous and wage workers are not a genderless 'given'. Divisions in the working class are described as being partly constructed through the operations of the state, for instance, through social security. This seems to undermine the earlier argument that analytic categories will simply 'reflect' genderless distinctions imposed by capitalism.

A more generous reading of the paper however would be that the group saw these tendencies as being in tension. It is clear from the paper that the operation of right-wing policy is by no means neutral in terms of gender; it works through a gendered working class, to some extent redefining or reconstructing gender divisions in the process, and is not gender-neutral in its effects. For instance, the removal of employment opportunities for women, together with the way social security rules are being changed or applied, has the effect of sending (especially married) women 'back into the family' and economic dependency, and out of the labour force altogether. The apparent neutrality of Thatcherism can be demystified in terms of gender as well as in terms of class. Whether or not that happens is a matter of politics and the political strength of feminism, not an inevitable outcome of capitalist logic. But while I would not accept all of the *explanation* in the Sex and Class Group's paper for the separation of gender and class questions, what they point to does seem to be true. The problem of feminism being 'added on' is a real one when it comes to policy and strategy. If gender divisions do emerge, they emerge as a separable dimension, 'women's issues'. They may be given space, but it is often hard to see how they fit into a general programme. Judith Hunt, for instance, in her recent discussion of feminism and the Alternative Economic Strategy, indicates a sense of unease on this score. Somewhat apologetically, she remarks that some of the points in her article may help to popularise the Alternative Economic Strategy among women, but 'may not be necessary to a mathematical economic recovery'. This unease points to the fact that we are just not used to thinking about 'economic recovery' in terms of its gender-specific implications. Yet many of the points Judith Hunt is discussing—saving jobs, creating new ones, raising wage-levels—are quite central to what 'economic recovery' means to us; only they are gender-specific jobs and wages. Somehow the consideration of gender divisions in terms of a package of 'women's issues' makes them difficult to integrate with a coherent core of economic policy; they are posed as policy options at a different level of specificity.

As the Sex and Class Group paper remarks tangentially, what the separation of a package of 'women's issues' is likely to result in, is to place them under the heading of 'social policy'. The way this is manifested in particular statements is actually quite complex. In the Labour Party NEC's policy statement to the 1981 conference, 'The Socialist Alternative', gender division at work does indeed appear as a problem of *'women* and work'. There is a mention of men assuming childcare responsibilities, but the consequences of this are not followed through in terms of hours of work; shorter hours are for 'study, longer holidays, earlier voluntary retirement'. At least the problem is mentioned as part of a programme for full employment, so that job access, training, flexible working hours and equal pay all appear under this heading. However, the more extended discussion of 'equality for women' with more specific proposals set out, appears under the title 'A New Social Strategy'. It covers training, recruitment, employment protection, maternity leave, equal pay, working hours and day care for the under fives. Most of these are, of course, economic questions rather than social ones in that they concern employment. The document itself links the effects of the economic recession with the social effects on women of the Tory cuts in public services; it carefully points out that 'a desire to improve the status of women and provide equal opportunities for both sexes must guide all our policies across the range of economic and social issues'. But the reporting of the pamphlet in the press amplifies the greater attention given to 'women' under the 'social strategy' heading. Thus The Guardian reports: 'As part of its social policy the document seeks to extend the laws on equality and to spend more on education. It suggests more training opportunities for women, improved maternity leave, a strengthened Equal Pay Act, more flexible working hours, and more creches.' What is remarkable about this is that an issue like equal pay (i.e. concerning women's wage levels) thus appears under a 'social' label even though pay is a squarely economic concern and one that has always been at the centre of labour movement activity. The construction that the Sex and Class Group puts on this facet of policy formation (though not arguing from this particular instance) is that it simply reflects a low priority for women's pay and jobs. Women's pay and jobs may be seen as improvable after economic recession has been overcome; but not as part of that process.

What it might also reflect is the idea that women's subordination can adequately be dealt with as a matter of adjusting 'inequality'. It may not be conceived of as structurally grounded in production. Feminists cannot doubt that better legislation on equal pay is necessary, possible and urgent. But it has been obvious that one of the major stumbling-blocks to equal pay under the present legislation has been the pervasiveness of job-segregation. Equal pay cannot be fought for only at the level of the law, but equal pay needs to be more radically tackled in terms of the work women do, how their skills are defined and so on. It is not just a matter of 'equal rights'. This is not of course to say that better equal pay laws together with a programme of positive discrimination at work might not be effective, or that the individualistic approach of the present law could not be changed.

Putting issues like women's pay and training into the realm of the 'social' and out of the realm of 'economic policy' does matter: it plays down the extent to which these are things that need to be fought for at work, by unions and others. Otherwise, it may seem as though the problems women encounter as workers are only imported from their status as housewives and mothers; as though the construction of gender takes place somewhere else, and never at work.

Although that is important, there are aspects to such a practice which are less sinister than seeing it just as a 'relegation' of matters affecting women's position. Part of the argument for insisting that gender divisions in the working class do matter, is that in many ways people *are* primarily defined as men and women and not as workers. Feminists have rightly insisted on the centrality of the family in structuring a relation to waged work for women which is different from that of men. The importance of the family, the prime target of 'social policy', for structuring women's position in and out of work is another reason for grouping women's issues under that heading. It is a reason less inimical to feminism, indeed it is concordant to an extent with the emphasis of much socialist feminist work. No doubt, to give too much emphasis to the direction of feminist analysis itself in reflecting on the apparent separation of economic questions and gender divisions, would be to assume too great a role for theory in constraining the formulation of policy. The constraints on policy formation are mostly a matter of politics and thus the political weight of feminism and feminist groups. But it might be worth making a brief remark about feminist explanations of women's work, in the context of that separation of economic questions and gender divisions.

4. Feminism in Theory

A central project of the recent wave of feminism has been the excavation of the apparently private areas of life, and the sphere of politics and the public has been brought into these previously strictly private areas. In the analysis of women's paid work, explanation has relied heavily on questioning the equation of all work with waged work under capitalism. This analysis has pointed out the importance of domestic labour and its division in creating the different relation of men and women to wage labour. Looking at why women are a form of cheap labour or at why married women seem to be used as a 'reserve army' of labour, explanations have invoked economic dependence in the family. This is carried over into the labour market to account for women's disadvantaged position. But while what is intended is to bring out the connections between home and work, a possible reading of such arguments is that they suggest a separate location of women's oppression—in the home. The features that characterise women's waged work—in particular, transience, low pay, unskilled status—receive a unitary explanation that originates elsewhere than in the workplace. It comes from women's general position in the family. This is also true of explanations of the particular nature of job segregation as a carry-over of women's 'traditional', i.e. domestic, tasks.

Other feminist work has looked at the way gender divisions are actively created in the workplace. The concern here is about a possible reading of gender divisions in waged work as being really a 'domestic' matter. It has focused on the construction of gender divisions in the labour process, through labour organisations. Work on the 'family wage' has emphasised it as a demand based on historical choices in the labour movement; work on job segregation has looked at the definition of skill and skill-levels as something not objectively given but the outcome of the struggles of workers with ideological assumptions about gender; work on the labour process has argued that 'women's work' when viewed from the workplace is less of a unitary phenomenon than it appears when viewed from the home, and so on. Sometimes, writers have explained the focus of their work by voicing explicitly their anxiety lest the left should construe feminist arguments as a license to consign improvements in women's position to 'changes in the family'.

But in addition to feminist analyses primarily concerned with the construction of gender within the home or else at the workplace, it is worth noting that a striking characteristic of much recent socialist feminist analysis is its emphasis on the interrelations—between work, the family and reproduction, the state—of the determinants of women's position. Although this is of course a strength, it gives rise to a sophisticated explanation of women's oppression of a rather tantalising complexity. Paradoxically, this complexity might actually reinforce a tendency to see gender divisions as an inseparable package of women's issues— although that is an argument one could not push far. But the complexity of analysis emphasises the links between different issues, so that to disaggregate them into different policy areas can seem inadequate, and does not do justice to the links.

5. Economic Equality: Social Policy and the Economy

This complexity is perhaps particularly apparent in feminist work in the area of social policy. In order to continue considering the hiving-off of gender divisions into an apparently separate 'social' sphere, the paper now turns to social policy and how this policy area relates to the problem of achieving greater economic equality for women. To argue that social production should itself be seen as a sphere where gender division is constructed and correspondingly that 'economic' policy should not be seen as gender-free, is not to say that social policy is an irrelevant area for integrating questions of gender division, or feminist demands with socialist ones. The place of social policy as a whole in a socialist programme is also something that needs to be discussed. It is an area where the interpretation of the economic and the social is equally important—and less contentious. The interpretation of social policy issues in relation to the economy —the importance of relating the social security system to the labour market, say—has been a concern of left analysis of social policy issues. The issues socialist feminists have raised in social policy have also emphasised their relation to the economy, especially perhaps in the case of social security and taxation. This is also an area where some restructuring is currently taking place, where there have been fairly widespread discussions of change, and which has come under an intense ideological focus recently. Social security especially represents that welfare state consensus is no longer subscribed to by the radical right.

There is little doubt that the 1980 Social Security Acts were meant to worsen the position of claimants relative to wage earners. These Acts untied the uprating of long-term benefits from the increase in average earnings and untied short-term benefits increases from the rate of inflation. This is either interpreted as an attack on working-class living standards as a whole, or as an attempt to divide the working class by increasing the distance between those in and out of work. Feminists to some extent want to add that the claimant/worker division partly masks a gender division since the majority of claimants are women. Thus in any conflict of interest over claimants' living standards between those in and out of work, the weight of feminist opinion would therefore presumably be behind prioritising benefit increases.

However, the benefits system does not on the whole deal in gender categories as such. The way women's and men's position in social security —and in the tax system—is differentiated is mostly by assumptions and rules about household structure and marriage. Most feminist analysis and campaigning around tax and benefits has been about challenging these assumptions and rules, in relation to the way they reinforce the problem of women's economic dependence on men. In fact, the major way in which the problem of getting economic equality for women has been posed within social policy has been in these terms—'equality' has been addressed as the removal of economic 'dependency' on men, bolstered by social security and tax.

I want to look at projected feminist solutions to the task of achieving economic equality for women and at the implications of construing this as a problem either soluble within social policy or else as one requiring more directly economic changes. The question of economic equality could be set up in social policy terms either as accomplishable by changes within the state's redistributive mechanisms themselves; or else social policies could be seen as only being effective insofar as they produce more directly economic change. A direct improvement in women's position as workers would be an example, necessitating changes in the division of labour at home. To set up the alternatives in this way, as legal/financial changes, versus changes centred on production, does not reflect a simple polarisation of feminist debate. In this area especially, feminist analyses are overwhelmingly aware of complexities and links between work, family and the state. But here two approaches are looked at which differ in their relative emphasis; this enables us to see whether the polarity between legal/financial changes on the one hand, and changes centred on production on the other, lead to any differences of analysis.

A main line of feminist argument has been, as noted above, one posed in terms of economic dependence on men. The pervasiveness of either full-time domestic work or else badly-paid often part-time waged work for women, it is argued, leads in the first place to such dependency, structured round the assumption that a man is 'the' breadwinner. This assumption that wife and husband are one economic unit headed by a male breadwinner, with a female dependent, is agreed to be in at least some ways reproduced or reinforced in the social security and tax systems. Such coherence as the social security and tax systems have in relation to gender, is argued to be the practice of aggregating the incomes or welfare 'needs' of wives and husbands and treating them as a single economic unit on that basis, in which the wife is assumed financially dependent on the husband. Although the systems are complex and have evolved in a fairly piecemeal and even haphazard way, to see 'aggregation' as the main principle through which women's dependency is structured, means that certain aspects of the systems which do not fit the 'dependency' paradigm can be seen as anomalies rather than evidence of contradictions in tax and benefits provisions. For the tax or benefit unit thus structured round the nuclear family, women's access to the unit's benefits or allowances is generally through the husband; though with exceptions such as Child Benefit. The feminist response to what's seen as a coherent policy of 'aggregation' has been to demand the 'disaggregation' of tax and benefit units, i.e. their individualisation. This is seen as removing state support from a family-system-with-dependent-wife. An argument of this type appears in 'Disaggregation Now!', an article in which Rights of Women and the Campaign for Legal and Financial Independence outline their objections to part of the DHSS report on supplementary benefits, 'Social Assistance'. The state system itself is seen as being able potentially to provide a measure of independence, and hence greater economic equality, for women through access to state benefits. Thus Rights of Women argues that 'genuine equality is inextricably linked to the provision of financial independence for women. . . the only route to such independence is through disaggregation—every adult being entitled to claim benefit in their own right'.

Contrary to this line, an argument has been put forward casting doubt on the efficacy of an approach to economic equality focused on dismantling 'dependency' and pitched at the level of legal and financial demands on the state (Bennett, Heys and Coward in *Politics and Power* I). First, it is suggested that economic inequality in social policy should not be seen as a homogeneous problem of economic dependence on men, which focuses attention entirely on women's family role. A more fragmented analysis is justified by the complexities of the tax and social

security systems which are thought to be contradictory rather than
homogeneous as they impinge on women. Demands for 'disaggregation' as
the main means of attack on women's economic inferiority, the authors
argue, assume too much coherence in state policy. The contradictory
effects which proposed changes therefore may have are indicated by the
fact that demands for 'disaggregating' or individualising tax and benefit
units have been made by a wide variety of groups, not all feminist, and some
forms of disaggregation have been quite compatible with a traditional role
for women in the nuclear family. The Conservative Women's Advisory
Group paper 'Women and Tax' is illustrative of a demand for independent
treatment of women together with a strengthening of the family. It is
because of the lack of coherence in the operation of social policies in this
area that 'disaggregation' it is suggested, is not an unambiguously feminist
demand.

Second, a challenge is posed to the concentration on the question of
redistribution through existing structures of public expenditure, implicit
in the demands of groups like Rights of Women. The state's redistributive
mechanisms are seen as a relatively superficial layer for addressing inequalities originating elsewhere, in the division of labour in waged work
and in the home. This is linked to the view that social security and tax
policies should be seen as contradictory in their effects; these measures
reflect the way economic inequality is structured through paid and
domestic work, rather than themselves constructing it and giving it
coherence. In the opinion of Bennett et al making demands that tax and
social security units should be disaggregated is asking for social policy
changes that are limited within the sphere of social policy in their effects.
They would not see these social policy changes as affecting the ways
economic inequality is constructed in the primary spheres of home and
work. They conclude: 'As socialist feminists we have been led to the
conclusion that it is not simply a matter of changing the structure of cash
benefits to create surface equality with men. Such tinkering ignores more
basic inequalities and forms of discrimination. We need to place discussion
about tax and social security within the wider debate about the relationship between waged work, domestic labour and child care, and link this to
the debate on the nature of social policy and its potential for producing
a fairer distribution of social resources.' Overall, the thrust of the article
is that it would be better to concentrate on more socialised, non-cash
provisions especially direct provision of childcare, since this would have a
straightforward effect on the major source of inequality in the division
of labour at home. Pressing for 'equality' within state cash provisions is
interpreted rather as thinking of equality as a matter of overt discrimination against women that can simply be removed by changing the principles
for allocating tax allowances or benefits.

I would agree with the argument that pressing for 'equality' within state provisions is in a way a dangerous game to play. The idea of 'equality' can be tossed around and attached to changes which are purely formal and don't touch equality in fact. This would be true of some of the proposals in 'Social Assistance' for the 'equal treatment' of husband and wife in claiming supplementary benefits, for instance. It is also the case that, as the article points out, trying to establish 'equality' at the level of legal principle almost inevitably cross-cuts other sorts of inequality of concern to us as socialists as well as feminists. Some proposals that have been made for the individual taxation of married women's investment income would exacerbate class bias, and so on.

Nevertheless, to situate 'disaggregation' as a demand that is entirely limited within the operation of social policy does not seem entirely right. The structure of tax and benefit units does not necessarily only concern demands about equality in redistribution by the state. The arrangement of allowances and benefits around 'dependency' for (married) women, insofar as that is a principle, does feed back on the labour market and so does affect the way inequality is structured through waged work. This will not necessarily be brought out in discussions of 'disaggregation' produced in response to particular government documents, or as campaigning demands, as the 'Disaggregation Now!' article for instance was produced. It is apparent in the brief discussion of social security in the CSE Sex and Class Group paper previously discussed, however.[1] This suggests that the operation of social security should be seen as a way in which the state constructs gender divisions in the working class by defining who needs to find work and who is allowed to rely on state benefits. Social security is in that perspective partly responsible for constructing the labour force and divisions within it. To argue in this way, that the state does create gender divisions in the working class and does it through supporting a family form with a wife normally dependent on a husband's wage, also connects with the labour market in that it's congruent with demands made by male workers for a 'family wage'.

Defining women as their husbands' dependents, in supplementary benefits for instance, not only denies them access to benefits in their own right, but there is a corresponding lack of obligation to sign on for waged work which means that, in the strict sense, they are defined out of the proletariat. This confirms a semi-proletarianised status for married women and contributes to their not really being counted into the labour force. A married woman's work status might depend on that of her husband in another way. Given women's predominantly low pay, a benefit for a dependent wife with a low level of 'disregard' of her earnings may result in her not finding it worthwhile to work if her husband is unemployed. There are several possible reasons for the fact that fewer wives are employed where husbands are out of work, and any explanation that smacks of 'voluntary unemployment' is rightly to be regarded with suspicion; but the operation of benefits rules may partly affect *who* is unemployed. In a minority of cases, married women's relation to the labour force may be defined through dependence on a husband's work status in this sense, as well as through assumed dependence on his wage. Disaggregation of benefit units would make married women's proletarian status more straightforward. Feminist demands for disaggregation do not necessarily work entirely within a conception of social policy as an area separate from the economy, and at an unambiguously more superficial level.

Taking a view of social security and tax which is more fragmented, as do Bennett, Heys and Coward, does have the advantage that it pays relatively more attention to the way women's inferior position in state redistributive provisions reflects their inferiority *as workers*. The contributory, National Insurance benefit scheme is analysed as a system of 'worker-based' benefits which to some extent reproduces women's inferior position as workers. This brings into question the emphasis that has been prevalent in the labour movement, on securing better contributory benefits for maintaining an income—and replacing earnings—when employment is interrupted. This emphasis on access to benefits through acquiring rights rather than through means-testing is an understandable priority. It is not so much that this strategy discriminates against women, as that it fails to deal adequately with providing a non-wage income for women; women tend disproportionately to have a work history of interrupted employment due to domestic work and they also fall disproportionately into low-paid categories. Earnings-related benefits in particular cannot be relied on to provide equally for women reproducing as they do an earnings hierarchy where women tend to be at the bottom. This problem is not limited to women; earnings-related supplements have not been much help to the unemployed as a whole as longer spells of unemployment have undercut the ability to meet contribution conditions. But the problem is exacerbated in the case of many women so that fewer have been able to claim Earnings Related Supplement and payments have been smaller in amount too.

In the present situation where Earnings Related Supplement has been abolished from 1982 and the system of National Insurance is being undermined by a massive reliance on supplementary benefits, a return to the status quo of contributory benefits with an element of replacement of an individual's normal earnings looks very tempting. But it should not be forgotten that contributory, worker-based benefits are problematic for women. If the long-term aim of socialist strategy is to get women into full-time waged work on the same terms as men, the same arguments in favour of contributory benefits would apply. Not only does that rely on the economy's being buoyant in general, however, but it also presumes a large scale change in the division of labour at home. This raises the question of what change in a socialist direction would be. It might also be seen as raising more awkward questions about full-time employment for everyone as a socialist objective and whether 'full employment' is simply an aim to be gradually extended to more women on the same terms or whether the incorporation of women into the labour force requires the objective itself to be rethought.

The view put forward by Bennett, Heys and Coward, however, not only casts doubt on the potential of contributory benefits for having much effect on economic inequality. The article points out a dilemma involved in relying on cash benefits at all. If 'worker-based' contributory benefits reproduce women's inferiority as workers, the alternative of non-contributory, non-means-tested benefits do at present confirm a full-time domestic 'caring' role for women. Child Benefit for instance falls into this category and the article suggests that although it gives women some financial independence, the benefit is allocated to women on the assumption that responsibility for childcare is theirs, and that it therefore reinforces this division of responsibility. Any higher allowance more related to the costs of childcare would be even more likely to tie women to the home and keep them out of the labour market, for instance if it took the form of a 'home responsibilities' payment. In any case, even if campaigns to give women greater access to benefits and to increase the level of child support were successful, this would still leave childcare as a private concern, and a woman's responsibility. Direct provision of childcare would be a more socialised form and would not tie women to a 'caring' role in the same way.

In a sense, this emphasis on privatised childcare as the crucial barrier to women's status as workers is borne out by the current interpretation of the 'availability test' which can be used to 'disqualify' unemployed workers from receiving their contributory benefits. Benefit officers are reported to be operating this test so as to assume on principle that women with young children are so restricted in the hours or locality of work they can offer that they have no reasonable chance of finding a job. The significance of this is that even when women have been working long enough to qualify for contributory benefits, their status as mothers can itself be used to override their rights as workers. A document which notes this interpretation of the 'availability test' (the results of which, it claims, cannot be quantified) is 'The Payment of Benefits to Unemployed People', a discussion document jointly sponsored by the Department of Employment and the DHSS. It goes on to consider whether, as in Northern Ireland, a woman with young children should be required to produce a declaration from a 'responsible adult' that they would child-mind if the claimant found a job; highlighting the reinforcement of privatised childcare even more. However, simply to argue that childcare should be socialised instead does not really answer the problem of how to reach a position where it is widely agreed that social policy should have that aim. An advantage of trying to break down the assumptions about women's child-care responsibilities and assumptions of dependence within the present benefits and tax systems is that at least it begins from our present position.

This is also true of attempts to improve the allocation of cash benefits in the means-tested sector, notably supplementary benefits. This is the sector of the cash benefits system where the assumption of women's economic dependency is at its most monolithic, notoriously assimilating the position of all women cohabiting with men to that of wives, under the 'cohabitation rule'. Bennett, Heys and Coward however point out that there are other intractable problems as well as 'dependency' in trying to build on cash provisions in the means-tested sector; a comparison is required of 'needs' of households of different compositions and of their costs of living, involving assumptions about the 'economies of scale' of living in households of varying size and age. A system of individually-based means-tested benefits—and individual taxation—would still have to address the question of 'needs' and 'costs' although there is no objective basis for assessing them. Attempts to derive 'equivalence scales' for this purpose have so far proved econometrically dubious. But in fact this is not only a problem internal to the tax/benefit system. It is involved in any comparison of living standards as such. Therefore, it is something that a society attempting to move towards socialism would have to consider, and to 'disaggregate' or individualise recipient benefits and tax units at least has the merit of making discussion of those comparisons explicit.

6. Conclusion

Feminist demands for disaggregation of tax and benefits units, taking women's economic dependency as their focus, argue that changes in the taxation and social security systems themselves can have some effect on women's economic inequality and can affect it in a coherent direction, basically by changing the supply conditions for female labour. Questioning the usefulness of those demands as a central means of combatting inequality brings into sharper relief the fact that economic inequality is partly constructed through women's position as workers: simply getting women into the labour force is not enough. Women's inferior position in the labour market may be reflected in an inferior position in benefits provision. Changing women's inferior labour market position could be seen as a problem of reflating the economy as a whole and of securing women's participation on the same terms as men; for example by direct provision of childcare facilities. On the other hand, it may also raise more awkward questions about the need to rethink full-time, full employment as an aim in order to make women's participation in the labour force possible. Whether they are posed in terms of 'dependency' or not, feminist demands for greater economic equality make it clear that we cannot think of social policy changes as neatly segregatable from the economy. Feminist concerns cannot be simply tacked on as an after-thought to socialist analysis.

NOTE

1.   See also Mary McIntosh (1981).

REFERENCES

Bennett, et al (1981) 'The Limits to "Legal and Financial Independence": A Socialist Feminist Perspective on Taxation and Social Security', *Politics and Power* no. 1. Routledge, Kegan Paul, London.

Conference of Socialist Economists Sex and Class Group, Plenary paper, 1981 Conference.

Department of Health & Social Security, 1978, *Social Assistance*.

Hunt, J. 'Women and the Alternative Economic Strategy', CPGB *Economic Bulletin* no. 8, Spring 1981.

Labour Party National Executive Committee 1981 *The Socialist Alternative*.

London Women's Campaign for Legal and Financial Independence and Rights of Women, 1979, 'Disaggregation Now! Another Battle for Women's Independence', *Feminist Review* no. 2.

McIntosh, M., 1981, 'Feminism and Social Policy', *Critical Social Policy* no. 1.

Rayner, Sir D., *The Payment of Benefits to Unemployed People*, March 1981, DE & DHSS.

DISCUSSION

Irene Bruegel

There are two particularly valuable points in Jill Rubery and Roger Tarling's paper that I would like to consider here. First, their examination of the thesis that women's labour is more 'disposable' in times of recession across a number of countries is to be warmly welcomed. By showing that the experience of British manufacturing industry cannot simply be generalised to western capitalism as a whole they warn us all of the dangers of trying to 'read off' a theory of capitalism's (or patriarchy's) utilisation of female labour from the experience in one instance and raise tantalizing questions for feminist analysis. Can we in fact talk of women and recession within the terms of some overarching theory of patriarchal capitalism or is it more a question of analysing the particular constellation of contradictory forces within patriarchal capitalism which obtain at any given place and time? Rubery and Tarling do tease out very well the conflicting forces which make up any aggregative picture, but I would like to know more of how they would explain the differences in the patterns of women's experience across different countries. In particular, how far strong unionisation amongst men appears to make women more vulnerable to recession and how far differences between countries relate to any differences in women's ability to resist.

Second, Rubery and Tarling argue, rightly, that the impact of recession on women goes far beyond a rapid rise in unemployment. The deterioration in the conditions of wage labour and indeed, domestic labour, is a price women are being made to bear for economic crisis.

I agree with their view that the struggle to improve women's wages and conditions of work remains as important as ever and that there is a real danger of that struggle being undermined by high unemployment, but I wonder how far the problem of 'selling' conditions for jobs is peculiar to women. Over the last year, as unemployment has risen, real wage levels have fallen for most groups of workers, unorganised and organised. Are there any grounds for expecting women to be especially vulnerable to accepting wage cuts and deteriorating conditions? Are they a soft underbelly in the monetarist offensive?

Rubery and Tarling suggest two reasons for a greater vulnerability to wage cuts amongst women. First, that they are less well unionised than men and, second, that there are no social security payments to form a floor to their wages. I think there are some problems with both these arguments.

95

Lower rates of unionisation certainly make for lower pay and lower wage rises in times of expansion, but in a period of recession (and union bashing) it is not clear how far lower (but rising) rates of unionisation are a particular handicap to women maintaining their wage levels. Two questions arise; how are union mark-ups affected by recession? How are union wage bargaining strategies affected? Is the emphasis back to the male wage as the family wage or more towards the 'rate for the job'? Is there, indeed a single answer?

The second reason I find more difficult. It is clear from the number of men who do work for wages below the supplementary benefit level that the rational calculus implied by Rubery and Tarling operates only imperfectly. Indeed, one can argue that women have a far more rational and instrumental approach to wage labour than men who, because of their socialisation into masculinity, are often prepared to accept a job at (almost) any price. If all the studies of participation rates are to be believed, married women provide a much more wage-elastic supply of labour power. They do operate with a very definite floor to the wages they accept. Since it is unthinkable for child care costs to be met by male earnings, women with young children will only work when such costs can be met. Moreover the social security system ensures that wives of men on benefit only work in those few instances where wages are sufficiently high to overcome the clawback effect. The cuts in public expenditure which have surely raised the time input required for domestic labour, have probably raised the minimum wage required by a married woman to enter wage labour, given that there is little evidence that men have increased their share of domestic work with recession. Thus, for married women, the response to declining wage offers is as likely to have been withdrawal from the labour market as much as the response by men has been to remain unemployed. Thus, there seems to be no *a priori* reason to expect women to accept declining wages more readily than men.

In a recent study Daniel found, indeed, that the reservation wage of the unemployed women was higher in proportion to their last wages than was the average reservation wage for men (which was actually lower than their last wages). Moreover, there was little difference between men and women in the acceptability of a job which involved a cut in pay compared to their last job.

Evidence from the New Earnings Survey is that while women's hourly earnings fell relative to men's between 1977 and 1979, they rose between 1979 and 1981, even after allowing for the effect of declining overtime hours on men's earnings. In the light of Rubery and Tarling's argument that wage data underestimate the impact of recession on wage levels because of a 'creaming' effect, it is interesting to note that, after 1979, women's hourly earnings rose relative to men's even in the NES matched sample, which includes only those in the labour force at both dates.

Thus on the evidence we have so far, it would appear that the recession in Britain has had as devastating effects on men's real wage levels as on women's. Nevertheless, men's hourly earnings remain much higher than women's.

While I think Rubery and Tarling do well to alert us to the possibility that women may be especially vulnerable to cuts in real income with recession, particularly when the only growth area of the economy seems to low-paid, poorly organised women's work, this, like women's greater vulnerability to job loss, does not seem to be an unambiguous process. Certainly, women will lose income *vis à vis* men as the recession deepens, because for many women the loss of paid work spells the loss of any independent income, but whether those *in work* will be subject to greater proportionate cuts in wages is a different question. I have suggested that, paradoxically, the reinforcement of the domestic division of labour in recession may have contributed to women's lesser vulnerability on this score while heightening their vulnerability to job loss.

REFERENCE

Daniel, W.W., *The Unemployment Flow*, Stage 1 Interim Report, Policy Studies Institute 1981.

DISCUSSION

Veronica Beechey

The papers by Jean Gardiner and Sheila Smith and Jill Rubery and Roger Tarling address important questions which socialists and feminists who are concerned about the position of women in the present crisis must consider. First, they are concerned with how women's employment is being affected by the recession. Second, with what strategies can be used to combat the effects of the recession on women, and to further the struggle for women's equality with men. In these brief comments I want first to address a conceptual question which is raised directly by Rubery and Tarling's paper concerning the analysis of women's employment in the recession. I shall then consider some of the problems of political strategy which Gardiner and Smith raise.

The major problem which Rubery and Tarling address is to what extent the recession has lessened women's employment opportunities. They argue that the effects of the recession on women's employment opportunities are more complex than a simple industrial reserve army thesis would suggest, that although women have been more vulnerable to cyclical fluctuations in manufacturing industry between 1971 and 1981, their employment opportunities continued to rise in state and private services, at least through the mid 1970s, and that there are now few sectors where employment opportunities for women are expanding.

Clearly declining employment opportunities constitute a severe problem for women. I think, however, that it is a mistake to constitute the decline in employment opportunities as the sole problem which women face in the recession. A second question which is in my view equally important is how the recession is affecting the organisation of the labour process, and what effects it is having on the constitution of women's jobs and men's jobs within particular forms of labour process. I do not think that an analysis in terms of the distinction between primary and secondary labour markets which Rubery and Tarling use gives a *purchase* on this second question. First, because it is far too general. The category of secondary workers in particular encompasses many different kinds of work—unskilled and semiskilled work in manufacturing industry, clerical work, and all kinds of service work in state and private industries. Second, because it ignores the structure of the labour process, and the ways in which the organisation of particular forms of labour process is being affected by the processes of restructuring in both the capitalist (manufacture and private services) and state (public services)

99

sectors of the economy.

An analysis of the restructuring of the labour process at this more specific level is essential for understanding the important question of the ways women's and men's jobs are being restructured in the recession. Rubery and Tarling explicitly state that they are not concerned with occupational segregation or access to higher paid jobs on the grounds that 'it is the expansion of job opportunities, the moderation of the impact of family commitments on access to wage employment (through for example the expansion of part-time work) and improved minimum terms and conditions of employment that have been of greatest importance to working-class women in the post war period'. It is of course an empirical question whether their assertion that these have been the most important issues for working-class women in the post-war period is correct, and I do not know of evidence which would either substantiate or refute it. However, what is clear from statistical evidence is that the increase in the level of women's employment in the twentieth century, and particularly in the period since the Second World War has not been accompanied by any significant breakdown in occupational segregation and that vertical segregation has actually increased between 1911 and 1971. There has also not been any overall improvement in the relative earnings of women workers (despite a small short-term improvement between 1970 and 1977, which has since begun to be eroded), as Gardiner and Smith point out. Thus the entry of more women into paid employment has not been accompanied by any lessening of inequalities between women and men in employment.

I am emphasising this point because I think that one implication to be drawn from Rubery and Tarling's paper is that reflation of the economy and the creation of more jobs would counter the effects of the recession on women's employment. While such a strategy might give women greater access to jobs, there are no grounds for believing, on the basis of post-war experience, that this would lessen the inequalities between women and men in employment. Furthermore, it does not follow from the fact that if more jobs exist that women will be recruited to them, because the existence of occupational segregation within the labour process means that women are drawn into employment in ways which are structured according to gender.

In order to further women's equality with men it is necessary to demand not only the right to work but the right to work in conditions which are compatible with women's continued domestic responsibilities, as Jean Gardiner and Sheila Smith point out. It is also necessary to develop strategies to deal with occupational segregation. Positive action programmes which endeavour to counter institutional discrimination against women in the education system and training programmes, and occupational segregation within the labour process, would seem to be particularly important in this respect.

Finally, it is essential to devise means for breaking the vicious cycle in which women are trapped, caught between low-paid work in the labour process and financial dependence upon men in the family. I am less optimistic than Gardiner and Smith about whether the Alternative Economic Strategy (AES) can be developed in such a way that it can encompass these demands and whether a left government committed to implementing an AES would take them seriously. I think that feminists have little choice, however, but to engage with the proponents of the AES and to try and persuade people to take feminist demands seriously. If Gardiner and Smith are right in their assessment of the problems women face in employment, and if I am correct in thinking that some of these problems (e.g. the length of the working day and the organisation of the working week, systems of payment and occupational segregation) are rooted in the very organisation of the labour process, then a strategy which is primarily concerned with conditions in the labour market will be limited in its effects. The tricky problem is that a strategy which is directed towards the organisation of the labour process quickly comes up against a whole lot of sacred cows, and must ultimately involve challenging not only capital's control over the labour process but also trade-union strategies which embody assumptions of the family wage. It is vitally important that socialists and feminists who are committed to women's equality with men take such questions seriously. Otherwise the sceptical feminist view that the AES has little to offer women will indeed be vindicated.

DISCUSSION

Economics—A Case of Men's Studies Modified?

Barbara MacLennan

Mr. Bagehot felt so strongly the inapplicability of the assumptions of the system to the greater part of the world, that he actually limited political economy to England at its present state of commercial development, and to the male sex in England. . .[1]

The general problem with the papers to be discussed today and the papers on the Alternative Economic Strategy due for discussion tomorrow is that none, but the three in this section, deal with women.[2] And so the complaint, made independently in the paper by Jean Gardiner and Sheila Smith and in that by Sonja Ruehl, that women's issues are just tacked on to policy statements ('tacked in' would be a more appropriate metaphor, if it were women's doing) is unfortunately justified even in the programme of the Socialist Economic Review Conference itself. Certainly no seamless web of social and economic understanding is to be obtained from the conference papers. The tacking is strained; the seam does not hold; and indeed the gap is all too visible. Is it men who are responsible for this?

It is not just the outcome of discriminatory research that ignores women[3]: men are not mentioned either; and the reason is that people are not mentioned. This is a grave shortcoming since though there may not be agreement on whether it is primarily democratic planning, democratic socialism, bourgeois democracy or social democracy that is to be the object of analysis and strategy it must surely be democracy of some sort. And democracy (*cracy:* rule, *demos:* of the people) has to do with people. Its neglect may be explained by the conception of the Alternative Economic Strategy as something devised by the big battalions, institutions like the Labour Party or the TUC and labelled as such by the Cambridge Economic Policy Group or even the London Group of the CSE, excluding analysis presented last year in this very conference. If it seems like Manchester chauvinism to claim that had this year's authors read the papers by Pat Devine on 'Principles of Democratic Planning' and by David Purdy on 'Government-Trade Union Relations', they would have gleaned some idea of what democratic planning could be[4] and discovered how ordinary people might get involved in the provision of vital services,[5] then so be it: on that basis, they might have advanced the analysis this year. The problem is how decision-making is to take place in reality. In the women's movement new forms of democratic process have arisen with

103

the abandonment, so disconcerting to outsiders, of those familiar forms of organisation that tend to concentrate power. Ways of nurturing democratic participation might have been suggested by consideration of the women's movement were there not a *cordon sanitaire* between the bulk of the papers and the ones in this special section.

If the Socialist Economic Review is to be taken seriously it cannot afford just to discard the papers that are produced each year and drift aimiably but aimlessly on to pastures new or back to pastures old—women this year: youth next year? If there is disagreement there must be engagement with the contested issues: if there is agreement then we can build on what has already been written. And why not regard this as a contribution to the further elaboration of the Alternative Economic Strategy? Why exclude our own work from the development of this strategy?

Recently the TUC held two special conferences: one in November 1980 on Positive Action and one in April 1981 on Shorter Working Hours. The resolution on positive action, as Jean Gardiner and Sheila Smith say, is all very fine but the consultative document *Unemployment and Working Time* produced in February 1981 for the conference later in the spring contained not a jot of recognition that even equal treatment for women, far less positive discrimination in their favour, was official TUC policy. Instead of being treated as the norm for the general working population women are set aside in a special category.

The issue of shorter working hours arises with particular force in relation to unemployment and this is conceived of as a general economic problem perhaps even more as a men's problem than a women's problem despite the evidence regarding female unemployment as presented by Jill Rubery and Roger Tarling and also by Veronica Beechey. The TUC document fails to engage directly with the problem of unemployment among women and, in the few references that it does make to working women, it simply takes the burden of their domestic responsibilities as given.[6] Whereas the duration of hours of work, including overtime, worked by male manual workers in low-paid jobs is recognised as deriving, not from choice but from their oppression at work, there is no recognition that the pattern of hours of paid employment worked by women stems from their oppression in the home and is no more a matter of choice for them. Despite the TUC's recording of agreements which reduce 'full-time' work to as little as 31-and-a-half hours per week (Times Newspapers) the objective of equal treatment for 'part-time' workers, who may work as many as 30 hours per week, is obfuscated in a single disingenuous sentence: 'Differences between full-time and part-time workers will tend to be reduced to provide a basis on which negotiating rights and conditions can be evened out.'[7] This formulation implies that the desired outcome will automatically follow rather than demanding a vigorous campaign:

1. To rectify the shameful neglect by the trade unions in the past of

those in part-time employment;

2. To promote part-time jobs, integrated with work in the home and in the community at large, for men and women alike; and

3. To achieve eventually a more balanced life for all.

Attitudes may be changing but the prospect of men in the British labour movement putting their hearts and minds into a campaign for the reduction of hours of (paid) work so that they can increase their hours of (unpaid) work in the home, though not to be written off, is nevertheless somewhat utopian. There is an analogue here with the striking tautology presented by Gardiner and Smith that if women's relative pay is to rise then men's relative pay must fall.[8] Though the economic prospects for effecting this without a fall in men's absolute income may not be great; and though the issue of control over family finances may be more intractable than the appearance of shared income in some households might indicate; and though inequalities of job opportunity constitute a formidable problem originating not in anything one might call the market but rather in the home and other institutions, so permeating through society at large; nevertheless, the immediacy of personal experience, dichotomised from general social attitudes, may make it more difficult to effect a redistribution of labour time in the home than to effect a redistribution of income, between men and women. The way to the former will most likely have to take in, en route, other preserves of male dominance—among them, the preserve of knowledge.

The personal is undoubtedly political but individual self-knowledge has to be extended to social knowledge in order to achieve that under-standing which is indispensable to sensible policy formation: knowledge is power—or potential power. There is too much mythology and too little data: too much focus on the short run and too little consideration of history or the long run. A striking example of the revolutionary impact of research is the long-run data analysis of Dr Catherine Hakim which laid a foundation, not just for changing the answers, but more for changing the questions about the social and economic process. In the place of questions regarding women's increasing participation in the labour force were substituted questions about the processes that had earlier led to women's exclusion from the labour force around the turn of the century and about the persistence of job segregation.[9] It is not just a matter of gathering more facts but also of perceiving that the process of collecting information may, in itself, act as a social catalyst within those privatised areas of life that are so difficult to influence directly by legislation or social and economic policy. The opportunity of establishing anything about women's lives was lost dismally in the last census. More needs to be known about the divison of labour in the home and how this varies internationally, between different regions, different occupational groups, different ethnic communities, within the context of different personal relations and (dare one suggest it?) between different classes. The census, to be completed in every household, can draw into public discourse, by judicious choice of questions, issues that are not normally talked about; it can make people self-conscious about their own practice; and can itself be a force for change. Ignorance of how other people currently live makes it difficult to recommend sensible policies by which they might gain that control over their own lives which is the objective of democrats.

This leads to consideration of other vehicles for change. Over the issue of shorter working hours, the TUC posed to member unions the question of whether there should be resort to legislation since this seemed to have been more successful in other countries than their own rugged reliance on collective bargaining. (Interestingly, the only previous breach of faith in collective bargaining noted by the TUC, refers to protective legislation relating particularly to women. Does this signify recognition that collective bargaining may be less effective for the weak than for the strong?)[10] But for women these processes themselves must be the object of reform. Some modest advances have recently been made with respect to women's representation on the General Council of the TUC and with respect to the status of resolutions from the Women's Conference of the Labour Party. Even though it does not conform to the best democratic practices of the women's movement, the campaign for increasing the number of women in parliament is to be supported despite taking the present bizarre form of the organisation that arranged a talking shop on a boat trip to Denmark in the summer of 1981. Campaigns for changes to give women voice on what they want for themselves within the unions, within political parties, within parliament and within quangos, such as the EOC and other public bodies, are needed alongside the campaigns for measures such as shorter working hours and equal job opportunities.

The variety of ways in which society can be changed is something that the multifarious activities of the women's movement has demonstrated, thus extending conceptions of political action. Small groups are involved in innumerable different ways endeavouring to transform relations of production and reproduction so as to establish democratic control over them:

1. Women's co-operatives;
2. Experiments in self-insemination;
3. Fictional portrayals of how women experience life as it is lived and how it might be lived with changed relations of production and the transformation of relations between the sexes.[11]

These are worth mentioning just to give an inkling of the scope of activities appertaining to this purpose.

In the transition to socialism, the fundamental issue is to decide *what* goods and services are to be produced in society and, perhaps even more importantly, *how* these are to be produced in the sense of what relations of production are to prevail in their provision. In intervening in the dynamic of capitalist development, the issue presents itself in the forms 'What is capitalism good at?' and 'In the provision of which goods and services would capitalist control have too high a social cost?'. Is it to be bingo-halls or libraries? Should fish and chips be provided by multinational food chains, by small-scale private enterprise on the corner, or in private kitchens where, within orthodox marital relations, there is exchange of service for subsistence? But more immediately such considerations would influence the assessment of proposals for either an increase in child benefit in the form of a cash payment or for the provision of nursery services by capitalist enterprises, by trade unions or by local community groups.

This raises the issue of the attitude of capital to women's liberation. Neither the particularly severe effects on women of the general economic policy of cutting public expenditure nor the effect of policy that appears to be directed specifically against women, such as the erosion of maternity rights in small firms, necessarily signify a coherent ruling-class strategy against women. They signify rather the priority of other objectives, just as the use of the concept of the family wage, on the side of organised labour, signified the prioritisation of wage increases for men. Of course, the forces of conservatism on the side of capital are particularly strong; but, as was demonstrated by the relative success of the campaign to maintain access to abortion, which drew on support from the medical profession as well as from the trade-union movement in a way that was not as coherent as to merit the description 'Broad Alliance', such forces need not prevail. Capitalism itself is sufficiently flexible to accommodate women's emancipation from, for example, marital economic dependence. The prospect of drawing more women into the labour force, so extending their proletarianisation while providing child-care facilities at the work place, is viewed with equanimity by 'progressive' capital.[12] There is scope for determining what will eventuate.

This issue of how goods and services are to be provided leads me to a note of dissent from Gardiner and Smith's proposal of parental leave for child care. Certainly it is better than proposing such provisions for women only. But increasing numbers of women are choosing to have children out of wedlock, free from the oppression of marriage. The proposal for parental leave would disadvantage such women as compared to couples and would reinforce the kind of family relationship which anyway shows an increasing tendency to break down, as people aspire to greater personal happiness and fulfilment. Instead, an entitlement to a year or two of child-care leave for all adults, to be taken as desired, would facilitate spreading the responsibility for the care of children beyond the bounds of biological or legitimated adoptive parenthood. Anyone who had not benefited by the age of, say, 55 would be allowed to take alternative leave for some other form of self-development and enjoyment. And if it seems inappropriate to regard child care in this light then that is a measure of the extent to which society has yet to be transformed.

For political economy in which women figure, the definition of economics used in orthodox economic theory will not do. To understand society and to transform it, the provision of goods and services within the home is as much a matter of concern as capitalist production of goods and services or the role of the state. Women's productive activity spans both what is conventionally defined as 'economic' and what is excluded as 'non-economic'; but the two are symbiotically related both in capitalist development and in the transition to socialism. To effect a total social transformation, the variety of campaigns sustained in the women's movement has much to suggest for the development of the Alternative Economic Strategy.

NOTES

1. Cliffe Leslie, *Essays in Political Economy*, 1888, p. 207.
2. In Michael Bleaney's 'The UK Economy—An Overview', there is a fleeting reference (p. 3) to the 'sharp increase in female unemployment'; while only in oral amplification of his paper 'The European Economies: An Overview' did John Palmer suggest, among a number of possibilities for transcending national boundaries, the development of a women's campaign on the lines of the movement for European Nuclear Disarmament.
3. For an account of the way that the occupations of women were excluded from the record of the census in the 19th century, see Dr Catherine Hakim's paper, 'Social Monitors: Population Censuses as Social Surveys', delivered to the British Association for the Advancement of Science, 1981. See also, *Social Trends*, 1974 and *Radical Statistics*, no. 20, February 1981.
4. See 'Principles of Democratic Planning' by Pat Devine, Manchester University, *Socialist Economic Review*, 1981. Cf. 'A "Right" Criticism of the AES', by David Lipsey, *Socialist Economic Review*, 1982, Merlin Press, who apparently did not read last year's papers.
5. See 'Government-Trade Unions Relations' by David Purdy, Manchester University, *Socialist Economic Review*, 1981, Merlin Press.
6. TUC Consultative Document, *Unemployment and Working Time*, February 1981, pp. 12, 20.
7. *Ibid.*, p. 12.
8. *Supra*, p. 32.
9. *Op. cit.*, p. 13.
10. The reprimand of the EOC which according to the TUC, took the wrong line on protective legislation, its very first subject of investigation, is effected in a self-congratulatory vein that would be more appropriate if the TUC had acted on its principles and done more to extend that protection to men. See Gardiner and Smith, p. 40, for their assessment of collective bargaining. Cf. *Hear This Brother* by Anna Coote and Peter Kellner, on collective bargaining and trade union support for the Equal Pay Act, p. 13.
11. Marge Piercy's *Woman on the Edge of Time*, 1976, and Charlotte Perkins Gilman's *Herland* (written in 1915, published 1979) are good examples of fiction about how life might be lived.
12. See CBI publication, *Working Time—Guidelines for Managers*, 1981, p. 12.

A 'RIGHT' CRITIQUE OF THE ALTERNATIVE ECONOMIC STRATEGY

David Lipsey

I begin with a sub-Wilsonian reminiscence. In 1975, I was political adviser to Anthony Crosland at the Department of the Environment. The Labour government was then facing up to the first bout of deflationary measures, following its profligate first year in office. I was horrified by the scale of cuts for which we were being asked—not that they were severe compared with what we have seen since—and I wrote a minute to Crosland arguing, on one side of a sheet of paper, that we should go over to the Alternative Economic Strategy. It arrived back on my desk next morning; across the top the magisterial hand had written: 'young Lipsey is evidently becoming frivolous'.

With hindsight, this seems to me a fair judgement. What worries me is that so many advocates of the Alternative Economic Strategy—and I accept that the New Cambridge school has been a prominent exception—have adopted a frivolous approach to it. They have exaggerated its capacity for good; under-estimated its capacity to make things worse; misused it; and, most culpably of all, failed adequately to refine the argument and tackle the fundamental difficulties. In consequence a Labour government which carries out such a strategy could unleash a new disillusion which would be permanently damaging to the Labour Party, the labour movement and the country. The term 'Alternative Economic Strategy' has lost precision. Used by some Labour spokesmen, it means little more than that they reject Mrs Thatcher's TINA: 'there is no alternative'. In a stronger version, as advanced by Michael Foot and (in a rather more left-wing form) by Denis Healey, it comprises a substantial reflation along conventional lines, with a mix of devaluation and import controls used to deal with the implications for the balance of payments. But this is still nothing like the kind of AES advocated, for example, by the CSE London Working Group,[1] which is presented as a transitional strategy to a fully socialised economic system. In part, the difference is rhetorical. The London Group surrounds—some would say, drowns—its reflationary recommendations in a sea of phrases about the 'collapse of capitalism', the 'demise of market forces' and the rest. If this makes its broadly reformist recommendation more acceptable to its target group, never mind.

But there is a real difference too. I think we should do well to distinguish two AESs, if you like 'AES Mark One' and 'AES Mark Two'. 'Mark One' is really a form of neo-Keynesian; 'Mark Two' is neo-socialist. The first of these, a reflationary, if you like reformist, strategy, is one to which on

109

balance I adhere. Certain problems which could arise with alternative economic strategies surely do not arise with this one. It seems to me highly unlikely to provoke the wrath of 'British capitalism', whatever that may be; indeed, given a couple years more monetarism, industry at least will be begging for it. The City of course, won't like it. But the main weapon they have in their hands is to sell sterling, thus depressing the exchange rate. If a Labour government does not panic before such blackmail, it is more likely to be helpful to the strategy than the reverse.

Import controls however are likely to be the main instrument in preventing the reflation from destroying the balance of payments. Unconstrained, half the impact of any conventional reflationary stimulus to the economy is likely to leak out into imports. So given the scale of reflation needed to get us back to anywhere near full employment, no devaluation which would not lead immediately to intolerable inflation is likely to enable us to do without import controls. But we would be less than honest if we claimed that there was any certainty that import controls would radically improve our economic performance.

The first problem is a technical one. Import controls, if they extend to raw materials or semi-manufactures, will require substantial changes to the factor mix in production—for example, substituting home-made energy sources for imported sources. These problems would be quite severe in the case of some industries where the production process, and not just ownership, is multinational—for example, the motor car industry. Of course, this damage could be averted by excluding semi-manufactures from controls, but only at the risk of increasing evasion.

One possible way of tackling this difficulty would be to institute a kind of 'import controls through the market' by creating a shadow foreign exchange market. The foreign currency value of our exports could be estimated; that sum (and no more) made available in foreign currency by the authorities for purchasing imports; and the price of foreign exchange would then rise to choke off any excess imports. Such a scheme would at least merit detailed examination.

The second problem is that of international retaliation. Now, it is possible to show—as Godley and Cripps have shown—that in a purely economic sense, retaliation would be an irrational response on the part of other nations. The argument goes: reflation will increase our national wealth. Though the *proportion* of it going on imports will diminish, *total* imports will increase because our GDP will increase. But which of us feels confident that we shall persuade President Reagan—or for that matter, Helmut Schmidt—of that fact? The problem is made more difficult by the fact that those countries with whom we run a big manufacturing deficit—not as is commonly believed Japan, or the rapidly developing countries, but those of Western Europe—are precisely those where the geopolitical consequences of widespread protectionism will be perceived as most deleterious. This need not be an insuperable problem. We may know better when we have had a chance to observe how the Mitterand government copes with the pressures that will arise from its policies. The labour movement could make it easier for itself if it conducted itself between now and the next election as if it had an understanding and a concern for our present allies, and a genuine commitment to the internationalism of the Socialist International.

The third, and to my mind the most serious issue posed by 'Mark One AES', is inflation. Directly, import controls will reduce competition at home, and thus lead to some increase in prices. Indirectly, the whole policy will, we hope, bring down unemployment very rapidly. This will restore the hideously damaged organisational strength of the unions, and could lead to a burst of wage-induced inflation. I will say something more about this when I discuss the second form of alternative economic strategy below. But it is clear to me whether you study the speeches of Michael Foot, or of Denis Healey or of Peter Shore, or the documents that have gone to the Labour Party-TUC Liaison Committee, that they recognise, even if they cannot yet spell out, the need for an incomes policy. I only hope that the movement will allow them to work out the details in time. The debacle of the 1974 'social contract', 35 per cent inflation, and the rest cast a shadow over the whole term of office of the last Labour government, without doing anything whatsoever for the living standards of ordinary working people.

Even with such an agreement on incomes, I do think it important not to overestimate what 'AES Mark One' might achieve. It would be unwise for the Labour Party to go into the next election promising an economic miracle. There should be a substantial one-off benefit from the 'AES Mark One'. At the moment, the economy is clearly operating at far below its present potential capacity. A reflationary strategy should enable the economy to operate at substantially nearer that capacity, and we should have substantially less unemployment and substantially more wealth than we now do.

I used to believe that we could expect a further effect. As demand grew, I used to think, so too the underlying rate of productivity would grow. The promise of steadily increasing demand would lead to higher productive manufacturing investment. The knowledge that employment was reasonably full would enable negotiation once more to take place on productivity; unions who embarked on such measures could do so confident in the knowledge that their members would have other jobs to go to. I hope this is still the case. I fear, however, that defensive mechanisms are now very much more developed on the labour side; and I fear also that management is quite capable of reacting to reduced foreign competition and easier home markets by going back to sleep. Those elements in the programme of a future Labour government which could increase productivity are a massive programme of training and retraining. These by their nature are slow acting.

My optimistic assessment of 'AES Mark One' is that our GDP would rise quite substantially. Unemployment would fall; productivity would resume an upward trend, though a slow one, and, thanks to an effective agreement on prices and incomes, inflation would be roughly what it is now. The increase in national wealth could be substantial, but it would be one-off. The AES would not, of itself, increase the ceiling of our productive capacity; it would merely enable us to run out economy at a level closer to that capacity. Pessimists, however, are entitled to argue that the international response to our controls on the foreign balance would cause serious economic dislocation, including perhaps, some areas of physical shortages of raw materials; that the limits of our economic capacity will turn out to be lower than we hope; and that import controls will permit a wage-induced inflation to get a hold which it then becomes very hard to break. Being by nature an optimist, I would be inclined to give it a go, if only because, should it fail, the choice could lie between another prolonged experiment with monetarism—this time, *with* water cannon; or of moving to a highly controlled economy, also with water cannon; or attempting a Friends of the Earth 'solution' with more poverty all round.

There is a problem for a 'right' analyst in moving to the next stage, the examination of 'AES Mark Two'. It is a problem of language. If one chooses to conduct the argument in conventional 'bourgeois' terms, then one stands at risk of being accused of missing the point. But to conduct the argument in its chosen terms, may mean conceding points that one does not want to concede. For example, I now find it hard to give any substantive meaning whatsoever to the term 'capitalist'. How then do I debate with those to whom the supposedly 'capitalist character' of our economy is its essential feature?

This is particularly hard since 'AES Mark Two' is Janus-faced. To the present Labour Party, it presents itself as a strategy for transition to socialism. Critics can therefore legitimately question whether it adequately assesses the opposing social forces which would be brought into play in the quest for such a transition; and many conclude that it does not. But it does not partly because it has much in common with 'AES Mark One'; that is to say, it is essentially reformist, trying to make what we have work a good deal better, and founded round the non-Marxist concept of mediating conflict rather than the Marxist one of forcing it to a head out of which a new synthesis will spring.

So, to which Janus should one address oneself? Should one return to past battlefields in political philosophy? Should one take the AES for what its rhetoric sometimes suggests it is, a proposal for the transition to a society where the social conflict endemic to 'capitalism' has ceased? Or should one confine oneself to those propositions within statements of the

AES which purport to be economic and empirically testable and discuss them?

Let me stick with the empirical. The first thing that strikes me is that the proponents of the AES have wholly failed to say how they intend to integrate their belief in national planning, with their commitment to workers' control at the shop floor or plant level. The London Group say: 'In the development of planning suggested [sic] by the AES, the involvement of workers at the point of production, and of workers and their families in localities, would enable planning to be democratised from the outset.'[2] Earlier the London Group had recommended a National Planning Commission. Would someone explain how this Commission, working in London or perhaps Glasgow is going to be 'democratised' by the involvement of workers at the point of production? Either the Commission will tell the workers what to produce, in which case they are not behaving democratically. Or the workers will tell them what they will produce, in which case there is precious little planning.

The omission of this crucial link in the argument is all the more curious since it has been a central feature of all arguments about Eastern European economies. Experience suggests that such economies can evolve in one of two ways. They can be based on 'top down' planning, with more local bodies acting as subordinate institutions to aid the fulfilment of the plan. The trade unions also become part of this apparatus of planning and control. Or they can attempt more of a 'bottom up' approach, as in Yugoslavia, in which central institutions play a broadly indicative and predictive role. Since it is logically impossible in such a system *both* to allow local units to determine what they produce *and* to lay down national plans for the detailed use of resources, the market plays a much bigger part in such a system. We could conduct an interesting debate on the merits of these two approaches. What does not make for interesting debate is to proceed as if you could adopt both at once.

The trouble is that AES economists really have not settled what their critique of the market actually is. It is, say the London Group, 'an instrument of class power'; we need to change from 'production for profit towards production for social need'. This sort of rhetoric leaves open more problems than it answers. If we are against production for profit, where is surplus to be generated for social and other investment? If we are to produce for 'social need', who is to define this? Can we be sure that it will produce a fairer outcome than the market? Will not inequalities of political power to command resources prove worse in practice than the inequalities produced by the market which gives greater weight to the desires of those with most income and wealth? You do not make something democratic merely by saying it is democratic. Until these questions are answered —if they can be—the AES will be accused of being a strategy for a *dacha* society.

The other major sin of omission on the part of the AES is any considered approach to inflation. If the strategy is designed to be transitional, and not merely a way of heightening 'contradictions', it will have to produce an answer to the problem of inflation. In fact, it is remarkably thin on the subject. Sometimes it falls for the temptation implicit in the rhetoric of assuming that any increase in money wages can be accommodated from profit. In fact, according to the latest CSO figures, gross trading profits in the first quarter of 1981 amounted to £6026 million out of a GNP at factor cost of £51,445 million. If it were possible to transfer the whole surplus to real wages and salaries, net of tax, they would rise by about ten per cent—scarcely more than they did in the last eighteen months of the last Labour government.

An attempt has been made to avoid this dilemma by arguing that Britain has a large sector comprising multinational companies. These multi-nationals, it is argued, syphon off large sums of profit abroad, and there-fore, if they are nationalised a much larger profit pool would be made available for popular use. That there is a problem of the control of multi-national companies, I have no doubt; but I do doubt if it is sufficient to bear the weight alternative economic strategists place upon it. First, why should multinationals seek to get their profits out of the UK? It is fre-quently argued on the left that British taxes are unduly generous to the multinationals. 'AES Mark One' reflationary policies (for example, Blake and Ormerod, *The Economics of Prosperity*)[3] rely on considerably higher revenues from tougher company taxation. But if our tax system is generous, then, *ceteris paribus*, firms will want to show their profits here.

Second, where the government has become deeply involved in industries, either by nationalising them or supporting them in other ways, they have never found a deep pool of profits waiting to be tapped. Indeed, it is highly implausible that they should; firms which are highly profitable want the government to step in like they want a hole in the head. Third, one only has to read company reports the world over to realise that the multinationals are not the prosperous and powerful institutions they appeared a decade ago. The reason is simple. To become highly profitable, they had to play the trick of producing cheaply in countries with low wage rates to sell dearly in countries with buoyant markets due to high wage rates. And over the decade, there have been few such easy markets.

If the AES is to have a chance of working, therefore, it must be much more forthright and honest about what this will require in terms of the planning of money incomes. This will be made easier by the fact that in the economy which the next Labour government inherits, there ought to be some scope for increasing real incomes, though the priority objectives of a socialist government should surely be to restore public spending and to increase investment. If these intellectual problems of the AES are resolved, I do not think we need to be too worried by political fears for the AES. For example, fears of military intervention have been expressed. Now it is possible that the next Labour government will run into problems with the military. If, for example, we ask them simultaneously to accept defeat in Northern Ireland, a ditching of Trident, a slashing of defence expenditure and a precipitous charge down roads that lead out of NATO, I dare say there will be more than mumbling in the barracks. But I do not think that most military men would recognise an AES if it hit them on the nose.

Where the AES could run into political problems is if after the next election, Labour looked to be undertaking what one might describe as a democratic coup. Let us suppose that at the next general election, the Tories are reduced to perhaps 27 per cent of the vote; the Liberal/Social Democratic Alliance gets 32 and Labour 35. The workings of our electoral system are such that that would give Labour an overall majority. Suppose also that it was clear from poll and other evidence that we had won this majority on the backs of Tory unpopularity (as indeed a high Social Democratic/Liberal vote would suggest). Suppose that soon after the election, our electoral college decided to substitute a more left-wing leader for Michael Foot. In that case, an insubstantial mandate and an unenthusiastic country, it would be wholly unrealistic to believe 'AES Mark Two' could be implemented. Those who criticise the performance in office of past Labour governments are frequently insensitive to the constraints that will apply to future Labour governments. 1945 gave birth to a successful Labour government because there was a genuine popular enthusiasm for much that it was trying to do. For this popular enthusiasm, the committed support of a few hundred thousand labour and trade union activists will be no substitute. Most existing statements of the AES we have seen so far might be designed to prevent any such enthusiasm from developing. They are couched in an inpenetrable sub-Marxist jargon; and they appear at one and the same time to lack precision *and* vision. They lack a reference point in ordinary people's experience.

Of course, people are desperately concerned to see a return to full employment. But they want something else too. They want to know how socialists intend to give them back a sense of control over their own lives. They want to know what the values are that will inform a socialist society. They find no answer to these questions in slogans about capitalism, nor comfort in National Planning Commissions. And although they are demo-crats, the thing they want least of all is a society where they pass their weeks in works committee meetings, and their weekends in draughty church halls considering the policy papers prepared for cabinet by the National Executive Committee of the Labour Party.

The present economic crisis could open up enormous opportunities for socialists. I have a horrid feeling that we are going once more to pass them up by talking to each other in language that we understand, instead of talking to those whom we need to convince in language that has resonances for them. And as Bertold Brecht wrote with savage irony of the East German regime in June 1953, it is not open to us to elect a new people because the existing one has failed to come up to our expectations. Even Labour Party conference cannot reselect its voters.

NOTES

1.   CSE London Group, 1950, *The Alternative Economic Strategy*, CSE Books/ Labour Coordinating Committee, London.
2.   *Ibid.*, p. 85.
3.   Blake, D. and Ormerod, P. (eds.), 1980, *The Economics of Prosperity*, Grant McIntyre, London.

A 'LEFT' CRITIQUE OF THE ALTERNATIVE ECONOMIC STRATEGY

John Harrison

What Critique of What?

No single, authorised version of the AES exists. The London CSE group accurately described the Strategy at the time of writing their book as 'a field of debate, a consensus on the basic components and structure of economic strategy within which there is an urgent need to develop and debate more detailed policies' (LCSE, *The Alternative Economic Strategy,* 1980, preface). That is still a fair description. Much debate has since occurred, but no consensus has emerged. Commentators construct frameworks in which to classify different versions (e.g. Sharples, 1980; Cobham, 1981), and, within the Parliamentary Labour Party, Benn and Healey—who clearly disagree on many important points—both claim to support *the* AES. This presents problems for a critique—just what should I go for?

One way out would be to deal with a particular formulation (preferably one sanctioned by an important labour movement body). The TUC's *Plan for Growth* (TUCER 1981) comes to mind. But I think that would be a cop-out. Lenin's dictum that you should confront the best formulations of your opponents' ideas seems better advice. So I will take what I see as the best arguments for the type of AES I want to criticise. But which AES is that?

Different versions can be located on a spectrum ranging from Keynesian through to radical. The essential criterion is the extent to which they want to take company level decision-making powers away from capital. So the Cambridge Economic Policy Group's position—which is basically that reflation plus import controls would be enough to solve Britain's economic problems—is very Keynesian. Radical versions ascribe a key role to: extension of public ownership (of financial institutions and profitable manufacturing companies); compulsory planning agreements (with heavy sanctions for non-cooperation); and the tougher variants of 'workers' democracy' (including a major role for combine committees and the like in tripartite planning agreements, the compulsory establishment of Main Policy Review Boards with 50 per cent worker representatives and wide-ranging powers, extensive 'open the books' legislation, and so on). The London CSE's version is a good example. This classification is obviously rough and ready, and you often need to read between the lines when applying it to 'official' pronouncements. But I find it useful.

This paper is basically concerned with radical AESs. This is not because they are dominant—the TUC's is moderate and the Labour Party's is still up for grabs. It is mainly because they are the more robust, better argued variants. Also, most SER readers probably support them. Finally, they are the more potentially dangerous for the labour movement because they constitute the greater challenge to the status quo. This last point takes us to the nature of a left critique.

There are at least as many criticisms of the AES as there are versions. But most left critiques boil down to one of two arguments:

1. AESs are ultimately devices for stabilising capitalism with no socialist content.

2. AESs are dangerous because attempts at implementation would unleash a vicious assault on the labour movement.

It is obviously consistent to hold both positions about *different* versions of the Strategy. The only way I can see of consistently holding both positions about the *same* version is by arguing that it depends on the balance of class forces at the time of implementation, and that this cannot be predicted in advance. I find this unconvincing. A precondition for the implementation of any particular variant is surely that the balance of class forces lies within a particular, fairly narrow range. Government policy is heavily constrained by class struggle.

I think the first position is basically wrong. Obviously some Keynesian AESs do not have—and are not intended to have—any distinctly socialist content. The Cambridge Economic Policy Group, for example, does not offer its programme as a prescription for a socialist transformation. It sees it as a way of making UK capitalism work better. But the real issue is whether Keynesian AESs could achieve what their advocates claim. I think not in present circumstances. Briefly, once anything approaching full employment was achieved they would fall foul of low profitability and a vicious wage/price spiral. (This obviously implies a view about the nature and severity of Britain's economic problems which I cannot develop here.)

Some Keynesian AES-type measures might find a place in a recovery programme following a major working-class defeat. But this is not what most advocates of the 'stabilisation' thesis have in mind. More importantly, their use would be largely incidental; it would be the defeat, rather than the measures then implemented, that really saved capital's bacon.

The argument that radical versions could simply prop up capitalism depends on substituting a facile syllogism for serious analysis. The syllogism runs: the AES is not socialist because it leaves the bulk of industry in private hands; the AES seeks to solve Britain's economic problems; therefore the AES is a device to shore up British capitalism. In reality, since radical AESs are violently opposed by the capitalist class, they could be implemented only in the context of a major working-class offensive, including the election of a very left Labour government. That would be a situation in which capital was knocking at the knees; not one in which it was being shored up.

Even some radical AES measures might be included in a recovery pro-gramme following a working-class defeat. If independent trades unions had been smashed and replaced by puppet state organisations, for example, then elements of 'workers' democracy' might be introduced (that—and not the co-option of TUC bureaucrats into some NEDO-type system—is what real corporatism is about). But, again, it would be the defeat that had really saved capital. And the whole scenario is a million miles away from the here and now of Bennism.

The other left critique—that the Strategy would prompt a nasty reactionary backlash—is much more on the ball. There is every likelihood that a government hell bent on implementing a radical AES would meet capitalist resistance on a scale for which it was quite unprepared—and which the strategy could not deal with. If the government did not either back down or go well beyond current AESs then economic and social chaos would result. This would discredit left policies in many people's eyes and create conditions in which right-wing forces could seize power (probably via a military coup) and inflict an historical defeat on the workers' movement.

The rest of this paper develops that argument. It looks at two important aspects of the UK economic activity: the connections between the home and international economies, and the domestic activities of the private sector. It takes the form of a critical assessment of the best relevant radical AES writings—those that take the threat of capitalist resistance seriously.

Trouble on the Foreign Exchanges

The UK's integration into the international economy is rightly regarded as a major problem for anti-capitalist policies (whether of a radical AES or any other kind). The best pro-AES discussions of the difficulties I have found are the relevant sections of the London CSE book and Rowthorn's contribution to the Cambridge Political Economy Group's 1974 pamphlet *Britain's Crisis: Causes and Cures* (reprinted in R. Rowthorn, *Capitalism, Conflict and Inflation*, 1980). This section is basically a commentary on these pieces.

An obvious starting point is the issue of import controls and retaliation. It should by now be agreed that the 'conventional' left argument that import controls will promote retaliation because they 'export unemploy-ment' is misplaced. Expansion of the home economy and 'planned growth' of imports would, in principle, generate more jobs in sectors exporting to the UK, not less. But export volumes are not the only motive for retaliation. In the context of a radical AES, import controls would rightly be seen abroad as breaking the rules of the international capitalist game and as a move towards socialism, and so would be opposed. Both London

CSE and Rowthorn recognise this.

The severity of the difficulties posed by retaliation (or an all-out boycott) would, of course, depend in large part on its scale. It is reasonable to suppose, as Rowthorn does, that the most hawkish response will come from the US. But the UK could probably ride out a unilateral US boycott OK. So the main issue is how many other governments the US could pull behind it. Anyone aware of the UK's trading pattern knows that the EEC countries are key here.

There are two types of AES proposals to deal with this problem. One is medium- to long-term measures to reduce the UK's vulnerability to trade sanctions. Those usually mentioned are: more deals with Third World and Eastern bloc countries, and diversification to reduce dependence on foreign supplies (especially foreign-based multinationals with UK subsidiaries). London CSE add:

> The negotiation of bilateral and multilateral trade deals with other countries which have suffered from the international trading system in the way that we have [presumably other weak industrialised capitalist countries. . .] (and a) campaign for international agreement amongst socialists on the need for a new system of regulation of trade which allows us to move collectively away from the policy of competitive deflation encouraged by the present regime. [LCSE 1980, pp. 100–101.]

This is fine as far as it goes. But it neglects two key problems. One is the extent to which the UK can or should withdraw from economic relationships with Western Europe (a much broader issue than EEC membership). If Britain broke from the capitalist bloc while the rest of Western Europe did not, this would become a crucial question. I know of no serious work on it.

The other problem is what short- and medium-term policies offer the UK the best chance of averting disruption by foreign governments and restructuring its international economic relations in the ways suggested. This issue is discussed by London CSE and Rowthorn.

Both agree that an effective approach must combine mobilisation of international working-class opposition to a boycott (especially within the Western European labour movement) with more technical-economic measures. Neither discusses the crucial issue of mobilising support abroad in any detail, and nor does anything else I have read.

London CSE and Rowthorn also agree that the most pressing problem will be an attempted exodus from sterling. London CSE point out that this will almost certainly start in the run-up to the election, and be in full flood by the time a left government takes power. Both agree that exchange controls for UK residents—whilst desirable—are inadequate as a total response. They could not even prevent UK citizens from moving into foreign currencies. London CSE, writing after Thatcher's abolition of exchange controls, point out that it would take time to reassemble a unit capable of administering the controls. Rowthorn stresses sabotage and evasion of such controls. Both note the likelihood of a leakage from capital to current account via 'leads and lags' and transfer pricing. Both also acknowledge that even 100 per cent effective exchange controls on UK residents could not prevent a major run on the pound because of massive foreign holdings. (Neither point out the likelihood that the US would organise an assault on sterling to either force the government to change tack or bring it down.) So both advocate a temporary suspension of convertability. So far, so good.

London CSE then seem in difficulty as to how to proceed:

> Beyond that time [the temporary suspension of convertibility] it is a question of looking at options. One option would be to restore exchange controls on capital movements by UK residents and try to reduce the impact of overseas capital movements on the economy. One step would be to remove the overhang of sterling balances using North Sea oil revenues or liquidation of UK assets overseas. . . A second step would be to tighten up on 'leads and lags' through exchange controls. A more radical option would be a total suspension of convertibility for capital movements so as to freeze overseas investments in the UK, but this would involve a variety of costs and may allow leakages through current transactions. The final option would be to permanently suspend free convertibility of sterling so that allocation of foreign exchange for purposes of purchasing imports would be a responsibility of a body charged with the planning and direction of foreign trade. Allocations for investment purposes, or withdrawal of overseas investments in the UK, would be subject to stringent controls. [LCSE 1980, pp. 111–112.]

End of section. Nothing about the practicality or desirability of the alternatives listed. A few pages away there is an acknowledgement that multinationals would be difficult to control via planning agreements (p. 108). So things are left up in the air. Problems are acknowledged, but nor confronted. We are not told what to do.

Rowthorn goes further, arguing that:

> Without the active cooperation of other states it would not be possible to develop a foolproof or even adequate system of controls on the operations of international capital. Since a left government is unlikely to receive such cooperation it would sooner or later, and probably sooner, be driven to more radical measures. Much of the international business of the city would have to be run down and most of the rest taken over and administered directly by the Government. Equally, many international firms would have to be taken over. . . both foreign and domestically controlled. [Rowthorn 1980, p. 82.]

He also notes that foreign investors would want to wind up operations quickly and get their money out. He advocates a policy of encouraging controlled withdrawal and paying compensation, whilst using the threat of expropriation and debt liquidation as a bargaining counter against reprisals. The money could perhaps come from the requisition and disposal of UK assets abroad. The scheme is obviously not watertight and there is no guarantee that a crippling boycott can be avoided. But it is the best I have seen.

What conclusions emerge? Many are uncontentious: the inherent difficulty of the problem, the need for more work on it, the crucial role of popular support abroad, and so on. But the ones I would like to stress are the importance and difficulty of controlling the foreign exchange operations of international firms. These are recognised by both London CSE and Rowthorn. The key difference between them is that Rowthorn is prepared to accept the policy consequences, and grasp the nettle of widespread state takeovers. London CSE are not, and so lack a clear policy. This illustrates the general point that radical AESs must get a good deal more radical if they are to overcome capitalist resistance.

Economic Resistance at Home

Keynesian AESs see the creation of a suitable macroeconomic climate (sometimes together with financial incentives at micro level) as sufficient to solve Britain's economic problems. Radical versions see planning, in the strong sense of *direction*, as required. This is a crucial difference between the two approaches. The key tool—or instrument of direction—envisaged in radical AESs is the compulsory planning agreement:

> . . . an agreement negotiated annually, but for a five year period—which would cover the main strategic decisions taken by [the largest 100 or so] companies on investment levels and location, employment, price policy and the like. It would be negotiated between management and government with the trades unions playing an important role. The government would have available a variety of sanctions and incentives to enforce agreement including allocation of selective aid, discretionary tax relief, control of funds channelled through a National Investment Bank and Investment Reserve Fund, public purchasing policy, planning permission and permission for price increases. . . A final sanction of nationalisation in cases of obstinate non-cooperation would also be available. [LCSE 1980, p. 7.]

In the context of a radical AES, the term 'planning *agreement*' is a misnomer. There is little chance of government and management objectives coinciding (general coincidence would, of course, make the agreements redundant). And government views must prevail if corporate decisions are to be brought into line with overall objectives. So far as government management relations are concerned, the role of planning agreements is as an instrument of *direction*. They are a surrogate for the nationalisation of the 'commanding heights'—an alternative way for the government to bring the activities of large enterprises into line with broader economic objectives.

The argument that corporate and government priorities would diverge is not a general one about the ultimate incompatibility of social objectives and the pursuit of private profit. It is an argument about the particular circumstances—economic and political—in which a government attempting a radical AES would be operating. (This is why arguments for planning agreements based on comparisons with the French experience of the 1960s are largely irrelevant.)

Any government coming to power in Britain will inherit a major economic crisis. It will face a situation in which the net outcome of firms' decisions, made on profitability criteria, has for years failed to meet major social objectives (full employment, adequate economic growth and so on). The gap between what firms and the government regard as optimal economic behaviour will not be marginal and negotiable (as in France for much of the period of 'indicative planning'). It will be huge.

And quantity turns into quality. When the gap between government and company targets is small, 'negotiations' need not be heavy affairs. Government can accept managerial authority and restrict its role to manipulating some of the variables management considers when making decisions (state contracts, tax liabilities, regional subsidies and so on). All very civilised.

But it is a different ball game when the criteria of profit and social need diverge markedly. Once manipulation of financial variables is insufficient to close the gap, 'negotiations' become more serious. For what is now at issue is: who decides when agreement cannot be reached? Capital or government? *Who has real control?* This is not something on which capital will concede easily.

Moreover, the political climate will hardly be conducive to capitalist confidence and a spirit of cooperation with government. It will be one which has seen a major leftward shift in British society, bringing to office a government committed to a programme considerably more radical than any adopted in recent years by the PCI (traditionally the most dangerous spectre haunting Western Europe). Probably the closest analogy is the programme of the Allende government in Chile.

The attitude of the bourgeoisie is all too predictable. It has been well summarised by Rowthorn:

> . . . the AES would arouse intense hostility in capitalist circles, both at home and abroad, for it would threaten powerful vested interests and would be *correctly* perceived as a prelude to something more extreme. . . [it] will be seen as a declaration of war by major capitalist interests. [Rowthorn 1981, p. 8.]

How will capital react to this 'declaration of war'? Again the answer is predictable. It will engage in what, following Chile, has come to be called 'economic destabilisation'. Likely measures include: the scrapping of investment programmes (an 'investment strike'); loss of confidence in all but the most short-term contracts; attempts to convert assets into forms which are liquid, easily transferable abroad and concealable; and an unwillingness to lend (perhaps especially to the government).

There are various motives for capitalist destabilisation. One is economic self interest in the face of extreme uncertainty. Another is to pressure the government into ditching its programme. Another is to discredit the government and try to bring it down. Yet another is to keep in with organisations which have some control over you (such as banks threatening to foreclose on a loan or parent companies abroad acting on 'advice' from their governments). Taken together, they are pretty powerful. The economy would begin to come apart at the seams fast.

London CSE acknowledge the difficulty:

> The final difficulty with the strategy of planning agreements is perhaps the most fundamental. It can be argued that as long as Capital remains in private hands it will do all it can to subvert attempts at planning and to resist the imposition of social control. Capitalist opposition to a thorough policy of planning could certainly be anticipated. Moreover it is not difficult to see that any measures taken to deal with this problem through the exercise of more direct control by the government or the trade unions would simply harden the opposition of Capital and could result in an all out investment strike. Traditionally it is in the financial sphere that the economic effects of these political conflicts are most obvious—capitalists refuse to buy government debt and shift their capital overseas. [LCSE 1980, p. 73.]

An admirable summary of the problem. How do they propose to deal with it?

> Whether this opposition could be overcome is a matter of judgement: We believe that it could, provided the rationale for planning was broadly understood and supported and provided the workforce of the companies involved were committed to its implementation. [LCSE 1980, p. 73–4.]

End of discussion. What does this mean? What is the basis for believing that opposition could be overcome? Just how could widespread support for planning overcome capitalist sabotage?

Clearly the broader and more committed the support for planning, the harder it would be for a left government to capitulate at the first sign of resistance. This is important. But it does not tell us how the resistance could be overcome. As London CSE point out, further moves by the government 'would simply harden the opposition of Capital'. So what then?

Part of the answer is that the government could wheel out the sanctions at its disposal. In a situation of widespread destabilisation many of these would probably be worthless (e.g. the threat to withhold planning permission). But others seem more powerful—most importantly nationalisation. Surely a government armed with that weapon is certain of victory?

I think that depends on both the sense in which the government is armed with nationalisation and the use to which the weapon is put. Take the latter point. Weapons may be used as deterrents or tools of combat. If the threat of nationalisation proved sufficient to quell capitalist resistance then it would clearly have given the government victory; it would have enabled it to impose the planning agreements. But a situation in which capitalist resistance were overcome only by widespread nationalisations would be a different kettle of fish. It would be a victory for the government, but not the AES. Success would have been achieved only by going beyond AES-type measures.

This brings us to the other matter: in what sense would a left government be 'armed with' the nationalisation weapon? It is common to distinguish between formal and real ownership of means of production (the former consisting of possession of legal title; the latter of effectively controlling productive use). The same distinction can be applied to weapons.

A left Labour government would have some formal right to nationalise. (By asking the Labour leader to form a government, the Queen would have signed a kind of gun license. This would include small print. A gaggle of Law Lords and judges would then point out the illegality of touching the gun—let alone firing it—whilst certain constitutional niceties they had dreamed up remained undecided.) But real control is what matters.

Would the government be able to enforce state takeovers? This issue is crucial both to the extent of capitalist resistance—if capital were certain that the government could and would nationalise any company that obstructed then it would know that sabotage constituted suicide, and might well then go along with government proposals—and to the chances of overcoming it. Government decisions are normally executed by the state apparatus. Would it cooperate in the situation envisaged? I doubt it. I think it more likely that top civil servants would either resign or strike (i.e. refuse to act until the constitutional situation had been 'clarified') and that the Civil Service would be effectively paralysed in key areas. Would the situation then be hopeless?

It would certainly be difficult. The government would be virtually powerless and capital encouraged to redouble its efforts to topple it. But there is one powerful force the government could call on—the workers in the companies concerned. They could take over the factories and deal directly with the government. This kind of 'nationalisation from below' would almost certainly be the only effective way to counter economic destabilisation.

London CSE come close to this view in their final few words on the matter ('providing the workforce of the companies involved were committed to its implementation'). But they fail to think through—or at least spell out—the key implication, which is, once again, that the underlying objectives of the AES can be achieved, and capitalist resistance defeated, only by embracing measures which go well beyond those currently envisaged.

Final Remarks

This paper has many limitations. It considers one weakness of one type of AES only—the failure of radical versions to deal adequately with the problem of capitalist resistance. Even this is discussed only partially. Little is said about non-economic resistance, nothing about what right-wing organisations might be up to and nothing about the response of the military. The paper also fails to develop an alternative in any but the most general terms. These are important omissions. Another possible criticism is that it is all old hat. Certainly there is nothing original in it. But that is neither here nor there. It is necessary to repeat important criticisms time and again until they are adequately taken on board.

Capitalist resistance has not yet been properly taken on board. Many AES supporters still ignore it or dismiss critiques based on it out of hand as 'ultra-left' or 'economistic'. Others, including the authors discussed here, accept that it is a problem but cannot really come to terms with it. This is not basically a weakness of the authors; it is inherent in the strategy itself.

The fact of the matter is that it would be *harder* to implement a radical AES than a fuller take-over. In fact, it would be damned near impossible. The kind of halfway house envisaged—in which capital is stitched up in compulsory planning agreements whilst the bulk of industry remains in private hands—represents the worst of both worlds for the labour movement. It goes far enough to provoke capitalist destabilisation but stops short of the key measures needed to combat it.

REFERENCES

Cobham, D., 1981, 'The Socialist Economic Review Project: progress in the economics of the left', *Politics and Power* no. 3.
London CSE, 1980, *The Alternative Economic Strategy*, CSE books.
Rowthorn, R., 1980, *Capitalism, Conflict and Inflation*, Lawrence and Wishart.
Rowthorn, R., 1981, 'The Politics of the AES', *Marxism Today*, January.
Sharples, A., 1981, 'Alternative Economic Strategies: Labour Movement Responses to the Crisis', *Socialist Economic Review 1981*.
TUC, 1981, *Economic Review*.

DISCUSSION

Tony Millwood

The papers by Lipsey and Harrison each present an essentially political critique of left-wing versions of the AES, though from conflicting standpoints. Both take as their target the work of the London CSE Group[1] and criticise it not for its economic analysis but for its judgment of the political consequences of introducing a radical AES of this type.

Lipsey accepts the desirability of reflating the economy and the necessity for protecting the balance of payments by import controls, being rightly sceptical of the adequacy of devaluation for this purpose. The chief difficulties he identifies with this limited ('Mark One') AES are opposition by foreign governments to greater discretionary state control of trade, and inflation, and he sees the need internationally to develop an alignment of socialist forces to accommodate our import controls and internally to develop an incomes policy. The weakness in Lipsey's strategy is that no attention is given in his analysis or his policies to the fact that a large section of the economy is in private hands and while it might welcome some respite from monetarism the chance that it can be expected to provide the investment and employment that the current situation requires is slim. Past reflations (1963–4 under Maudling, 1972–4 under Barber) provide little ground for optimism. The need to exercise social control over the private sector not only to promote investment but also to develop creative answers to problems of job sharing, equal opportunities, regional imbalances, new technology and the energy crisis, to name but some, is now more acute than ever. Private capital is becoming ever more concentrated and a source of unaccountable, undemocratic social and economic power that responsible socialists must address.

Lipsey draws attention rather sharply to the inadequacy of arguments in support of the view that we can have both planning and democracy, and accepts the view that the two are inherently opposed. It is an important argument for it is a major political obstacle to the introduction of planning. It is trite but true to say that much more work needs to be done by socialists to develop both a theory and practice of democratic planning, but that such is possible need not be doubted.

Harrison has provided a cogent analysis of what he identifies as the main obstacles to the implementation of a radical AES. The scenario he depicts is one where a 'very left Labour government' is elected and seeks to exercise substantial control over the activities of private capital as well as introducing the macroeconomic policies shared by the 'soft' and 'hard'

127

versions of the strategy. He believes that such a strategy would be violently opposed by the capitalist class, which would mobilise international resistance in the form of a possible trade war, an assault on sterling and an investment strike. In these circumstances the government would have to backtrack and accept defeat or take more radical measures centred on expropriating private capital. His conclusion is that the labour movement should therefore start with a policy of widespread nationalisation. Proponents of a radical AES should take Harrison's particular criticisms seriously: it is important to develop measures to prevent the collapse of sterling, and to consider such options as suspension of convertibility as well as the reintroduction of exchange controls; it is important to develop an alliance internationally between political forces opposed to monetarism and deflation. However I think Harrison overstates his case. The AES is a strategy of radical reform, contingent upon gaining consent and support from a significant section of the British public. This qualification is a double constraint: it limits how far-reaching the initial measures envisaged in an AES can be; it also provides a limitation on the forms of opposition that the capitalist class can wisely undertake if they wish to prevent a more hostile, anti-capitalist attitude to develop. Harrison's scenario of a rapid polarisation is not incredible but in my judgment it is not a likely one. There are in Britain today a broad array of social groups and interests among whom an alliance can be built around a package of economic reforms whose central theme is to develop forms of social control over economic forces. I think it unlikely that were such an alliance to be built with the AES as an important element the response of the ruling class will be to give up the argument and resort to destabilisation. Rather, in my view they will seek to split the alliance and seek to prevent the reforms from gathering momentum. It is these developments, and not Harrison's breakdown, that the left will have to respond to.

NOTE

1. CSE London Working Group, 1980, *The Alternative Economic Strategy* (CSE Books/LCC), London.

COLLECTIVE BARGAINING, INFLATION AND INCOMES POLICY*

Brian Burkitt

1. Introduction

British capitalism faced a profound crisis during the last decade, when a general recession amongst western industrial nations was superimposed upon a long-term relative decline in Britain's economic performance. The symptom of these problems that aroused most public concern, at least until recently, was the persistence and the frequent acceleration of inflation. Consequently attempts at developing an alternative economic strategy cannot avoid focusing upon the origins of inflationary pressure and possible methods of alleviating them. This chapter argues that an important source of post-war inflation has been the conflict between capital and labour for a greater share of available resources. Inflation is therefore seen as a specific manifestation, within the British historical context, of the class divisions that capitalism always generates.

2. The Pivotal Role of Unemployment in Capitalism

A unique feature of British experience between 1940 and 1970 was the long-term maintenance of full employment. However, unemployment is not an accidental blemish but an integral component of a capitalist economy. It fulfills the crucial function of facilitating accumulation by maintaining industrial discipline and dampening the distributional conflict always latent in capitalism. It does this by implanting the fear of job insecurity, so that workers' scope for action in pursuit of their interests is severely restricted. Under a regime of full employment, dismissal no longer plays its disciplinary role; the social position of the employer is partially undermined, while the self-assurance of the working class grows. Therefore continuous full employment poses problems for capitalism, because it permits distributive conflict to be more intense and to some extent more equally matched. Less advantaged groups became more effective in disputes, gaining not only immediate advantages but also a stronger position for future bargaining. Cost push inflation arises not because of new influences on wage earners and their organisations, but because of the weakening of old inhibitions imposed upon them. Workers have learnt from capitalism the practice of exploiting market positions to the full, if necessary by using the power of organisation. The absence

---

* I am grateful to David Currie, David Purdy, Malcolm Sawyer and Margaret Wilkinson for their helpful comments on an earlier draft of this paper.

129

of unemployment enables trade unions to struggle increasingly successfully for higher money wages; capitalists price their products so as to preserve or extend their profit margins and inflation ensues.

Acceleration of inflation from the mid-1960s can be plausibly linked to the changing composition of the labour force. Each year workers conditioned into acceptance of employer authority by the lack of jobs during the inter-war depression were replaced by those whose experience was confined to full employment—by 1968 only 25 per cent of UK employees had been members of the workforce before 1939. Moreover, inflation itself tends to destroy the conventions that legitimate the existing distribution of income and wealth, as the role of bargaining power becomes more visible. Inflation therefore is the product of a deep-seated distributional conflict that was prevented from erupting in the past by the continual threat and the periodic occurrence of unemployment, which acted as a deterrent to union militancy. Organised labour secured an increase in its bargaining power without any change in its subordinate status, leaving the structure of industrial authority intact. The resulting price-income spiral contains no obvious brake in an economy propelled by actions in accord with self interest.

Writing during the Second World War, Kalecki (1943) argued that full employment capitalism needes new social and political institutions to reflect the increased power of the working class; 'If capitalism can adjust to full employment, a fundamental reform will have been incorporated in it. If not, it will show itself an outmoded system which must be scrapped.' The persistence of cost push inflation indicates that the necessary adjustments have yet to be made. The decisive barrier to full employment is not deficient demand but the socio-political requirements of an economy primarily dependent on capitalist motivations. The monetarist revival of the pre-Keynesian concept of the 'natural rate of unemployment' is based on this barrier but presents it as a technical constraint within a given set of market relationships.

3. The Mechanism of Cost Push Inflation

Cost push analysis is based on the assumptions that the economy is not perfectly competitive and that organised groups attempt to obtain a higher share of real national income by manipulating the money prices over which they exert influence. Unless price and income decisions are centrally coordinated, no mechanism ensures that the rival claims on income (those negotiated by unions in the wage bargain and those pursued by capitalists in their pricing policy) are equal to the resources available. If they are greater, conflict between capitalist pricing and collective agreements creates inflationary pressure. This can be illustrated by an upward movement of the aggregate supply curve; as aggregate supply increases from S1 to S2 to S3 in figure I, full employment output (Y1) can be maintained only with a rising price level (P1 to P2 to P3). If governments attempt to hold prices closer to P1 by preventing any increase in demand beyond D1, unemployment results as output falls to Y2 and Y3, while there is still more rise in prices.[1]

Figure I

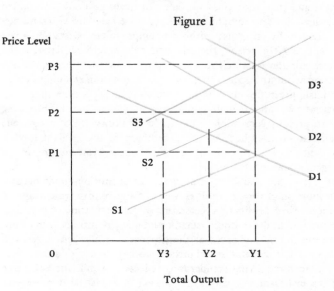

Total Output

Such a situation can occur once the framework of a perfectly competitive economy is abandoned, because the possession of bargaining power enables suppliers of commodities and productive resources to exact higher prices even at the cost of lower sales and employment. Whenever a small number of corporations dominate an industry, they can choose between alternative combinations of high prices and small sales or lesser prices and larger sales. Trade unions often enjoy similar discretion in a choice of higher wages and fewer jobs or lower wages and more jobs. Nor are markets for services exempt from seller domination.

Under a regime of market imperfections and administered prices, income changes may be self-financing; if a general increase in money wages occurs, industry supply schedules, and hence aggregate supply, move to the left. However, higher wages increase aggregate demand (from D1 to D2 to D3 in Figure I) so that a new price-output equilibrium is reached. Because a money wage change implies upward movement of both aggregate supply and aggregate demand, the general price level is not uniquely determined by their equality and equilibrium can be attained at any level of money wages and prices.

Therefore cost push inflation can arise from distributional conflicts in the labour market, which is inherently imperfect and occupies such a prominent place in the economy that general increases in money wages and salaries may create the additional demand required to sustain them. Monetarists argue that such class warfare can never generate a sustained inflation, unless the government is prepared to create the extra money needed to finance the cost push without unemployment. Certainly, apart from the 1971 to 1974 period, there is little evidence to suggest that the velocity of circulation is sufficiently flexible to allow rising prices for any lengthy period without a substantial increase in the money supply. However, cost push pressures may impel governments to permit monetary accommodation via unanticipated increases in public sector borrowing or policies to prevent depression. The supply of money is not exogenous as in monetarist theories but may be a function of the level of money income. It then plays a permissive rather than a causal role with regard to rises in the general price level.

A faster rate of accumulation implies that consumption goods occupy a smaller proportion of total output. However, the extent to which capitalists can increase their profits by accelerating the accumulation of capital is severely restricted under modern socio-economic conditions, when any attempt to raise the rate of profit at the expense of real wages is resisted by trade unions. The extreme reluctance of workers to accept a deterioration in their acquired living standards is reflected in militant collective bargaining for higher money wages. The threat of industrial disputes can be averted by wage increases, but if prices are raised correspondingly, the level of real wages is not restored and the original situation is repeated. Prices and incomes may chase each other upwards and this spiral becomes the inflation barrier[2] to raising the real value of profits. The conflict between the desire of capitalists to invest and a refusal to accept the level of real wages which that planned investment entails results in an upward movement of prices and money incomes which persists until capitalist expenditure, on investment or consumption or both, is curtailed.

4. The Statistical Relationship between Collective Bargaining and Inflation

Attempts have been made in recent years to assess whether the variability of the rate of change of inflation over time is associated with changes in trade-union bargaining power, measured in a number of different ways. They yield conflicting results, partly because of differences in the specification of the models and of the variables. Moreover, the concept of union bargaining strength is multi-dimensional, so that attempts to measure it are at best approximations.

Hines (1964) produced econometric evidence that the rate of change of unionisation was a significant explanatory variable of the rate of change of money wages in the UK between 1893 and 1961. He suggested that this relationship reflected trade-union militancy manifested in simultaneous recruitment campaigns and wage claims. Hines's research provoked considerable discussion by, for example, Stoney and Thomas (1970), Wilkinson and Burkitt (1973) and Purdy and Zis (1974). Subsequent studies indicate that the unionisation model has a lower statistical significance and is subject to greater variation than Hines claimed, but the rate of change of unionisation usually remains significant despite a varying economic environment, in the wage determination equation. The lack of theoretical precision surrounding the role of unionisation, which implies that causation could flow in either direction, makes discrimination between conflicting explanations difficult. Ultimately in the present state of knowledge one's choice of hypothesis is a matter of judgment. Evidence from studies in which some index of strike activity is used as a proxy for union power is similarly inconclusive; Armstrong, Bowers and Burkitt (1977).

At industry level variations in union strength may not produce relative wage changes, because trade unions may influence the overall level of money wages while maintaining a stable wage structure. Criteria of horizontal and vertical equity can generalise the advances in living standards gained by one industry to other sectors. Much UK and US research verifies the existence of a wage transfer process, but the precise role played by trade unions requires greater analysis. In attempting to preserve living standards and differentials they may use collective bargaining to achieve a target real wage and to resist any diminution of this level. Henry, Sawyer and Smith (1976) developed such a model of union behaviour.

The weight of evidence suggests that trade-union bargaining power can affect money wage movements and impart an inflationary bias into the labour market. In seeking to maintain their members' real living standards unions escalate the reaction of wages to price changes, while their presence appears to facilitate the generalisation of key wage bargains. The effect of other union activities remains not proven. These conclusions must be assessed in relation to the problems encountered by research in this area, notably the difficulty of constructing sensitive proxies for cost push forces. It seems unlikely that such a complex socio-economic phenomenon as the modification of relationships during a period of continuous full employment can be analysed by simple econometric techniques. It is certainly difficult to measure the association between inflation, the collective permeation of the economy and different intensities of ideological confrontation, but if a general theory of inflation is ever constructed it will incorporate broad socio-political interactions of this kind.

5. *The Policy Problem Created by Cost Push Inflation and the Alternative Economic Strategy*

When inflation arises from cost push forces, conventional reliance on demand management proves ineffective unless deflationary policies are pursued vigorously for a considerable period, so that control of inflation may involve permanently high unemployment or recurrent slumps. Over the past decade all western governments faced a deteriorating trade-off between rising inflation and rising unemployment, under which fiscal and monetary counter-inflationary measures entailed a heavy loss of output and jobs. The current disastrous experiment with monetarism, which essentially seeks to recreate the pre-1940 environment in which individual but not collective acquisitive ability could be exercised without restraint, demonstrates this clearly. It is an inefficient as well as an unjust policy, since more commodities could be produced by existing resources but the system of economic relations and decision-making rules prevents the economy from reaching maximum potential output. The costs of deflation in terms of lost production and employment far outweigh the cost which inflation imposes upon society. Governments need to cope not merely with inflationary symptoms but with the underlying distributive conflict creating them.

Current discussion of the Alternative Economic Strategy must be located within this context of capitalist crisis. The AES is designed to create a popular alliance based on a new vision of social organisation which can generate a comparable shift in late twentieth century British society to that achieved during and immediately after the Second World War. Although considerable controversy surrounds details of the AES, its broad approach can be indicated by a number of its general propositions. These include a policy of reflation including some commitment to expand public spending; measures of industrial and labour market intervention including a variety of forms of planning and control of the allocation of finance; regulation of trade and international capital movements; and direct action to determine price, and more controversially cost movements. The AES is put forward as a set of proposals that can ensure economic growth, take Britain a long way towards full employment, provide improved living standards, reduce inequality and achieve these objectives in a way that extends democracy in all spheres of life. However, how to contain the price level while maintaining full employment is the most important economic policy issue of the day. The only alternative to the deliberate creation of unemployment is conscious control of the level of prices and money incomes. Direct regulation of cost push forces could form part of the AES by being an integral feature of the new social and political apparatus to accommodate the increased power of the working class at full employment that Kalecki (1943) called for.

6. The Historical Experience of Prices and Incomes Policy

The stated *aim* of all prices and incomes policies is to obtain a given, lower rate of change of the level of internal prices, either to secure price stability for its own sake or to obtain a balance of payments equilibrium at full employment. The *instrument* of incomes policy is direct control of the relationship between the rates of increase of money wages and average productivity of labour. This relationship in conjunction with the target rate of price change implies an implicit or explicit government policy with regard to income distribution and a set of assumptions about other economic variables.

The success of previous UK incomes policies as an anti-inflationary device, in both the short and the long term, is still a topic for debate. The methodological problems involved in testing for their effects are formidable. A recent study by Henry and Ormerod (1978) indicated in four recent 'policy-on' periods the rate of increase of money wages was reduced below the level which it would otherwise have been. Their long-term success is more open to doubt, although the available evidence suggests that the price level has not been permanently lowered by the UK periods of restraint. The policies which appear to have exerted short-run effects were the Wilson controls introduced with the deflationary package of July 1966, the Heath freeze in the winter of 1972–73, its successor in 1973 and the social contract measures between 1975 and 1977.

Each of these policies reduced the level of real earnings to below what it would otherwise have been. Wage increases were kept lower than the prevailing rate of inflation, leading to a loss of real income as higher costs already in the pipeline were processed through the economy in the form of raised prices. Unless prices adjust simultaneously to any new level of wage increases, this short-run real income loss is an inevitable feature of any form of wage restraint. Evidence from UK econometric models indicates that at least two years pass before the real income of workers is restored to the level it would otherwise have reached in the period immediately following the introduction of wage controls.[3]

This historical background explains the hostility of many trade unionists to proposals for an incomes policy as part of the Alternative Economic Strategy. In the past Labour politicians paid lip service to the concept of a planned growth of wages as part of a plan for all incomes, but the policies they applied amounted to little more than attempts to secure cuts in real wages. Whenever the rate of change of money wages is lower than the rate of change of productivity plus the rate of increase of prices, the share of wages in the national income falls. In effect, the government accepts as an unchangeable institutional datum the saving habits of capitalists and strives to preserve profits; capitalists' consumption remains untouched, whereas the share of workers is adjusted to whatever level is consistent with the equilibrium of aggregate demand. By guaranteeing the profit margins consistent with investment requirements, the state essentially nationalises part of the product, which is handed over to capitalists through a transfer of wealth from one class to another; workers are compelled to restrict their consumption in order to facilitate investment, yet they possess no rights in the ensuing accumulation of capital. In all previous versions of incomes policy the standard of living of workers depended on circumstances beyond their control, for productivity depends less upon effort than upon the age and type of equipment in use which is decided by managers.

7. Prices and Incomes Policy, the Alternative Economic Strategy and Economic Democracy

It would be wrong for trade unions to cooperate in any form of wage restraint, until its overall impact is seen to be benefiting working people. However, post-war experience indicates that wage militancy alone cannot achieve a permanent shift in the balance of class forces. The need for the labour movement to develop a wider strategy becomes even more urgent in face of Mrs Thatcher's far-reaching reactionary policies. Could a comprehensive prices and incomes policy be an element in this strategy? Such a policy implies the creation of a social contract under which different classes reach sufficient agreement about the distribution of income and wealth to refrain from attempts at securing immediate advantages at each other's expense. Price and income regulation can undoubtedly achieve its objectives if applied rigorously. Partly as a consequence of its use in the British war economy, prices rose by only 6 per cent between 1942 and 1945, a remarkable record given existing claims on resources. However, prices and incomes policies are easily evaded in a decentralised economy, unless evasion is deterred by a consensus on shifts in distribution or an army of enforcement inspectors. Equitable treatment for all types of income is the sole foundation for achieving acceptability, but numerous loopholes exist. Wage regulation is circumvented by upgrading staff, greater fringe benefits, additional increments and overtime working. Price controls can be evaded by changes in product quality, the terms of sales credit and the development of black markets which increase profits per unit of sales. Moreover, tax avoidance, the use of expense accounts, the existence of incremental salary scales and the ability of the rich to buy expertise to circumvent fiscal or legal measures, all maintain the position of the relatively privileged. Such differential advantages in a mixed economy are embedded in the structure of property ownership.

The underlying causes of an inflation arising from administered prices and distributional conflict can be ameliorated only by modification of price setting procedures and collective bargaining. Trade unions will not accept restraints on their ability to raise money wages for more than a brief crisis period unless tangible benefits are secured in return. Burkitt (1980) outlined the framework of a prices and incomes policy with a specific commitment to redistribution; its major features involved price controls, an equitable system for determining differentials, regulation of wage drift, synchronisation of public sector settlements, a government commitment to full employment and economic growth, development of the social wage, coordination with other aspects of government policy and a more equal distribution of wealth. However, in a mixed economy the framework within which governments regulate pay depends upon a number of variables that they do not control, such as the volume and direction of investment, corporate strategies and the balance of foreign trade. Since failure to determine these variables ultimately undermines the acceptability of prices and incomes policies, this dilemma can only be resolved by a major extension of collective planning of economic activity.

To secure even minimal consent to wage restraint, prices and other incomes have also to be controlled. Dividend restraint is relatively painless except for small shareholders. So long as the economy continues to grow, large shareholders receive their lost income back in the form of rising prices for their firm's assets.[4] Restraint on prices and profits, however, involves heavy costs. High profits are essential to obtain greater output and productivity, because profits are both the source of, and the incentive for, investment. They are the motive force behind production and must be allowed to vary to encourage competition, efficiency and innovation. The notion of a 'fair' profit is nonsensical. The only fair profit under capitalism is the highest possible. Profits fuel the accumulation of capital, so that growth will not occur if they are curtailed.

Here lies the dilemma of incomes policies. They must treat all classes on conventional criteria of fairness if they are to gain acceptance, but if equally fair to wages and profits they defeat their main purpose. Permanent controls on profit lead to the erosion of the private sector and the eventual socialisation of investment, as the government is increasingly compelled to provide the output and employment that private capital is unwilling to supply. No effective planning is possible so long as the 'commanding heights' of the economy are in private ownership and under private control. The public appropriation of these strategic points does not create power but transfers it from the private domain, where its operations cannot be effectively controlled, to the public domain where they could be. Without extensive public ownership, government can only exhort capitalists' co-operation and it obtains such cooperation only by following policies that support capitalists' interests. These do not include an irreversible shift in the distribution of power and wealth—hence the bias towards greater inequality under previous incomes policies. Without institutional reforms, income control is either spurious (a wage freeze sold through public relations) or it destroys capitalist motivations without providing workable substitutes.

Therefore restraints on collective bargaining to control inflation can be acceptable to socialists only in the context of an alternative economic strategy which embraces an increase in nationalisation and the introduction of effective industrial democracy. If workers are compelled to accept a given level of consumption to facilitate economic growth, the least they should obtain in return is that a corresponding fraction of the capital stock be placed under their control. Moreover, the right of workers to influence the choice of productive techniques becomes crucial once the link between money wages and productivity is institutionalised. Britain currently faces an urgent need to modernise its physical capital, but this can be achieved by substantial investment which ultimately must derive from some form of wage restraint. Trade unions are unlikely to accept a wage freeze for capital accumulation which accrues to the bourgeoisie. However, if the capital growth resulting from wage restraint went to workers, the TUC and its members might look at an incomes policy in a new light. The Swedish proposals for employee investment funds,[5] which essentially socialise capital growth are relevant in this context; not only do they produce a gradual socialisation of the economy, they also provide a practical solution to the immediate problem of providing new sources of capital formation. Such a policy would be a daring one for a Labour government to adopt, but the alternative method of industrial regeneration is to carry out a regressive redistribution in the hope that capitalists will then find reinvestment attractive.

In capitalist democracies working-class power has been kept at a largely passive level. Civil liberties, universal suffrage and the right to organise enable labour to disrupt but not produce alternatives. Incomes policy might play a crucial role in a strategy to extend trade unions' decision-making capacity, greater restraint in pressing pay claims being exchanged for a full share in industrial decisions. A suitable slogan for this development is 'no moderation without participation'. How radical it would prove to be (e.g. the extent of the transformation of existing hierarchies of authority; the size of concessions secured in exchange for wage restraint) depends on the strength of the labour movement and on the structure of a particular advanced capitalist economy. Thus West German unions have offered considerable moderation for many years in return for a limited degree of participation, while the involvement now demanded by Swedish unions is potentially far-reaching. Swedish proposals for employee investment funds focus crucially upon control of investment that affects the balance of class relations; the state's dependence on capital's assessment of its own needs for future growth constitutes the main basis of capitalist hegemony. Erosion of capital's sovereignty over investment would undermine its power base, although it remains problematic whether capital would allow this to occur through a peaceful democratic process. Certainly the long-term implications of such a strategy encounter resistance as a threat to the status quo, for its internal logic involves progressive departures from market principles in the regulation of the economy. This open ideological hostility will be supported by groups advancing their parochial short-term interest, so that a range of doctrinal and practical influences will attempt to block the collectivist solution.

Rather than visualising democratic planning in terms of an institutional structure, with new state agencies grafted onto or even replacing existing ones, economic democracy must be seen as a process of building upon and extending the existing forms of popular control that have been forged in the community and the labour movement. Purdy (1981) provided some striking examples of how such developments can be achieved. Democratisation consists in advancing collective bargaining to new areas of company policy, such as investment, the design of tools and equipment, employment policy; to granting rights of access to information; to securing worker-representatives on company boards; to giving greater powers and responsibilities to local community groups in running certain aspects of the social welfare services. A Labour government would have a vital role to play in passing enabling legislation and in allocating resources, but its role should be that of a partnership with popular organisations based on the workforce and the community.

8. Conclusion

Free collective bargaining is unable to control all the variables determining the relative shares of labour and property in the national income, because it deals inevitably with money rather than real wages. However, the bargaining position of trade unions was strengthened by the years of continuous full employment between 1940 and 1970 and by the consequent change in the character of relations between employers and employees. Should capitalist accumulation depress real wages below the workers' minimum acceptance level, unions press for higher money wages under the threat of strike action, and an inflationary price-income spiral commences. Therefore cost push inflation is endemic to a capitalism that endeavours to operate without unemployment. In the words of Devine (1974): 'Chronic inflation is a necessary feature of a social reality in which workers are impelled to struggle to realise their rising aspirations, cannot be prevented from struggling and the system cannot, necessarily cannot, meet these aspirations. . . Inflation is a product of the capitalist system in its present stage of state monopoly capitalism.' It is at this juncture that the main economic contrast between left and right approaches can be situated. The right believes that the underlying tensions of British society can be resolved by the operation of market forces in the climate of an economic crisis and under the stimulus of unemployment; the left argues for a lasting solution through state economic intervention in the context of a general democratisation of institutions.

To reconcile price stability with full employment, a prices and incomes policy is indispensable. However, government wage controls invariably operate against working-class interests in a capitalist economy, because its living standard becomes removed from the influence of collective bargaining and becomes dependent upon forces beyond trade-union control. The relationship between money wages and productivity is institutionalised, but the choice of productive technique, which largely determines productivity in the individual firm, remains securely under management control. These reflections suggest that if the dilemma posed by cost push inflation is to be resolved on an equitable basis, more extensive communal ownership of the means of production allied to some form of economic democracy extending labour's authority into higher spheres of control relations is an essential precondition. Certainly the effective implementation of any but a regressive prices and incomes policy rests upon a change in the power structure and a contraction in the sphere over which the profit motive holds sway. Under such an institutional framework the contradictions of capitalist accumulation could be avoided; investment is financed not from individual incomes but from a collective levy to which all contribute and from which all receive the benefits. Incomes policies would then cease to be a means of providing capitalism with a respite from its problems at the expense of real wages, but would become one instrument in a framework of socialist planning, under which all economic variables are subject to democratic determination. Effective control of cost push inflation can only be a part of a general social control of inequalities.

NOTES

1. Neoclassical economists confronted with Figure I would examine the consequences of movements along the curves for changes in their position (the accelerationist issue) and might query the actual extent of market imperfections in the goods and the labour markets. Under attack, they rely on the Laidler and Parkin (1975) thesis that imperfections can affect not the rate of change of prices but the 'natural' rate of unemployment. Many of the practical problems associated with monetarism arise because the supply curve of Figure I is approximately horizontal, except in the very long run. Many factors combine to produce this rigidity—the changing composition of the labour force, internal labour markets, advertising, economies of scale etc.—but the author believes class conflict to be crucial.

2. Burkitt (1979) discussed the operation of the inflation barrier in greater detail.

3. See, for instance, the evidence contained in the Cambridge Economic Policy Group's *Economic Policy Review* 1981.

4. Since institutional shareholdings now account for a substantial proportion of total shareholdings, the reaction of such institutions and their policy-holders must be taken into account when assessing the impact of dividend restraint.

5. Employee investment funds attempt to ensure that capital growth accrues to workers as a group. Companies have to transfer a portion (10 to 30 per cent) of their profits in the form of newly issued shares to employee investment funds administered by the relevant trade union. The transferred portion of profit would be new equity capital and would remain in the firm for reinvestment. Unions would enjoy the voting rights of the stocks. Stephens (1979) estimated that in 50 to 60 years the huge majority of Swedish capital would be collectively owned under this scheme.

REFERENCES

Armstrong, K.J., Bowers, D. and Burkitt, B., 1977, 'The Measurement of Trade Union Bargaining Power', *British Journal of Industrial Relations.*

Burkitt, B., 1979, 'Wage Restraint and the Inflation Barrier', *Review of Radical Political Economics.*

Burkitt, B., 1980, *Trade Unions and Wages—Implications for Economic Theory*, Bradford University Press (2nd Edition).

Cambridge Economic Policy, 1981, *Cambridge Economic Policy Review*, Gower Publishing.

Devine, P., 1974, 'Inflation and Marxist Theory', *Marxism Today.*

Henry, S.G.B., Sawyer, M.C. and Smith, P., 1976, 'Models of Inflation in the United Kingdom', *National Institute Economic Review.*

Henry, S.G.B. and Omerod, P., 1978, 'Incomes Policy and Wage Inflation: Empirical Evidence for the UK 1961-77', *National Institute Economic Review.*

Hines, A.G., 1964, 'Trade Unions and Wage Inflation in the United Kingdom 1893-1961', *Review of Economic Studies.*

Kalecki, M., 1943, 'Political Aspects of Full Employment', *Political Quarterly.*

Laidler, D.E.W. and Parkin, J.M., 1975, 'Inflation: A Survey', *Economic Journal.*

Purdy, D.L. and Zis, G., 1974, 'Trade Unions and Wage Inflation in the United Kingdom: A Reappraisal', in *Inflation and Labour Markets*, ed. D.E.W. Laidler and D.L. Purdy, Manchester University Press.

Purdy, D.L., 1981, 'Government-Trade Union Relations', in *Socialist Economic Review* 1981, Merlin Press.

Stephens, J.D., 1979, *The Transition from Capitalism to Socialism*, MacMillan.

Stoney, P.J.M. and Thomas, R.L., 1970, 'A Note on the Dynamic Properties of the Hines Inflation Model', *Review of Economic Studies.*

Wilkinson, R.K. and Burkitt, B., 1973, 'Wage Determination and Trade Unions', *Scottish Journal of Political Economy.*

WORKING PEOPLE AND THE ALTERNATIVE ECONOMIC STRATEGY

Owen Jones

1. Introduction

The purpose of this short paper is to take a critical look at the way working people as a whole—and not just trade-union activists—are referred to in discussions around the Alternative Economic Strategy (AES). The paper is therefore not about economics as such, but rather about some of the wider political implications of a left economic strategy. It will be argued, however, that weaknesses in the role attributed to working people threaten to undermine the chances of the AES achieving its stated economic objectives.

Although the paper confines its attention to working people as a class, a comprehensive political strategy for socialism would clearly have to recognise the many divisions *within* the working class along national and racial lines, as well as the crucial issues of gender division and gender oppression. The reason for spending some time looking at class strategy is simply that if we failed to win the support of working people for the AES, the viability of the strategy as a whole would be called into question. The paper makes the assumption that the AES will do little towards solving Britain's long-term social and economic crisis if it is not based on the support of working people *as a class.*

2. The Concept of Mobilisation

> 'The revolutionary war is a war of the masses; it can be waged only by mobilising the masses and relying on them.'
>
> *Yen Han*

It is usually accepted in discussions of the politics of the AES that it will not be possible to implement the AES unless it has a broad base of popular support. The concept of popular 'mobilisation', in particular, represents one of the most important ways in which proponents of the AES have attempted to respond to the need for a political strategy to support the AES.

Unfortunately this concept is not always used in as precise a way as a coherent political strategy would require. We often seem to be working with more than one concept of mobilisation, and more than one concept of who is to be mobilised. In fact, at one extreme, the concept of 'mass' mobilisation sometimes appears to assume most of the characteristics of

143

a wholesale social revolution. This must be considered an unlikely consequence of introducing the AES: indeed if such a revolution were possible, it is open to doubt whether the AES would take the relatively limited form it does.

A class strategy should be judged by similar criteria to those normally adopted for the AES itself. Thus on the one hand, it should be genuinely transitional in the sense of being capable of realisation. A transitional class strategy is not merely an alternative to monetarism, but also to the notion that nothing can be done to advance socialism short of a complete social revolution. At the same time, it should promote a qualitative, and not merely quantitative, advance in the condition of ordinary working people. No assumptions should be made about the existence of a latent socialist majority amongst working people, waiting to be mobilised by the right choice of policies or political leaders. The majority of working people in this country are not socialist, and a socialist majority will have to be constructed. This will require a strategy which offers concrete advances while simultaneously promoting a sense of hegemony amongst working people—that is, a sense of their ability to order society according to their own values as a class. Considered in this light, mobilisation is a more complex and uncertain concept than is sometimes implied.

Although obviously the advocates of an AES would welcome the *maximum* political support, in practice the strategy is clearly aimed primarily at activists—shop stewards on the one hand, and campaign activists on the other. Mobilising widespread support amongst this group is probably what most often counts as mass mobilisation, allowing for the ability of activists to transmit enthusiasm for the strategy to a wider range of ordinary people.

What is the reason for this particular conception of the people to be mobilised by the AES? The most probable reason lies in the underlying notion that the AES will provoke a confrontation with capital, and that the organised backing of local activists will therefore be vital to the enforcement of the strategy. There appears to be some confusion, however, about the most likely scenario involved. Some versions appear to envisage a *direct* confrontation between labour and capital, presumably taking the form of strikes, sit-ins, community resistance etc. But victory under these conditions seems implausible. The most likely form of opposition by domestic capital would be an investment strike: and the most likely form of opposition by overseas capital would be a sterling crisis. It is not clear at all whether local activists, however well mobilised, would be in a position to do anything directly to resist attacks in those forms.

Other accounts appear to concentrate on the relationship between labour movement activists and a Labour government which was coming under pressure from capital. Here the purpose of mobilisation is to ensure that the leadership does not capitulate. This implies that it is state power which will be decisive in enabling labour to defeat capital, but that democratic accountability inside the Labour Party is an essential pre-condition. This is a more plausible analysis, but it narrows still further the concept of mobilisation with which we started. It implies the need for an autonomous tendency inside the Labour Party, capable of organising majorities in favour of left-wing policies; but that is not necessarily the same as the mobilisation of working people at large.

Apart from differences concerning the groups to be mobilised, there are also differences over the basis for mobilisation. One recurring strand in writings about the AES is the notion that broad popular support may be mobilised around the achievement of simple material gains for working people. Perhaps it is worth reminding ourselves of the obvious point that the AES is basically an economic strategy, in which has been observed a potential for gathering political support. In the main, the policies which make up the AES have been selected on the basis of their coherence as economic arguments. Indeed one feature of the AES is that it is normally presented as a totality, with interdependent parts—by implication obeying an inner logic, rather than being framed from the start as a broad popular package of measures. It is not surprising, therefore, that one of the most commonly cited elements in the mobilising potential of the AES is essentially economistic. The AES is expected to generate support because it holds out the hope of more jobs, higher living standards and better public services.

An economistic programme is not without its advantages, if that means a programme which attempts to resolve the economic crisis in favour of working people, and offers them real economic benefits. A strategy which did not offer hope of a return to full employment, for example, could hardly claim the support of working people. Nor should we underestimate the importance of manifestations of popular support for the AES, however elementary their basis. Such manifestations do have a role in a bourgeois democratic system. In some cases they might make it very difficult for capital to intervene against a Labour government. Intervention through the armed forces, or through the agency of the EEC, are two examples where expressions of popular will in favour of the AES could be highly effective.

It should also be said that attaching the label 'economistic' to the AES is not altogether fair. For an AES to be implemented at all, working people would first have to vote a left Labour government into office. That would necessarily occur before anyone had received any material benefit at all from the strategy. One aspect of the potential electoral appeal of the AES is its plausibility and coherence: it relies on convincing people that a Labour Party aspiring to government possesses a carefully constructed programme in which likely obstacles have been anticipated, and which therefore stands a good chance of achieving its stated objectives. Therefore working people are not simply envisaged as the passive objects

of the AES: they are also being asked to think about the measures proposed, to evaluate them in the light of common sense and past experience,
and to exercise a positive judgement in their favour.

But ultimately the AES must be measured against its own, more
ambitious, criterion: that it should be capable not merely of attracting
popular support, but of starting a process of *mobilisation* amongst
ordinary working people. It is here that the familiar shortcomings of a
basically economistic approach immediately become apparent. We could
not necessarily expect working people to reward a Labour government
with continuing political support purely because it provided material gains.
We might just as easily find such an administration supplanted in time by
a renovated 'Heathite' Tory Party, or perhaps displaced by a technocratic
faction within the Labour Party itself—even assuming that the Liberal/
Social Democratic Alliance fails in its attempt to break the dominance of
the two major parties. Material advances are a necessary, but not a
sufficient, condition for the success of the AES. In this context the process
of mobilisation is too often confused with the gathering of political
support in a more general sense.

Proponents of the AES have in many cases recognised this, and added
proposals on industrial democracy in order to try and involve working
class activists in support of the AES. But although usually described as
'central' to the AES, in practice progress towards workers' control is
treated as totally marginal. This is especially true of official versions. The
1981 TUC Economic Alternative, for example, describes industrial democracy as a 'precondition for success'. Yet there is literally no discussion
of what this means.

What are the reasons for this phenomenon? One reason, no doubt, is
the existence of unresolved differences between the unions themselves
over what form industrial democracy should take. But another reason, as
it will be argued in more detail in the following section, is an almost
complete disjuncture in the analysis underlying the AES between what
happens in the labour process on the one hand and the course of the
economic crisis on the other.

It is often asserted, correctly, that an extension of industrial democracy
could involve working people in the implementation of the AES. But there
is a common conflation of propositions that: (a) industrial democracy is a necessary part of the AES, viewed as a genuinely transitional
strategy towards a non-statist version of socialism, and, (b) industrial
democracy is a mobilising force for the AES. Of course these propositions
are not mutually exclusive. But it is wrong to imply that adding industrial
democracy measures to the AES would guarantee broad mobilisation
behind it. This they certainly would not, if only for the simple reason that
most workers are not shop stewards, and that a large proportion of shop
stewards are themselves unenthusiastic about becoming involved in their

employers' decision-making processes. While industrial democracy pro-posals should clearly play an important part in the AES, they are unlikely to provide the basis for broad mobilisation.

The main task will not be to 'involve' working people in running their enterprise in the conventional sense. The path of 'involvement' and 'participation' can lead to the incorporation of working people's repre-sentatives, the subordination of working people's interests and the degradation of collective action. The alternative is to instead promote an increase in the organised collective power of working people in the labour process, particularly through trade-union structures, while at the same time encouraging the politicisation of that power. The distinction between the labour process and the wider area of strategic decisions is important here. The purpose of making this distinction is not to suggest that working people should not attempt to influence strategic decisions. Rather it is to acknowledge the constraints which are likely to act against such attempts in the foreseeable future, and to emphasise the sphere out of which hegemonic tendencies are most likely to develop successfully.

These constraints are present in both the consciousness and organisa-tional condition of working people. Thus, instead of a frustrated enthusiasm amongst working people for strategic decision-making, we find a deep lack of self-confidence. This is the product of a number of factors, including poor education, inexperience, and a basic lack of time and resources—as well as the ideological effects of a subordinate class culture. We are committed to a counter-attack on all these factors. But we should not expect progress to be rapid. Organisational solutions to the question of industrial democracy will fail unless this is recognised, and may actually retard development. Premature attempts at giving working people's representatives a 'share' in strategic decision-making and thereby in some sense 'mobilise' them behind the AES, are likely to result in their incorporation and isolation from working people. No system of accountability could do more than retard this process: accountability under present conditions would tend to be undermined by the absence of a proper basis for solidarity and collective action. Proposals for extend-ing workers' power too frequently rely on notions of democracy trans-planted directly from bourgeois forms—single representatives, votes in committees, etc.—rather than attempting to embrace, as far as possible, the concept of collective decision-making. This is precisely why, in practice, we have not seen the development of those organisational forms amongst the working class which are a logical precondition for any system of industrial democracy on the bourgeois pattern. Workers' combines are a case in point. Combines play an interesting role in discussions around the AES; they form the missing piece in a jigsaw puzzle involving the theoretical dictates of socialist planning on the one hand, and workers' intervention in strategic decision-making on the other: yet there are currently few combines which have the shape of the missing piece. Nor will the fact of identifying the political 'necessity' of their existence bring them into being, for the simple reason that their development is perpetually aborted under the constraints we have identified. Calling on trade unions (once more) to promote them will have no perceptible effect on the situation. Rather we have to examine the constraints with great care and attempt to create the conditions under which the development of combines might be not merely a logical 'necessity', but also the natural next step.

The purpose of these remarks is to begin to introduce some elements of scale into discussions about industrial democracy under an AES. There is a great danger of implying that dramatic changes may be brought about in the consciousness and organisational condition of working people simply by granting them formal legal powers over employers' decision-making processes; or at the very least, that working people would recognise the granting of these formal powers—even if they were not capable of exercising them effectively—as legitimating a wider political contract between organised labour and the state. Clearly neither of these outcomes is likely.

We should, of course, be encouraging the maximum progress towards industrial democracy—even if in the first instance this means implanting 'bourgeois' forms, because these may be better than anything which exists at the moment. But we may expect progress to be both slow and uneven. A few sections of the working class have already reached an advanced state of development, in which wholesale alternatives to management strategies are being placed on the agenda. But for the vast bulk of ordinary working people, the process may occupy several decades. This is not the stuff of a transitional strategy in the sense in which the term is normally used of the AES.

What are the implications of the preceding discussion for the mobilising potential of the AES? There is irrefutable evidence, based on past experience, that a radical economic programme would not be implemented if we relied solely on the political will of Parliament. Successful resistance to the opposition of capital requires that the programme should command the support of grass roots activists within the ruling party, and that a system of accountability be established to enable this support to be impressed on the party hierarchy. Second, the chances of success will be enhanced to the extent that our programme can offer real material advances to ordinary people, leading to expressions of popular support in the face of outside interventions. But none of this amounts to a social revolution. The concept of mobilisation has been used rather loosely to imply a potential for mass activity which probably does not exist. Proposals on industrial democracy in the AES, in particular, fall far short of fulfilling the role which is sometimes assigned to them: the extension of workers' control needs to be evaluated not in terms of whether it meets the requirement for 'involving' people in a predetermined strategy, but by the rather

different criterion of whether it advances or retards—in the longer term—
the development of a collective and hegemonic consciousness.

3. Working People and Explanations of the Crisis

This section looks at another aspect of the relationship between working
people and the AES: the role which is attributed to working people in the
evolution of economic crisis under capitalism. It will be argued that weaknesses in this area probably account for the incoherent and unhelpful use
of the mobilisation concept.

Working people often appear to play an ambiguous role in socialist
economic literature. This is true especially of socialist analyses of the
economic crisis. Official versions of the AES share this characteristic. This
is a worrying feature because it weakens the political credibility of the
AES, not least amongst working people themselves.

It is true that unofficial versions of the AES do attach some importance
to class conflict at the point of production. The London CSE Group,[2] for
example, suggest that it was stalemate in the class war which had, by the
end of the 1970s, deprived capital of the ability to undertake the drastic
restructuring then required. Sam Aaronovitch, however, in his account[3]
of the AES, tends to play this factor down, saying: 'How workers and
unions behave has some influence on technology and efficiency but for
the most part hardly a crucial one.' And in official 'TUC and Labour
Party formulations, even this marginal role for class struggle is apparently
discounted. The underlying causes of the economic crisis are either not
discussed at all, or else the crisis is explained in a superficial way, by
blaming the state for pursuing deflationary economic policies, and/or by
blaming capital for not investing enough in British industry.

Of course there is probably no such thing as a definitive account of
how capitalist crises are caused. Therefore in one sense it is useless
criticising official versions of the AES for not attempting to offer one. On
the other hand it is damaging to the credibility of the AES to imply that
there are no material or political consequences at all of the existence of
class formations inside the workplace, or of class struggle for control over
the organisation of production.

This still leaves us with the question of how significant a factor class
conflict is in explaining the course of economic crises. It might be that its
significance, as Sam Aaronovitch suggests, is only minimal. Again, there is
no definitive answer. But there are a number of reasons, some 'a priori'
and others derived from recent experience, which suggests that the issue
should be confronted openly in the AES itself, at the very least as a matter
of political necessity.

To begin with, there is the nature of capitalist crises themselves.
Recurrent crises are an essential feature of capitalist development. Their
resolution in favour of capital constitutes a continual process of renewal of

capitalist relations. Moreover crises are not necessarily discrete events, with a clearly defined beginning and end. The process of technological change involves a continuous, as well as continual, renewal of capital's control over the sphere of production, and over the terms of the distribution of surplus value. We should therefore expect to find significant effects where class struggle results in a slower rate of technological change, or a slower realignment of factor incomes, than the capitalist system demands.

Thus, on the one hand, the process of production is crucially a labour process, as well as a process of selecting, designing and developing capital equipment. The labour process affects the speed of performance of tasks and its precision, predictability and quality, as well as the continuity of production. And in addition to class conflict over the labour process, of course, we have to consider the inflationary effects of class conflict over the distribution of incomes.

Apart from what might be called 'a priori' considerations, there is also some circumstantial, but significant, evidence from recent British history of the importance which both capital and the state attach to the defeat of worker resistance as a precondition for the resolution of the latest series of crises. Thus the state has made repeated attempts to achieve either voluntary or compulsory restraint over labour incomes. Indeed the power of capital to restrain these unaided is now in question. Even recessionary crises, it now seems, are only effective when intensified by state action. Similarly, there have been major attempts to reform labour law in such a way as to restrict the rights of trade unions to organise and take industrial action. And again it is significant that the state should be led to intervene in this way. It suggests that the problem for capital has reached an acute stage. Taken together, these are some of the most distinctive features of the British political economy in recent decades. Yet all of these events are incoherent unless we are prepared to give a proper significance to class conflict, worker resistance and the labour process generally. Official labour movement responses, however, often tend to treat the different attacks as unrelated. This is epitomised in the analysis offered of the Tory government's monetarist strategy which regards the strategy as 'irrational' and 'insane'. The significance of monetarism as a coordinated onslaught on the power of labour, leading to a permanent increase in the rate of exploitation, is thus ignored in favour of the idea that the government's policies are somehow calculated to destroy the whole of British industry.

Could it be argued that the general conditions confronting a Labour government implementing the AES would be any different? Could such a government, openly committed to resolving the crisis in favour of working people, safely assume a different response to measures designed to regenerate British industry? An economic environment of expanding demand and employment might clearly create a different *political* environment, in which working people were more willing in principle to accept an acceleration in the rate of technological change and perhaps also self-restraint in the growth of incomes. The difficulty, however, is that a reduction in unemployment might simply shift the balance of power back towards labour, with no guarantee that this power was used to back a policy of restructuring. Would an individual worker be able to distinguish the experience of restructuring under an AES from the experience of restructuring carried out during an offensive by capital? The costs of accepting restructuring might be reduced, but then so would the necessity for accepting it in the first place. So restructuring might be slower and less complete than the AES requires. In some cases it might be ineffective altogether. This is crucially important for the AES, which could be relying on a high, and perhaps forced, investment strategy for restoring industrial competitiveness.

4. Conclusion

Critics of the AES, who have suggested that it offers merely statist or technical solutions to the economic crisis, sometimes attribute this weakness to the reformist politics of those who are promoting it. However, this takes no account of the fact that in the AES workers and trade unions are also attributed with no significant role in the development of the crisis itself. As we have seen, the origin of the problem appears to lie in the way the development of the capitalist system is analysed. If workers and trade unions are thought to play no role in the evolution of the crisis, it is quite natural that they should not be mentioned in a programme for resolving it. The more fundamental question, therefore, is why the underlying analysis is so weak.

One reason may be a simple fear of appearing to 'blame the workers' for the economic crisis, thereby playing into the hands of bourgeois propagandists, and weakening support for the AES from labour movement activists. The time is overdue, however, for the movement to take a serious look at *all* the political implications of its traditional reactions to the issue. There is, after all, more than one sense in which we have to take the monetarist assault seriously. One of the striking features of the monetarist prescription was the initial popularity of its main tenets amongst traditional Labour voters. Moreover the ideological hold which monetarism exerts has proved remarkably stubborn, given its devastating results. This is evidence that Thatcher has not somehow 'mislocated' the debate. The fact is that in one sense she has located the debate in exactly the correct place—inside the sphere of capitalist production itself. Monetarist arguments may seem more convincing for appearing to confront basic class issues, while the AES appears as a false set of 'easy options' involving merely technical adjustments to state policies. The danger of cynicism amongst working people is clear enough; it could seriously undermine the chances of success for the AES, which on its own terms requires active popular mobilisation in some form. An acute danger lies in allowing, or even worse contributing to, the entrenchment of a subordinate class psychology: we might emerge from a period of intensified class conflict to find ourselves confronted not by a renovated state capitalism, but by a neo-fascist state backed by majority support amongst working people. We need an AES in which the implications for an effective class strategy have been thoroughly considered.

NOTES

1. The author is grateful to Fran Bennett and David Purdy for their comments on an earlier draft.
2. CSE London Working Group, 1980, *The Alternative Economic Strategy*, CSE Books/LCC, London.
3. Sam Aaronovitch, 1981, *The Road from Thatcherism*, Lawrence and Wishart, London.

DISCUSSION

David Purdy

The general logic of Brian Burkitt's argument is irresistible. Indeed the outlines of his analysis were already formulated nearly 40 years ago by Kalecki. The history of advanced capitalism since then has fully vindicated Kalecki's insights.

The post-war economy attempted to combine four elements:

1. a full employment, welfare regime,
2. the predominance of capitalist relations of production across the greater part of economic life, including, notably, foreign trade, the principal flows of loan finance and the volume, timing, character and location of investment in fixed capital,
3. decentralised and unregulated money wage bargaining,
4. a tolerable degree of price stability, important less for its own sake than as an index of the underlying state of social conflict over the distribution of real output among rival uses and users.

In the long run it is next to impossible to knit these elements together into a stable amalgam.

Controversy over economic policy has been largely dominated by the ways in which political parties, factions and social groups have responded to the resulting dilemmas. Two main approaches have evolved—the neo-liberal and the social democratic (as distinct from Social Democratic!). The former aims to replace the full employment, welfare state by a new/old regime under which all agents within civil society, and the various branches of the state too, are firmly disciplined by a system of supra-political, quasi-impersonal financial rules. The latter aims to mediate directly in the processes of inflationary conflict. Negotiated agreement between the state and industrial organisations representing workers and capitalist enterprises respectively, is intended to restrain the use of market power in the process of wage and price formation.

Both approaches have proved unpalatable to the left, though there must by now be many who in the light of Mrs Thatcher's monetarist counter-revolution doubt the wisdom of the left's previous hostility towards prices and incomes policies. Essentially, Brian Burkitt argues that these doubts are justified, but that what is needed in order to contain inflation and the social conflicts of which it is the symptom, is an incomes policy of a new kind. This would require as the *quid pro quo* delivered in exchange for pay restraint, a substantial shift in the balance of the mixed economy between private and public economic power, and simultaneously a progressive extension of popular democratic control over industrial and financial corporations and over the activities of the state.

My main criticism of this paper is that it does no more than reiterate positions developed over the past decade by others, including me. (See references.) The paper presents certain general principles and then comes to an abrupt halt. Now the restatement of general principles is still, regrettably, necessary in the prevailing climate of opinion on the left. For understandable historic and agitational reasons many sections of the left stubbornly refuse to acknowledge the social and political damage caused by the unions' deep-rooted attachment to a system of uncoordinated and decentralised money wage bargaining.

But those who have long been convinced on these matters have a responsibility to go beyond general principles. They must offer concrete proposals for achieving within the foreseeable future a progressive and workable social contract—or government-union 'understanding', call it what you will—making no attempt to conceal or minimise the warts which will inevitably disfigure the appearance of the enterprise. This has to mean a willingness to draw up reasonably precise bargaining agendas and proposals for institutional change, together with all the supporting activities of campaigning, publicity, education and training which the labour movement could realistically pursue both at central government level and within the workplace and community. Without the immediacy of such an interventionist approach the principles themselves will never be transmuted from ideas into a material force.

In 'Government-Trade Union Relations: Towards a New Social Contract' by D.L. Purdy[3] it is shown how in three specific areas of policy —(i) refuse disposal, recycling and conservation, (ii) the division of the time cake between different activities and between the sexes, and (iii) the negotiation of new technology agreements—agreement on pay restraint could be linked to immediate and tangible advances on other fronts. This kind of approach to a new social contract would not depend on any unrealistically and undesirably large upward shift in the trend of output growth, or indeed on any major piece of macroeconomic engineering. It would incorporate a gradual, but self-reinforcing dynamic leading steadily towards economic democratisation. It would help to replace the discredited image of the welfare state with a reconstructed relationship between state and people. Finally, it would enable the labour movement to project itself as the champion both of the general social interest—for example, in recovering for our species a balanced metabolism with our natural environment—and of the interests of social groups whose oppression derives from non-class sources.

This last point also highlights the central problem in Owen Jones' paper on the politics of the AES. Owen's otherwise laudable emphasis on working class self-activity and participation in planning and executing alternative economic policies, suffers from an uncritical use of the concept of collectivity. 'Collective' (-ism, -ivity, etc.) is normally used as the opposite of 'individual'. But *this* opposition does not coincide, as Owen's usage implies, with the opposition between hegemony and subordination. Collective action, consciousness, etc. are quite compatible with the maintenance of class relations of domination/subordination. They can no longer be seen, as they were by classical Marxism, as social learning experiences leading automatically to the transcendence of a subordinate mentality within the working class.

This is due to two factors. First, even if we confine attention, as the paper does, to the *class* dimensions of privilege/oppression relations in society, there are *degrees* of collectivism. Trade-union organisation is structured by the contours of occupation, workplace, enterprise and industry. The character of workers' collective action is influenced, even dominated, by these contours. This usually causes the general *class* character of such action to be submerged or remain latent. And even when a collective consciousness comes momentarily to encompass almost the whole wage earning population within a given national territory, this in itself offers no guarantee that the workers' movement will either set its sights on the reconstruction of the forms of the state, or develop the requisite capacities. So even if we allow that it is in the course of trade-union struggle that the working class 'experiences itself as a class', there remains a gulf between this form of collectivism and the achievement of hegemony.

Second, it is in any case impossible nowadays to restrict attention to *class* division. This line of social differentiation and conflict has always been intersected by others—deriving from the gender system, ethnic origin, national identity, the division between mental and manual labour and the generation gap. In the past it was plausible to argue that the class division carried decisive weight: for political purposes the other social divisions could be treated as secondary. Today such traditional arguments are wholly implausible, though the issue is strictly empirical and cannot be settled by *a priori* theory. It follows that class-based collectivism cannot provide the sole or even principal foundation for a socialist political strategy. Some implications of this conclusion are worked through for the case of gender-based politics elsewhere in this volume in the paper by Sheila Smith and Jean Gardiner.

It also follows that the contrast discussed in Owen's paper between 'bourgeois forms of representation and accountability' and 'collective decision making' is simplistic and unhelpful as soon as one departs from the archetypal case of the mass strike meeting. (It may not even help much for this case: what exactly is wrong with ballots on pay offers and set piece industrial action from the standpoint of democratic principles?) Direct democracy without the mediation of representatives is appropriate and feasible only for a certain number of issues. And even in small groups of people there are cultural and material limits of time and space to their participation in communal affairs. A communist society would be one which systematically and without violence adjusted the patterns of its social activity in the common social interest. In devising institutional procedures for first identifying, then implementing the common interest on any given issue, it is hardly likely that we shall be able to dispense with the experience accumulated by humankind of various systems of government and social control, including the experience garnered over the past century or so of 'bourgeois' democracy.

REFERENCES

Purdy, D.L., August 1974, 'Some Thoughts on the Party's Policy Towards Prices, Wages and other Incomes', *Marxism Today*.

Purdy, D.L., 'The Social Contract and Socialist Policy', in M. Prior (ed.), 1980, *The Popular and the Political*, Routledge and Kegan Paul.

Purdy, D.L., 'Government-Trade Union Relations: Towards a New Social Contract', *Socialist Economic Review* 1981.

Prior, M., and Purdy, D.L., 1979, 'Out of the Ghetto', Spokesman.

THE POLITICAL ECONOMY OF TAXATION AND THE ALTERNATIVE ECONOMIC STRATEGY

Lesley Day and Chris Pond

Introduction

Taxation has an important part to play in fulfilling many of the objectives of the Alternative Economic Strategy (AES): a reduction in economic and sexual inequality; a move towards more collective consumption; a shift from the 'private' to the 'social' wage. Moreover, the strategy envisages a substantial expansion of public expenditure. Even though tax revenues will rise automatically as economic activity recovers, it is likely that taxation will increase as a proportion of national income: 'fair collective payment through tax for collective provision of services'.[1] Yet there has been little discussion of the type of radical tax policy which is needed as an integral part of the wider strategy. Throughout much of the post-war period, the burden of taxation on working people has increased substantially. There is a need to ensure that this burden is not increased still further under the AES.

The purpose of this paper is two-fold: to contribute to the discussion of the type of tax policy necessary as part of the AES and to put those discussions into context, by examining the distribution of the tax burden through the periods of social democratic policies and what is now termed Thatcherism. The first part of the paper is concerned with what might be described as 'the political economy of taxation'. This provides a framework within which we consider, in the second part of the paper, a programme of radical tax reform within the AES.

1. Political Economy of Taxation

(a) Financing the welfare state. The growth of the welfare state, and its present crisis, has been a subject of increasing interest. Many recent Marxist writings have argued against the 'reductionist' view of the state simply as an instrument of the functional requirements of capital.[2] Policy outcomes, their form and content, will tend rather to reflect the dynamic of class conflict. Changes in policy may represent real benefits for working people as well as meeting the needs of capital. In its relatively autonomous position, the state can be an arena of struggle and 'arbiter' between the demands of organised labour for wage increases and social welfare and the competing and sometimes conflicting short-term interests of different sections of capital. Consideration has to be given also to the way in which economic and social agents within the state and on behalf of capital, perceive their interests at different historical periods.

157

This is not to be confused with a pluralist view of the state as the representative of the 'common interest' or with a view that the state in an advanced capitalist society is simply a 'tool' of the ruling class. Gains won by working people in the arena of the welfare state may be real for them and a threat to capital; some may also inadvertently be in the long-term interests of capital; others may be an imposition by the state which working people primarily experience as socially controlling.

It is not our aim to enter into the complexities of this particular theoretical debate. Rather we are concerned to set in context our discussion of the funding of these state activities through the taxation system, and to consider whether taxation itself may reflect the balance of class forces. One argument is that if the growth of state expenditure could be financed almost wholly by working people, its threat to capital accumulation would be minimised. As Gough argues: 'If the cost of the welfare state could be borne by the household sector, predominantly the broad working class, then its expansion would not necessarily harm surplus value and capital accumulation.'[3]

(b) The growth of wage taxation. An analysis of post-war changes in the formal incidence of taxation would certainly seem to suggest that the burden of financing increased state expenditure has been largely concentrated on the working class. Direct wage taxation (principally income tax and national insurance contributions) has increased considerably. Until the mid-fifties only those with above average earnings or without family responsibilities paid any income tax. After the early 1960s, the tax burden on wages began to rise steeply. By 1964 almost ten per cent of the average wage was taken in tax, and this proportion had doubled by 1970. By 1978/79 the 'average' family was paying 24 per cent of its income in direct taxes, a proportion which had risen to an estimated 26.5 per cent by 1981/82. Moreover, a larger proportion of the workforce became liable to taxation.[4] The period witnessed not only an increase in the overall level of wage-taxation, but a shift in the burden towards those at the lower end of the distribution as well.

Meanwhile, the level of taxes formally levied on capital (corporate and personal) appears to have declined. There is fairly general agreement, amongst the economic establishment as well as Marxist writers, that pre-tax company profitability, measured in terms of either the share or rate of profit, has declined since the early 1960s. Recognition of this may have been one factor encouraging governments to ease the tax liability of the corporate sector. An analysis by King, for example, concluded (for the period of the mid-1950s to mid-1970s) that: 'While there has been a long-run decline in the share of pre-tax conventional gross profits, this has coincided with changes in taxes and investment incentives which have left the share of conventional gross profits after tax virtually unchanged.'[5] Corporate tax liabilities have declined further since the mid-1970s. Faced with a severe company liquidity crisis in 1974, the Wilson government introduced an 'emergency' system of stock appreciation relief. This, combined with generous capital allowances, had the effect of virtually eliminating Mainstream Corporation Tax[6] for many of the largest commercial and industrial companies. By 1978/79 it was estimated that although the top twenty industrial and commercial companies had made gross profits of over £5,000 millions, more than half of them had paid no mainstream corporation tax at all.[7]

Despite improvements in true profitability, the stock relief system therefore resulted in reductions in companies' tax liabilities. An amendment to the stock relief system by the Conservative government provided further tax concessions to companies to compensate for the reduction in profitability that accompanied the deepening of the recession in 1980/81. These reductions in corporate tax liability have been offset to some extent by changes in employers' national insurance contributions.[8]

Local authority rates may also be considered as a tax on property. Although local authorities' expenditure has increased rapidly throughout the post-war period, their revenue from the rates has been declining as a proportion of total taxes. Although the ratio of rates to GNP remained roughly constant, within a five-fold increase in local authority revenue between 1966/7 and 1978/9 the contribution of rates fell from about one half to just over one third.[9] Local authorities have become increasingly dependent on central government for finance.[10]

Finally we should consider the formal incidence of taxation on capital in the form of personal wealth. The main form of UK personal wealth taxation has traditionally been the estate duty, payable on the value of estates passed on at death. After the Second World War heavy increases in the rates of tax payable on the largest estates were imposed. However, over the next quarter century the proportionate contribution of this tax to total direct tax receipts declined, from nine per cent of the total in 1948/49 to only four per cent in 1973/74.[11] The post-1974 Labour government was committed to a 'fundamental shift in the balance of wealth and power in favour of working people and their families'. They replaced the old Estate Duty with Capital Transfer Tax, the intention being to close many of the loopholes which had made the estate duty into virtually a 'voluntary tax'. Nevertheless, revenue continued to decline, from 3.9 per cent of all direct taxes in 1973/74 to 1.2 per cent in 1980/81.[12] A similar decline occurred in the revenue contribution of capital gains tax over the same period.

(c) *The final burden of taxation.* The formal incidence of taxation described above is relevant to our discussions in the sense that it may reflect attempts by governments to rearrange relative tax liabilities. However, attention must also be paid to the final burden of taxation.

Within orthodox neo-classical analysis a tax imposed on a firm (whether it be a profits tax, employers' national insurance contributions or local rates) may either be passed on to labour in the form of lower wages or higher prices, or absorbed in reduced profits. The final incidence will depend on the relative elasticities of demand and supply in the various labour and product markets. However, we are more concerned here with the incidence of taxation as between labour and capital. An increase in the concentration of capital increases its ability to pass taxes on to labour as lower wages or higher prices. Similarly, a strong and militant trade-union movement may be able to resist the lowering of the living standards of its members through the mechanism of wage taxation, by demanding higher money wages to compensate.

As Gough argues (although within a different theoretical framework): 'In the real world, the final burden of taxation is determined by the ebb and flow of class conflict and will vary with the economic and political strength of the contending classes.'[13] Gough's argument has two main components. There is a need first to consider whether state expenditure is necessarily a drain on capital and capital accumulation, and second to consider who ultimately pays the taxes to finance state expenditure. Unlike Fine and Harris, Gough does not argue that all taxes are always paid out of surplus value and are therefore detrimental to the interests of capital.[14]

First, Gough argues that part of welfare expenditure, paid for out of taxes flows back in the form of services and financial benefits to reproduce the working and the non-working population. In the same way that the worker reproduces herself/himself and the family by wages spent in the market, so welfare benefits and services perform a similar function. Part of wages, in the form of taxes, are therefore recycled through the state and are part of the value of labour power. Therefore, consideration has to be given to that proportion of tax revenue which is recycled in a form which is indirectly productive for capital ('social capital' as defined by O'Connor) in that it augments the rate of profit and accumulation in the economy: that spent on the socialisation of the wage system (the 'social wage'); or on increasing the productivity of labour.[15] That proportion which is spent on the maintenance of order and harmony in the relations of production (sometimes called the social control function) is not even indirectly productive for capital.

Second, there is the question of who ultimately pays the taxes. Gough argues that certain forms of state expenditure produce use values for labour. The suggestion is that if wages are reduced or do not rise so fast because part of welfare expenditure represents the 'social' wage, and 'if as a result of this taxes are borne by the working class, the total mass of profits may not be diminished'.[16] However, these two components of Gough's argument should be considered separately since, even if gross wages do not rise to offset the increase in wage taxation, expenditure on

what we have termed social control, and the maintenance of order, is a
drain on capital accumulation. Gough himself points out that: 'The greater
the size of the unreproductive sphere, the greater the likelihood that the
state will have an adverse effect on the capitalist sector.'[17]

(d) *Taxation and labour militancy.* One important aspect of the changing dynamic of the class struggle, and its effect on the final burden of
taxation, is the strength of the labour movement. In the period of relatively full employment during the post war boom years, labour's strengthened
position may have enabled it not only to demand improvements in the
social wage, but to offset the effects of increased wage taxation by demanding higher money wages.

Wilkinson and Turner have argued, for instance, that the pressure on
living standards imposed by increasing wage taxation (combined with
successive pay policies) stimulated a growth of labour militancy through
the 1960s and into the 1970s.[18] A relatively strong labour movement,
borne out of the full employment policies of the 1950s and 1960s, was
able to resist attempts to use taxation as a means of reducing the growth
in private consumption.

The early post-war years witnessed few improvements in real wages,
but tax reductions mitigated the effect of rising prices. After 1960, however, wage taxation began to bite deeply into private disposable income.
Although gross real wages rose by an average of 2–2.5 per cent a year
from 1960 to 1968, the pre-tax rate of increase was cut by half in the
first half of that period and by four fifths in the second half. One response
to this increase in the tax burden was the wage explosion of the late
1960s, with gross money wages rising at an annual rate of ten per cent
between 1968 and 1970, representing a real increase of 3.6 per cent per
annum, reduced to 1.3 per cent by taxation. Hence a wage-tax spiral
developed with governments attempting to hold down increases in real
wages by taxation or pay policies, and labour responding by demanding
higher money wages. During periods of full employment it does seem
that a strong and militant labour movement was able to partially neutralise
the effects of increased wage taxation.

In the early years of the 1970s, characterised by relatively high employment levels associated with a mini-boom, the increase in gross money
wages was enhanced by changes in wage taxation. But thereafter wage
taxation began to increase again. During the period 1972 to 1975, gross
earnings increased by 66 per cent and net earnings by 52 per cent, which
after inflation represented a *decline* in real net earnings of 0.75 per cent.[19]

Although a strong organised labour movement has been able to resist,
during some periods, a reduction in real net wages this is not necessarily
true for all sections of labour. The more vulnerable and less organised
were less able to protect themselves. The study by Wilkinson and Turner,
cited above, found that 'as the 1960s progressed, tax began to bite more

deeply into the earnings of lower paid workers'.[20] Indeed, they found that towards the end of the period deliberate union attempts to discriminate in favour of the low paid in terms of gross money wage rises were almost entirely cancelled out by the effect of taxation. The same was largely true during the mid 1970s.

(e) The corporatist response. One response to the wage-tax spiral described above was for the state to centralise and take firmer control of public expenditure. There was also an attempt to develop corporatist strategies seeking agreement between capital and labour on wages, prices, taxes and social wage. A combination of wage restraint and rising un-employment now prevented wage-earners from 'passing back' the burden of taxation to capital. This threw into sharper focus the extent to which taxes paid by working people were perceived by them to be in their interests and was perhaps reflected in an unwillingness to finance certain forms of state activity. Under these circumstances, resistance may develop, manifest as some kind of 'tax revolt' against those forms of public expen-diture perceived as not improving the taxpayer's own living standards. This may explain the increased resistance to shouldering the burden of the reproduction of the non-employed sector of labour. For example, we may see a clash of interests between the employed and the growing numbers of the unemployed; resistance to women in the workforce; resistance to child benefits being paid directly to the mother rather than as a tax allowance in the man's wage packet. Resistance in this form may divide the working class, set men against women, and this may be strength-ened and reinforced by the state in its attempts to control aspects of public spending which are not in the long-term interests of capital.

Thus the corporatist response of the mid-1970s helped to lay the foundations for Thatcherism, by creating an environment in which an authoritarian right-wing government could appeal to the working class with promises to cut public spending and reduce taxes.

(f) Thatcherism. The election of a Conservative government in May 1979 has been described as a decisive break with social democratic politics and its corporatist strategy. This ideological shift represents an attempt by what Hall calls 'an authoritarian populist government' to gather up and give voice to one aspect of working people's contradictory experience of the welfare state—its controlling and alienating form.[21] Thatcher promised to 'free' working people from the bureaucratic and controlling aspects of state collectivism and give them the 'freedom' to spend their wages as they wished. What we see is a re-emergence of the ethics of self-help, individual-ism and free market economics. The other side of the contradiction is that some welfare recipients have no alternative but to rely on its support.

One of the political platforms of Thatcherism, therefore, was to cut taxes and 'relieve' the economy of the burden of the unproductive public sector. Emphasis was placed on what was perceived as a growing resentment to high personal taxation. There were some reductions in income tax rates in the Tories' first budget of 1979, although these were accompanied by substantial increases in indirect taxes. However, the record of the Thatcher government to date has been one of *increased* taxation. In 1980 taxes absorbed 36 per cent of GDP, compared with 34.5 per cent in 1978, the last year of the Callaghan government. The 1981 figures are expected to show a rise in this proportion to 40 per cent, surpassing even the peak reached in 1975.[22] Nor was this increase wholly accounted for by indirect taxes. Personal income tax also increased. In 1978/79 the 'average' family was paying 24 per cent of its income in direct taxes. By 1981/82 such taxes were taking an estimated 26.5 per cent. Only those earning more than two-and-a-half times the average wage were paying proportionately less tax in 1981 than before Thatcher took office, and the number of taxpayers increased by over a million.[23]

Two reasons can be identified for the increase in the burden of taxation on the average wage-earner under Thatcher. First there were the increases in public expenditure associated initially with rises in public sector pay and later with the recession and the government's own policies. The Manpower Services Commission estimated that by the end of 1981 the revenue costs of the unemployed (increased benefit expenditure and reduced tax receipts) had reached £12¼ billion per annum.[24] Increased interest rates also raised the cost of financing public sector borrowing. However, the increased wage taxation may also be explained by a shift in the burden towards working people and away from capital. Personal wealth taxes were reduced very considerably. Indeed, capital transfer tax concessions virtually eliminated the small amount of revenue raised by the tax, while capital gains tax and the investment income surcharge were substantially reduced. The highest rates of income tax were cut dramatically in the 1979 Budget, sufficiently to ensure that the tiny handful to whom these rates applied still paid significantly less in 1981/82 than in 1978/79. The number subject to tax above the standard rate were halved (from 4 per cent to 1.8 per cent in the same budget).[25]

What are the implications of this for the Alternative Economic Strategy? One aspect of this strategy which is not well developed is the practical possibility of devising and implementing a radical tax structure which is progressive and ensures that an appropriate contribution is made by wealth holders and companies. Can the strategy shift the balance of power back towards labour and therefore make it less likely that the burden of taxation will fall upon them? Clearly, when considering the technical aspects of a changed tax structure we have to consider this not only within the full framework of the strategy, but in the context of the inevitable tensions that will emerge from the strategy which it has been argued can only 'partially transcend the capitalist logic'.[26]

2. Taxation Policy in the AES

(a) *The need for a radical taxation policy.* Tax policy within the AES must be carefully constructed to achieve the principal objectives of the strategy as well as to ensure that the burden of financing public expenditure is not concentrated on the working class alone. There is a danger that the support from working people necessary for the success of the strategy and which converts it from a simple technical construct, may quickly evaporate if their tax burden is increased still further. Such fears will undoubtedly be manipulated by the right in an attempt to mobilise working class opposition to the AES. We need a tax policy which will provide the extra revenue required without increasing the tax burden of the average working family.

This requires a thorough overhaul of the tax system to ensure that it operates in a way consistent with the objectives of the AES as a whole. In the following pages we describe one set of proposals for such a tax policy. In the space available it is not possible to develop all the details of the policy, many of which in any case must be the subject of democratic discussion. Our purpose is merely to provide the outlines of a framework in which that discussion might take place.

(b) *The shape of a radical tax policy.*[27] As we have outlined above, the increase in wage taxation which has characterised the past three decades has been achieved by increasing the number and proportion of wage incomes subject to tax, and by increasing the marginal rate of tax on those with earnings of less than twice the average. Meanwhile, the taxation of capital (including companies and private and institutional wealth-holdings) has declined. This reduction has taken the form, not of cuts in marginal tax rates, but in the erosion of the tax base of income and wealth, through the growth of allowances and reliefs.

The starting point for an alternative tax strategy is to broaden the tax base once more through the development of a 'comprehensive income tax' (CIT). Such a tax would replace the existing income tax with its multitude of different schedules and concessions for particular types of income, savings or expenditure. At present, income from earnings, self-employment, transfer payments, fringe benefits, capital gains, rents and other investment incomes, are all treated in different ways. This results in inequities and distortions of economic activity.[28] Tax liability differs not only according to the *level* of income, but to its *source* as well. And income from capital attracts a lower tax liability than income from employment. Under a Comprehensive Income Tax all incomes, regardless of source, would be brought within the same progressive schedule of rates. Some elements which are currently exempt altogether would be brought into tax.

Less than half of all recorded incomes, and perhaps one third of actual incomes received, are subject to tax.[29] The remainder escapes liability through either exemption, avoidance or evasion. The CIT is designed to broaden the tax base by removing most (though not all) the tax exempt-ions, thus making avoidance and evasion more difficult. Broadening the base of tax would in itself make the tax system 'fairer' and more pro-gressive while at the same time yielding revenue to finance reductions in tax rates on lower income groups. We would favour a smoothly progressive structure of tax rates. It would also reduce the distortion to economic activity encouraged by our present partial and selective tax system and allow a reduction in marginal tax rates, especially on earned incomes. Since high marginal tax rates are associated with adverse 'substitution' effects (including disincentives and evasion) the policy offers the possi-bility of a more progressive and more efficient tax system.

We should note, at this point, that a CIT is not the only possible direction for structural reform of the tax system. The Meade Committee on tax reform, who reported in 1978, also concluded that many of the inequities and inefficiencies of the present system resulted from an erosion of the tax base. Although they considered the proposal for a CIT they recommended in favour of a Direct Expenditure Tax which they believed would be administratively simpler to implement, and would encourage saving and therefore investment.[30] The Labour Party, in their recent Discussion Document on Taxation, proposed an expansion of the tax base but also raised the possibility of moving towards a Personal Expen-diture Tax as one option for structural change.[31] The type of expenditure tax envisaged in both cases would not be levied indirectly on the price of goods and services (as with VAT and excise duties) but directly on the total annual (or lifetime) expenditure of the taxpayer. In effect, it would be an income tax with exemptions for *all* savings.

The proponents of such a scheme argue that Britain is already halfway towards an expenditure tax in that some forms of saving—housing, pensions and insurance—are exempt from tax. Because the exemptions are selective, they create distortions and inequities which would be reduced if all savings were tax-free. Starting from the same point, and with similar objectives, proponents of a CIT argue that the distortions and inequities are better dealt with by removing *all* exemptions for savings. A progressive expenditure tax deserves careful consideration. However, we believe it to be less consistent with the AES than is the case with a CIT for the follow-ing reasons. First, the tax is based on the principle that savings are to be encouraged in order to provide funds for investment and to reward hard work and thrift. The AES recognises that Britain's current economic problems are less to do with a shortage of investment funds and more with depressed demand and excess capacity. Second, there are the implica-tions of such a tax for inequality and the progressiveness of the tax system. To exempt savings from tax would be to exempt a larger proportion of high incomes (since savings propensities increase with income). It would be possible to compensate for this by adapting the structure of rates, but a distribution of the tax burden from groups with high savings ratios (principally those in middle age) to those with smaller negative savings (mainly younger families with children and the elderly) would still be likely. Depending on the structure of rates chosen and the adoption of a compensating tax on wealth holdings, an expenditure-based tax could result in a shift in the tax burden and an increase in the concentration of personal wealth. Finally, the Direct Expenditure Tax inevitably narrows the tax base by exempting savings. Higher marginal rates of tax would be required to raise any given level of revenue than would be the case with a CIT. For all these reasons, a CIT is, in our view, a more appropriate route for structural reform within the context of the AES.[32]

(c) *Tax expenditure.* A wide range of tax concessions currently apply. They include the basic personal allowances (such as the single person's and married man's allowance and the wife's earned income relief), tax exemption of certain forms of saving (especially housing, pensions and insurance) as well as some forms of income (capital gains, fringe benefits and some social security benefits). They also include tax concessions to companies and wealth-holders, to the private health industry and private education. Some of these tax reliefs would be considered quite legitimate within any income tax system, representing exemption of the costs of acquiring a taxable income. But very many represent explicit incentives or subsidies for particular groups or activities.

From the point of view of the recipient, these tax concessions are analogous to benefits from the state paid in cash; from the point of view of the state, they are equivalent in their effects to explicit public spending. The revenue cost is the same as if the benefits were paid in cash, and the effects on the public borrowing requirement and tax rates are also the same. However, despite stringent controls on direct cash public expenditure, these 'tax expenditures'[33] are subject to no control or scrutiny whatsoever. As a result, they have a tendency to grow relative to direct public spending. Their growth reduces the tax revenue available for social expenditure and increases taxpayer resistance to such expenditure by forcing up tax rates.

These tax expenditures have an important part to play in the analysis described earlier. They have been the principal mechanism for shifting the formal incidence of taxation from capital to labour and, within labour, from the high to the low paid. We also noted the difficulty that the Thatcher government has experienced in trying to control public spending during a recession. But while direct public expenditure has proved difficult enough to control, tax expenditures represent an open-ended commitment to the provision of additional resources, as the Thatcher government is quickly learning to its cost. For instance, in 1979 and 1980, as it became clear that the strategy was going seriously wrong, the government was forced to raise interest rates. Since many forms of borrowing, from house purchase to corporate investment, are allowable against tax, the increase in interest rates simultaneously increased the level of tax expenditures. Between 1979 and 1981, the cost of mortgage interest relief alone doubled, costing an additional £1,000 million.[34] The growth in tax expenditures has contributed to the government's inability to meet its objectives of reducing the PSBR and cutting tax rates. Under a CIT, these tax expenditures would be brought within the overall framework of public expenditure planning and control with the objective, in the long term, of reducing both their extent and size.

Tax expenditures are of greatest benefit to high income groups and the owners of wealth.[35] Despite the considerable advantages of such a policy, we are in no doubt that an attempt to reduce current levels of 'fiscal welfare' would meet with resistance from those most affected, just as the labour movement has resisted cuts in social welfare. Moreover, the right would be quick to exploit working-class fears that the scheme represented an attack on their living standards and aspirations. It would be necessary to spell out clearly the purposes of the policy and the fact that each major tax concession withdrawn would be replaced either by a reduction in tax rates or an increase in cash expenditure. The approach might be illustrated with the example of housing, perhaps the most sensitive area. Mortgage interest relief now involves revenue foregone of approximately £2,000 millions, which would be sufficient to finance a cut in the standard rate of tax of almost three pence in the pound. Capital gains tax relief costs another £2,500 millions, equivalent to perhaps four pence on the standard rate.[36] A proposal to cut tax rates by these amounts for *all* taxpayers, while withdrawing tax concessions to the owner-occupying half of the population, might meet with considerable popular support (even from owner-occupiers themselves).

There is a tendency, in any case, for the tax expenditures to become capitalised in asset prices so that the recipient of the concession is no better off in the long term. It is likely that the removal of tax concessions to owner-occupation would be followed, in time, by some fall in house prices as effective demand was reduced. Current owner-occupiers would lose and would need to be protected or compensated; but future or aspiring home-owners would be no worse off.

Of course, it would not be appropriate to withdraw altogether all public subsidies which are currently provided as tax concessions. The state may wish to continue encouraging certain activities under an AES; investment by firms would most certainly be one of them. Tax concessions are only one way of providing such incentives and it is a highly inefficient way. Under the AES investment would be more extensively planned, through planning agreements and in the public sector. Where financial incentives to invest are considered appropriate these can be more effectively controlled and administered through cash subsidies and grants than through tax concessions.

Some of the tax concessions, such as those mentioned above, are explicit subsidies; many more are implicit in the sense that there is simply no requirement to submit certain forms of income for tax, or the state turns a blind eye. Capital gains, undistributed corporate profits, fringe benefits and some self-employment incomes are examples. Under a CIT, these forms of income would be brought within the tax net.

(d) *Implementing radical tax change.* The outlines of the policy should now be clear. Some examples of the effect of the proposed policy on different sectors helps to illustrate how this policy might be implemented. We begin with the household sector. Many commentators on the AES, acknowledging the effects of the decline in the tax threshold (made up of the basic personal allowances) have proposed relief for the low paid by raising the value of the allowances, at least to the level of the 'official poverty line' (supplementary benefit level). However, since the allowances exempt the first slice of *all* incomes and not just the incomes of the poor, the effect would be to give a tax cut to all income taxpayers alike. Indeed, the biggest tax cuts would be enjoyed by those on the highest incomes. The cost would be several times the amount required to take the low paid out of tax, and would reduce the revenue available for other elements of the strategy. Other ways of exempting those on the lowest incomes from tax need to be found. One alternative would be the conversion of the personal allowances into specific 'vanishing exemptions', designed to exempt those on the lowest incomes from tax but to allow the full taxation of incomes above a certain level. The withdrawal rate of the exemptions, and the schedule of marginal tax rates, would have to be carefully designed to prevent the creation of a 'poverty trap'.[37]

Another approach would be to convert the value of the allowances into a cash payment, as was the case with child tax allowances and child benefit. Every household would receive this tax-free cash payment—a sort of 'social dividend'—related to family composition but subject to no means-test or contribution test, and set at an adequate level. Tax would be payable on all incomes other than the social dividend itself. This proposal has the advantage that it leaves open the option of integrating currently means-tested social security benefits into the social dividend itself. One element of the personal tax allowances which should certainly be abolished is the married man's allowance which discriminates against working women and costs a total of £3,000m in revenue foregone. This revenue could be used to provide a substantial improvement in child benefits or to provide a standard 'responsibility payment', payable as a standard sum to those with the care of children or adult dependents.[38]

This is not the place for a detailed discussion of the structure of social security. Its finance, however, is relevant. At present a large proportion of that finance is raised regressively through the national insurance contributions. Combined with income tax, the contributions ensure that the marginal tax rate faced by those on low earnings is higher than that payable on high earnings and even on most investment incomes. Despite these regressive aspects of the scheme, the contribution principle has been defended by the labour movement in the belief that governments would not cut the benefits thereby financed at times of crisis. Thatcher has proved them wrong. Although the contributions have increased considerably in the recent past, the benefits have been cut. The separate national insurance contributions should be scrapped, the finance being raised progressively through general taxation. There may be a case for the retention of a separate social security tax on employers, but this should be related to the size of the total wage bill rather than to the earnings of individual workers. Benefits should be payable at a flat rate according to need arising from interruption of earnings and residence.[39]

Social security benefits themselves would be taxable, along with all other forms of income. However, since we assume that the exemption level for tax would be at least as high as benefit levels, those with no other sources of income would receive their benefits tax-free. Additional incomes would be taxed at the normal rate.[40] We should distinguish this proposal from Thatcher's policy of using taxation as a thinly disguised means of cutting benefits.

An increasingly important element of household incomes now virtually tax-free are fringe benefits. The Diamond Commission found that, even by 1978, the average managing director was receiving more than a third of his salary (a total of almost £11,000 a year) in fringe benefits.[41] The proportionate value of the benefits had trebled since 1974, largely as a means of circumnavigating pay policies. The last Labour government made a feeble attempt to tax company cars, but a car valued at up to £14,000 still attracts a maximum tax liability of less than £400 a year. Instead of trying to tax fringe benefits separately from salaries, as now, the employer should be required to include in taxable gross salary the full cost of fringe benefits provided for each employee, as if they had been paid in cash.[42] Far more stringent definitions should be applied to what companies may deduct from their own tax liability as 'business expenses'.

Recent years have seen a significant reduction in corporate tax liabilities which have tended to offset partially the decline in profitability. Tax concessions have been provided through over-generous investment and capital allowances, and through the system of 'temporary' stock relief described above. These concessions virtually eliminated mainstream corporation tax for most industrial and commercial companies and created serious distortions within the company sector. Firms in a position to do so began investing in stocks in the knowledge that the return on such an investment would be tax-free. As Sam Aaronovitch has explained: 'The taxpayer has been financing the expansion plans of the retailing giants under the guise of protecting them from the effects of inflation.'[43]

Up to now, tax concessions to the corporate sector as a whole have been justified as a means of offsetting the decline in profitability. Under the AES the context would be wholly different. Increased economic activity and growth would bring with it some recovery of profits, and the profit motive itself would be somewhat downgraded as the driving force of the economy. Although the revenue yield is unlikely to be massive, corporate taxation has an important role to play in relieving the burden of wage taxation. At present the taxable incomes of companies bear little relation to their true profits. Depreciation of capital equipment should, of course, be allowed against taxable profits, as with other costs of production, but the 100 per cent capital allowances now granted are unjustified. Investment incentives should be awarded under a system of investment grants (of the type operated between 1966 and 1970) rather than tax allowances. The provision of such subsidies should be conditional on fulfillment by the recipient company of agreements on planning, internal democracy and employment conditions. Undistributed profits should be allocated to shareholders and included in their income tax liability (as if they were partners in the business) along with their dividend receipts. There would still be a case for a separate form of corporate taxation (in addition to that paid by shareholders and creditors of the company on their income receipts) to reflect the benefits of incorporation, including economies of scale and the advantage of limited liability.[44] As Aaronovitch suggests, this should be levied progressively with higher rates of tax applied to larger profits.[45]

(e) *Personal and institutional wealth.* Most presentations of the AES include proposals for an annual wealth tax, in recognition that personal wealth is heavily concentrated. One per cent of the adult population owns a quarter of the private wealth, including almost three-quarters of the privately held land, company shares and government stock. Those forms of personal wealth which confer power on their owners are especially heavily concentrated. A dozen other non-socialist OECD countries already have a wealth tax, where they fulfill the role of increasing economic efficiency (by encouraging wealth-holders to use their assets to obtain the highest income). But the contribution to greater equality is small. To make any impact, the rates of tax would have to be sufficiently high to ensure that, combined with taxes on the income from wealth, the largest estates could not be preserved intact. Valuation might be difficult, but would be made easier by a system of self-assessment backed by the option of the state to buy any asset at the price at which it was valued by the owner.

Even a wealth tax intended to prevent the accumulation of personal wealth would take several years to have a noticeable impact on the largest wealth holdings. Most of the very rich acquire their wealth through inheritance. An inheritance tax, combined with an annual wealth tax and applied at steeply progressive rates (rising to perhaps 100 per cent) would have more effect. The tax should be payable by the recipient (instead of the donor as is now the case) and should, of course, apply to all life-time gifts. Current exemptions for trusts, agricultural land and national heritage should probably be withdrawn if the tax is to be workable. Such exemptions have merely been capitalised in the value of the favoured assets.

These taxes would be concerned with the capital value of wealth itself. The income from wealth, including investment incomes and capital gains, would be taxable under the CIT, in the same way as other incomes. It would probably be necessary to tax capital gains as they accrued, rather than only when they were realised at sale. Otherwise taxpayers would find themselves subject to very high rates of tax when the asset was sold and would be encouraged to defer sale to postpone the payment of tax. As in the case of the wealth tax, annual valuation would therefore be necessary. The same returns could be used for both taxes. Control of institutional wealth, in the form of pension funds, banks and insurance companies, is perhaps even more heavily concentrated than personal wealth. The AES includes proposals for the democratisation of these institutions, but their tax status should also be carefully considered. Concessions to life assurance and pension contributions would be withdrawn under a CIT, to bring them into line with national insurance contributions. The funds themselves would be brought into tax by withdrawing their exemption from income tax and capital gains tax. We recognise the financial difficulties currently faced by the pension funds. Should the state wish to alleviate these difficulties this should be done through cash grants, not tax exemptions.

Much has been left unsaid about the details of the scheme. We have said nothing about the *rates* at which tax on the different sectors should be applied, only the framework within which those rates can be determined. The general objective should be to ensure that the structure of rates under the CIT should be smoothly progressive, but the relative burden of incomes, personal, institutional and corporate capital is a subject which requires careful discussion. Nor, in the space available, have we been able to devote sufficient discussion to the need for the eradication of the discrimination against women which persists in the tax system, or the need to shift resources towards families with children. We have also concentrated solely on direct taxation, ignoring indirect taxes and local authority finance. With respect to the first, our view is that indirect expenditure taxes, as far as possible, should be reduced to their regulatory role (discouraging, for example, certain forms of damaging or anti-social behaviour) and considered very much less as a source of revenue. In the case of local authority finance, it is essential to local autonomy that there should be an independent source of revenue. In our view, this is best achieved through some form of progressive income tax, perhaps supplemented by a property levy. Space does not allow us to develop these issues further here.

Conclusion

The programme outlined above offers the opportunity for a substantial shift of resources towards working people, and especially towards the lowest income groups. We have made it clear that we believe such a shift in the effective tax burden to be possible only within the wider context of an AES, and we have described a programme which we believe to be consistent with the objectives of the strategy. However, a radical tax policy such as this faces the same challenge as that confronting the AES as a whole. Would capital tolerate even a 'transitional' strategy of this type, in which its real rate of return was substantially reduced? Exchange controls would be essential to ensure that, if the rich left, they would travel light, without their wealth. Whether this in itself would be sufficient, we must leave as an open question. Not only must we discuss the form and content of the AES as a transitional strategy to socialism, but be constantly aware of, and prepared to confront, the resistance it will engender.

NOTES

1. London CSE Group, 1980, *The Alternative Economic Strategy: A Labour Movement Response to the Economic Crisis*, CSE Books, London.
2. For example see Gough, I., *The Political Economy of the Welfare State*, MacMillan Press Ltd., 1979, and *In and Against the State*, London Edinburgh Weekend Return Group, 1979.
3. Gough, I., 1979, *ibid.*, p. 106.
4. Pond, C. and Playford, C., *Carried Across the Threshold: Taxation and the Low Paid*, Low Pay Unit, 1981.
5. King, M., 'The United Kingdom Profits Crisis: Myth or Reality?', *Economics Journal*, March 1975. Over the period, King calculates, the effective rate of tax on companies (defined as effective tax to conventional gross profits) more than halved, from 37 per cent in 1950-53 to 14 per cent in 1970-73.
6. Mainstream corporation tax should be distinguished from Advanced Corporation Tax, which is effectively personal income tax paid by companies on behalf of shareholders.
7. Kay, J. and King, M., *The British Tax System*, Oxford University Press, 2nd Ed. 1980. Of the top 20 commercial and industrial companies, only nine paid any mainstream corporation tax. Between them these 20 companies had profits estimated at £5072m and paid tax of only £388m in 1978/79.
8. MacLennan, E. and Pond, C., *Insuring Poverty at Work*, Low Pay Unit, 1981.
9. Kay, J. and King, M., *op. cit.*, p. 143. Non-domestic rates fell from 28 per cent to 20 per cent.
10. Gough, I., *op. cit.*
11. Pond, C., Burghes, L. and Smith, B., *Taxing Wealth Inequalities*, Fabian Society, 1980.
12. *Wealth Tax Changes and the 1981 Budget*, Low Pay Unit, June 1981, Capital

Transfer Tax raised £460m in 1981/82, little more even in cash terms than in 1973/74 (£412m). Over the same period, income tax receipts quadrupled, from £7 billion to an estimated £28 billion. (H.M. Treasury, *Financial Statement and Budget Report*, HMSO, March 1981).

13. Gough, I., 1979, *op. cit.*, p. 126.
14. By defining labour as 'socially necessary labour' Fine and Harris conclude that: 'A tax on wages cannot effect a redistribution of values towards capital, for wage resources equal the value of labour power and the net value of wages cannot be permanently depressed below it.' They do, however, accept that in the short term there may be a shifting of the tax burden towards labour. Fine, B. and Harris, L., 1976, 'State Expenditure in advanced capitalism: a critique', *New Left Review*, 98 p. 106.
15. O'Connor, J., *The Fiscal Crisis of the State*, St. James Press, 1973.
16. Gough, I., 1979, p. 164.
17. Gough, I., 1979, p. 165.
18. Wilkinson, F. and Turner, H.A., 1975, 'The Wage-Tax Spiral and Labour Militancy', in Jackson Turner and Wilkinson, *Do Trade Unions Cause Inflation?* (C.U.P. 2nd ed.). See also Tarling, R. and Wilkinson, F., 'The Social Contract: post-war incomes policies and their inflationary impact', *Cambridge Journal of Economics*, 1, 1978.
19. Pond, C., Field, F. and Winyard, S., *Trade Unions and Taxation*, WEA Studies for Trade Unionists, no. 6, 1975.
20. Wilkinson and Turner, *op. cit.*, p. 78.
21. Hall, S., 'The Great Moving Right Show', *Marxism Today*, January 1979.
22. Williams, F., 'Sharp Rise in UK Taxes', *The Times*, 28 October 1981.
23. Pond, C. and Playford, C., *op. cit.*
24. MSC, *Manpower Review*, 1981.
25. Pond, C. and Playford, C., *op. cit.*, 1981.
26. Williams, M., Review Article: AES, *Capital and Class*, no. 14, Summer 1981.
27. This paper aims only to provide the broad outlines of such a strategy. More detailed discussion may be found in C. Pond, 'A Comprehensive Income Tax', paper presented to Government Economic Service Micro-Economic Seminar, May 1979, mimoed. The CIT is also discussed in the British context by J.E. Meade (Chairman), *The Structure and Reform of Direct Taxation*, Heinemann IFS 1977 and in the US context in J. Pechman (ed.) *Comprehensive Income Taxation*, Brookings, 1977.
28. An example illustrates the point. Average earnings now stand at approximately £8,000 p.a. If this amount of income were taxed as earnings it would attract a direct tax liability (income tax and national insurance contributions) of £2,376.50 (29.7 per cent): if treated as investment incomes (subject to income tax and the investment income surcharge) it would attract tax of only £1,809.75 (22.6 per cent) and if it were treated as a capital gain it would attract tax (if at all) of only £1,500 (18.8 per cent).
29. Inland Revenue Statistics, 1980, HMSO, 1981. ·
30. Meade, J.E., 1978, *op. cit.*
31. *Socialism in the Eighties: Taxation*, Labour Party, September 1981.
32. For a fuller discussion see C. Pond, 1979, *op. cit.*
33. The term 'tax expenditures' was first introduced in the US. For a fuller discussion of the concept see C. Pond, 'Tax Expenditures and Fiscal Welfare', in Sandford, Pond and Walker (eds.), *Taxation and Social Policy*, Heinemann, 1981.
34. HM Treasury, *The Government's Public Expenditure Plans*, HMSO, 1981.
35. See Pond, C., 1981, *op. cit.*

36. HM Treasury, 1981, *op. cit.*
37. The proposal is discussed in more detail in Field, F., Meacher, M. and Pond, C., *To Him Who Hath*, Penguin, 1977.
38. See Labour Party, 1981, *op. cit.*, and Hunt, J., *Women and the Alternative Economic Strategy*, in Economic Bulletin, no. 8, CPGB, Spring 1981.
39. MacLennan, E. and Pond, C., *Insuring Poverty at Work*, Low Pay Unit, 1981.
40. Many benefit recipients would consider this more favourable than the current regime, under which earnings rules can impose effective marginal 'tax' rates or additional earnings in excess of 100 per cent.
41. Royal Commission on the Distribution of Income and Wealth, Report No. 7, HMSO, 1979.
42. In evidence to the House of Commons Public Accounts Committee (12th Report, 25 June 1981) the Inland Revenue were unable to say how many forms were distributed for the declaration of fringe benefits, how many were returned or how much revenue was lost because of improperly completed or unreturned forms.
43. Aaronovitch, S., Smith, R., Gardiner, J. and Moore, R., 1981, *The Political Economy of British Capitalism*, McGraw Hill, p. 292.
44. See Meade, *op. cit.*
45. Aaronovitch, S., *The Road from Thatcherism: The Alternative Economic Strategy*, Lawrence Wishart, 1981.

DISCUSSION

Kerry Schott

Every variant of the Alternative Economic Strategy recommends additional government expenditure but as Day and Pond remark there has been little attention paid to questions about how this extra expenditure is to be financed. They focus on taxation, and this is probably the most important revenue source to concentrate upon. In theory governments can also raise revenue by borrowing and issuing bonds but the extent of this option is in practice subject to constraints. Furthermore, for a socialist left-wing government these borrowing constraints are likely to be relatively severe.

Bonds can be issued for sale in domestic and overseas capital markets and the more bonds that are issued the higher will be the interest rate. It is also likely, that however attractive the bond price may appear, there could be no buyers. No agent may be willing to lend money to the government whatever the return on the loan—and this is more likely to occur with left-wing governments which appear hostile to agents in the capital markets. Thus for any government, and a socialist government in particular, taxation revenues are of extreme importance.

But taxation of course is not simply about raising money; it is also about distributing resources amongst different groups in the society and these two functions may well conflict. A socialist government would want to distribute resources more equitably, at least partly via the tax system, and at the same time it would want to raise funds for the provision of additional public goods and services. It is these broad matters which are addressed in the latter half of the Day and Pond paper. The first half of the paper discusses previous tax policy in Britain within a Gough-O'Connor political economy approach and I will simply make one comment on this section.

The main purpose, in the context of this paper, in trying to understand the past political economy of taxation is to have some idea of the problems that a radical system of taxation will face. These are not simply economic problems but include the issues raised by attempting to change the social relations existing under capitalism by pursuing an Alternative Economic Strategy. Now the Gough-O'Connor treatment of the state does not seem to me to be particularly useful for this purpose. It leaves you with the hardly startling conclusion that capital will oppose a radical taxation policy but does not suggest how this conflict will translate into action, nor whether all factions of capital and all groups of workers will act in a concerted way. The main focus in Gough is on distributional struggles

175

between capital and labour over the economic pie, and simply shelving social relations and political issues, because the state is relatively autonomous, may be analytically easy but in practice it is not a great help or a good foundation for considering radical policy in any detail.

The particular policy that Day and Pond favour is a Comprehensive Income Tax in concert with some form of Wealth Tax. It is impossible to assess whether their policy preferences are desirable or not because first we would need to agree on what the wider objectives of the taxation policy were, what the equity implications were, and how much revenue the schemes would raise. All these matters need far more attention. As well as more discussion of what is wanted there is also an important role for detailed empirical work on the simple economic effects of the proposed policies. It is for instance well known that wealth in Britain is distributed far more inequitably than income and most proponents of a wealth tax stress not only its equity but also its high revenue raising features. If the wealth tax would raise lots of revenue then many of the problems associated with the income tax become less severe. But this is simply empirical—how much revenue would various schemes for taxing wealth raise? It would also be a relatively straightforward matter to work out the impact of the schemes proposed here on different types of households and this should be done so that the economic effects of different proposed tax rates and schemes can be assessed.

What also needs to be judged is the degree of opposition to a radical tax change. It seems rather naive to suppose that owner occupiers would welcome a removal of their subsidies, or that married men will welcome a removal of their tax allowances. These existing policies divide the working class, but removing discrimination of this sort will cause resentment in some quarters however ideologically sound it may be. At the same time as a radical tax policy is confronting capital, some workers are also being confronted and may well form quite unholy alliances to attack the new policy.

This raises the whole question of viability, and that certain air of utopia that surrounds Alternative Economic Strategies. No new radical taxation policy, or indeed alternative economic strategy generally can be introduced and maintained without solid working-class input and support for all its features. There must be more discussion and agreement about government expenditure, taxation, and the constraints on the state in a capitalist world before policies are implemented. This paper represents a start in this direction.

MONOPOLIES AND MERGER POLICY:
A NEW PERSPECTIVE

Keith Cowling

The merger wave of the late 1960s and 1970s completely transformed the industrial structure of the UK economy without the left having any well developed perspective of it. Probably the dominant view on the left was that the working class may be expected to share in the fruits of the efficiency gains that would undoubtedly result from the scale economies associated with merger, with the balance of power moving towards the working class given the more favourable conditions for union organisation within the giant firms which were created. This view always seemed to me to be rather naive and certainly completely neglected the implications for the working class of the rising monopoly power of the capitalist sector. The evidence suggests that efficiency has not improved following merger, and in many cases his disastrously declined. It also appears to be the case that wage share tends to fall as concentration increases and since the vast majority of mergers in the UK, as in the rest of Europe, have been horizontal, it follows that merger has in fact contributed to a shift in the balance of power away from the working class. This conclusion is reinforced by the macroeconomic implications of the monopolisation of markets which resulted from the merger wave.

After exploring theory and evidence on such matters the paper will argue that the left should adopt a rigorous anti-merger and anti-monopoly stance. The central plank of such a strategy would be the democratic control of the major centres of economic power—the giant corporations. The paper will explore various institutional arrangements aimed at achieving this. Demands for a tight ban on further merger activity where either participant is of significant size, would also be an important element in such a strategy given that economic and political dominance increase with size and thus make the achievement of democratic control that much more difficult.

Monopoly and Distribution

Increased market concentration will tend to imply an increase in the share of profits, and therefore a reduction in the share of wages, due to the fact that we expect the degree of monopoly $(p-mc)/p$ to rise with concentration, assuming profit maximising behaviour.[1] In two extreme cases this would not be true; (a) with perfect collusion at all levels of concentration

I am grateful to Mark Harrison for helpful discussions on topics raised in this paper.

the degree of monopoly and therefore the share of wages would be invariant to the degree of concentration,[2] and (b) changes in concentration may have no effect if the degree of monopoly is effectively constrained by the existence of potential entrants. Thus in the first case the monopoly outcome always prevails, and in the second case the competitive outcome could prevail despite the existence of apparently concentrated market structures. The first case is unlikely where we consider a substantial range in the level of concentration, given that there will always be gains to be made from undetected price cutting and the probability of detection may be expected to rise with concentration; and the second case will generally be ruled out, either because of the existence of barriers to entry, or because of investment in excess capacity as a credible deterrent to entry. Thus where competitive labour markets prevail, our expectation is that wage share will be lower the higher is the degree of concentration. But can we expect worker pressure for higher wages and better working conditions to mitigate or reverse this tendency? Kalecki (1971a), using a variant of the kinked demand curve hypothesis, has argued that this is possible in the case of oligopoly, and since this is a fairly general case his analysis warrants some investigation. The central point is that each firm in the oligopoly group will be reluctant to pass on wage increases won by union activity as price increases because of its pessimistic expectations about the response of rivals. Insofar as bargaining is firm by firm and insofar as spill-over effects of the wage settlements are unimportant or long-delayed then there is something in Kalecki's view, but with collective bargaining at industry level, or where individual bargains are rapidly transmitted over the whole industry, the impact on distribution will be limited. In tightly organised, concentrated industries we can expect a high degree of collusion over wage fixing via multi-employer agreements or wage leadership, so that wage increases will be rapidly passed on as price increases. Thus while union pressure may secure higher wages this is quite consistent with wage share remaining unchanged. What of the evidence? Levinson (1954) reports that for the US a five fold increase in union strength between the 1930s and 1950s led to a three fold increase in wages with no redistribution from profits to wages. For the UK, Hines (1964) has generated much-criticised but pretty robust results indicating a positive impact of union pressure on the rate of wage increase over the period 1892/1961, but as Pollard (1978) concludes, this only put the steam behind inflation without effecting a redistribution of income as between profits and wages.[3]

Recent cross sectional evidence would also support the notion that higher levels of concentration are associated with lower wage shares (Cowling and Molho, 1981). For workers collectively to increase their share of what is produced in a monopolising world requires that those in the monopolising sectors should increase their own wage share, rather than simply increasing their wage rates. Whilst there is some evidence that wage rates are higher in concentrated industries, there is every indication that despite this, worker pressure was unable to reverse the direct implication of higher levels of concentration for the distribution of income.

There remains the question of international competition. If wages are being pushed up by worker pressure, but international competition is making it increasingly difficult to pass on such increases in higher prices then the degree of monopoly will have been effectively reduced and the share of profits will tend to fall. This was the Glyn and Sutcliffe (1972) view—British capital was being crushed between the anvil of worker pressure and the hammer of international competition. Clearly this is a theoretical possibility, at least in a world of relatively rigid exchange rates, but it should also be made quite clear that the growth in intra-industry trade, e.g. imports of manufactures into the UK, does not necessarily imply a fall in the degree of monopoly within the UK, although it will imply the increased international competition for manufacturing jobs. The central question which has to be answered is who controls such trade? In contrast to the usual assumption which is (implicitly) made, imports are often under the direct control of the domestic monopoly/oligopoly structure, via its own transnational base or via agency or franchise agreements. The US car companies, like Ford, where intra-company, intra-European trade has been growing rapidly, are examples of the former, and Courtaulds, establishing arrangements with Scandinavian and Austrian suppliers of rayon following the creation of the European Free Trade Area, is an example of the latter. In neither case does the growth of imports represent any threat to the domestic monopoly structure and therefore to the degree of monopoly within the domestic economy. Although this is an area where documentation is difficult these are by no means isolated examples. Walshe (1974) examined 44 industries and classified thirteen as having significant import *shares*, but on further examination only four industries were classified as having significant import *competition*. Seven of the others were cases in which control over imports was vested in domestic (usually dominant) firms and the other two cases were where imports were unrefined and had to be processed by the domestic monopolies (oil and sugar). It might also be added that, as imports increase in importance, so it becomes a matter of increasing interest for domestic firms to obtain some element of control, and in some cases, where external suppliers gain control, monopoly control remains, but in different hands.

I would conclude from the above discussion that the relationship between the degree of monopoly in the domestic economy and the level of imports is a complicated one and the conventional wisdom that the degree of monopoly falls as imports rise can be very misleading. What of the evidence? Glyn and Sutcliffe (1972) purport to offer evidence in support of their hypothesis but it really cannot be interpreted this way, see Cowling (1978). Some recent econometric work focusing on the impact of import penetration on price formation in UK manufacturing offers little support for the Glyn and Sutcliff view, see Murfin and Cowling (1981), and the evidence provided by inter-industry profitability studies, which sometimes reveal a negative association between profitability and import penetration, can be interpreted in terms of a capacity utilisation effect, see Cowling (1981b).

It would appear therefore that the evidence so far available is not capable of refuting the hypothesis that the growth of manufactured imports has failed to reverse the tendency toward a higher degree of monopoly fostered by increasing domestic concentration. Indeed it is possible to take the argument a stage further and argue that the growth of such trade may enhance the degree of monopoly by serving as a mechanism whereby dominant domestic firms with transnational connections may more easily squeeze out smaller and weaker domestic rivals. Thus free trade leads to the increasing dominance of the transnationals and thus can contribute to a higher level of concentration and degree of monopoly in each domestic market.

To this point we have concluded that the tendency for the degree of monopoly to rise as concentration increases does not appear to have been reversed by worker pressure or import penetration, and therefore the underlying tendency for a rise in profit share and fall in wage share remains, together with its stagnationist tendencies (see next section). However, there is a further distributional issue underlying this. Much investment will be directed towards acquiring and maintaining monopoly positions—that is it will be devoted to distributional ends to be gained through market control. The competition for monopoly rents will create waste just as increasing monopoly results in waste due to the underutilisation of resources. Thus, given the degree of utilisation of resources, a system which allows the generation of monopoly rents will result in a diversion of resources from expanding the output of the system towards the redistribution of that output. Excess capacity (to deter prospective entrants), and excessive advertising and product differentiation through research and development would be cases in point. Thus not only will a world of monopoly tend to underutilise resources but the resources utilised will also be wastefully employed in the redistributive process.

Monopoly and Stagnation
As mentioned earlier the merger wave of the late 1960s and 1970s transformed the structure of the UK economy. As in the rest of Europe, mergers were principally horizontal in character, that is between firms operating in essentially the same markets. In 1968 approximately 82 per cent of mergers were horizontal, 91 per cent by value. The vast majority

were therefore contributing to the monopolisation of markets, and this was still true in the 1970s although the fraction was slightly smaller (over 70 per cent). As an indication of the magnitude of the merger wave, in 1968 (an admittedly peak year) expenditure on acquisitions exceeded £8.5 billion.[4] This represented the takeover in one year of at least 27 per cent of the total capital stock of the companies sector. Not surprisingly most estimates suggest a dominant role for merger in the evolution of both aggregate and market concentration, see e.g. Aaronovitch and Sawyer (1975), Prais (1976), and Hannah and Kay (1977). The substantial increases in concentration in most markets may be expected to result in the increase in prices relative to marginal costs and therefore to an increase in the share of profits plus overhead costs in value-added. What are the implications of this process for the evolution of the macroeconomy? The potential clearly exists for an increase in the share of profits but whether or not this is realised depends on the impact of the monopolisation of markets on aggregate demand. The immediate impact would be a downward revision in planned investment in line with the planned reduction in the rate of output within those sectors where the degree of monopoly had increased. The reduction in aggregate investment, in the absence of compensating adjustments elsewhere, would lead to a reduction in the level of profits in the total system, which would lead to further cut-backs in investment, and so on.[5]

Clearly any deficiency in investment could be made up by an increase in capitalist consumption so that aggregate demand could be maintained. However, this is unlikely to happen fast enough or to the required extent, given that capitalists receive their income less frequently than workers and also tend to have much lower propensities to consume. And in any case the substitution of capitalist consumption for investment could lead to problems in the longer run, since, given rising expectations among workers, accumulation is the key to social stability. Managerialism, reflected in rising intra-corporation consumption out of non-reported profits, could provide at least a partial antidote to such a realisation crisis, but contains its own contradictions. Although in aggregate, by tending to maintain demand, managerialism serves to maintain profits, it will still be seen as something to be minimised by those (stockholders) interested in the flow of reported profits. Given also that an increase in the export surplus or in the states' budget deficit will not automatically follow a rise in the degree of monopoly, a realisation crisis would appear to be a distinct possibility.[6] One other possible way out remains. Aggregate demand could be maintained by reducing workers' propensity to save via advertising and product innovation. Whilst this strategy has some attractive properties (see Rothschild, 1942) it would seem incapable of properly fulfilling this role given its essentially pro-cyclical character. Advertising and product innovation tend to mimic the behaviour of investment in general and so seem ill-equipped to fill the role of replacing investment within the structure of aggregate demand.

I would therefore conclude that although mechanisms are available to mitigate any stagnationist tendency precipitated by a tendency for the degree of monopoly to increase, none are automatic and each contains the seeds of further crisis.[7]

Policy
Given the distributional and stagnationist impact of the monopolisation of markets achieved by the merger waves of the late 1960s and 1970s, and still continuing today, it would seem that these processes should be of profound interest to the left in developing a strategy for the management of the contemporary capitalist system, but also having relevance to planning within a socialist system. This section looks at monopolies and mergers policy in the UK and makes some suggestions for change.[8]

Anti-trust policy is conventionally justified in terms of achieving social efficiency assuming full employment. It is assumed that the full utilisation of resources will be achieved via macroeconomic policy, whereas anti-trust policy, along with other microeconomic policies, will be aimed at the efficient utilisation of resources. Since these issues are not easily separable I want to take a broader view of social efficiency and anti-trust given that the existence and growth of monopoly/oligopoly will have implications not simply for allocative efficiency but also for the distribution of income and the tendency of capitalist economies to stagnate. Thus an optimal policy on monopolies and merger will have a macroeconomic and microeconomic objective and dimension. Social control over mergers, concentration and monopoly behaviour will be sought in order to control distribution and arrest stagnationist tendencies, as well as to avoid waste and secure an optimal structure of output.

The orthodox answer to the criticism that conventional anti-trust is not directed at issues of stagnation would probably be that these issues are better dealt with in terms of macroeconomic policy. This is certainly not self-evident a priori, but it is also necessary to point out that policies to secure full employment will be resisted at certain conjunctures, because of their implications for the balance of power between capital and labour, and what may appear as a way of controlling any potential stagnationist tendency may prove to be politically infeasible. The same may of course be true with an effective anti-trust policy, but it would seem important to at least establish the case and hopefully create a political climate for change.

Similarly on distribution it may be argued that this can be handled by appropriate tax policies. However, although technically possible, this ignores the essence of distributional issues—that they are necessarily the outcome of a power struggle. To change the balance of power, for example via the monopolisation of markets, is inevitably going to have an impact on the outcome. To argue that taxation changes are possible which will deflect this tendency is not a very interesting political or economic observation.

There are various possible approaches to the control of economic power via the state. Preventative measures, such as structural policies (e.g. mergers policy), may be introduced to control its emergence. If such structural policies are not ruthlessly pursued, then by imposing and enforcing rules the behaviour of the organisation possessing economic power may be modified. Profit rate control, price control, advertising control would be cases in point. If such rules proved unsatisfactory then a reversion to a more structural approach (e.g. divestiture or mitosis) would be a possibility. Alternatively a behavioural change may be sought via public take-over, either of the industry, or of a firm or firms within an oligopoly group. Given that the regulation of firm behaviour poses severe problems,[9] and given that public take-over is no obvious or immediate solution to the monopoly problem,[10] even if politically feasible, then it follows that structural policy has a potentially significant role to play in controlling the emergence and impact of monopoly power in the economy. If we put the possibility of divestiture on one side for the moment, then we are left with a requirement for an active anti-merger policy if control over the extension of monopoly power is to be established. However, whilst in the case of large economies, like the United States, there may be little to lose from such policies in terms of static or dynamic efficiency, in the case of smaller economies attempts to maintain relatively deconcentrated structures may be faced with substantial social costs.[11] To put the issue another way, merger activity leads with certainty to the acquisition of economic power, but this may be balanced by the possibility of real resource savings. This requires us to know more about any cost-savings which might have resulted from merger and provides a justification for much of the empirical work on the impact of merger.[12] Such investigation reveals a very consistent picture in which it is difficult to sustain the view that merger is in fact a necessary or sufficient condition for efficiency gain. Empirical results for the UK indicate that merger was generally consistent with either no change in profitability or with its decline, see e.g. Singh (1971), Utton (1974), Meeks (1977) and Cosh, Hughes and Singh (1980). These results are also consistent with those obtained for the conglomerate merger wave of the US in the 1960s, which have been recently surveyed by Mueller (1977). He concludes that for the US, 'mergers. . . have on average not generated extra profits for the acquiring firms, have not resulted in increased economic efficiency'. It is also interesting to note that Stigler's (1950) investigation of the earlier merger waves in the US led him to conclude that they were motivated by the desire for monopoly, rather than by questions of efficiency.[13]

Given that, at best, merger will leave economic power unchanged, the recent observations on declining or constant profitability must be construed as a strong indication of declining efficiency.[14] However studies of profitability may only reveal the tip of the iceberg. Given that most mergers in the UK have been horizontal, it is reasonable to suppose that monopoly power has generally increased and, therefore, that profitability may have been to some extent sustained by this. Thus in the case of merger leading to declining profitability, the decline in efficiency may have been greater, and, in the case of no change or improvement in profitability, there may still have been an efficiency decline. Some recent work attempts to decompose changes in profits following merger into efficiency and market power effects, see Cowling et al (1980). The message is the same—in general there is no evidence of significant efficiency gain following merger. Usually there are efficiency losses in the years immediately following merger, which might be regarded as transition costs, but these were generally uncompensated by subsequent efficiency gains which would not have been realised anyway.

These results, and the earlier arguments concerning the distributional and stagnationist consequences of the monopolisation of markets, would indicate that a rigorous anti-merger policy is called for. A total ban on merger would have the additional beneficial effect of shutting off an obvious avenue for circumventing restrictive practices legislation and would, therefore, contribute to the efficiency of existing legislation. To many observers such a policy may appear unattractive—why not let something like the existing Merger Panel (a group of civil servants from the various interested departments) or the Monopolies Commission assess each case on its merits? Surely it is irrational simply to apply a blanket refusal? My first response would be that the evidence really does not support this view. The evidence suggests that bad decisions have been made in the past—mergers have been allowed which in some cases have been disastrous and in other cases have simply allowed the emergence of substantial monopolies without any significant benefits. More fundamentally the whole approach has been biased in favour of acceptance since the parties involved have not been required to demonstrate that social benefits will result. The implication is that the array of policy options should be confined to a range, with an onus of proof on the merging firms to demonstrate social benefit at one end defining the mildest policy, and an outright ban at the other end defining the toughest policy. Within this range a variety of types of ban could be defined which might reasonably relate to the size of firms involved and their joint market share.

As noted earlier, attempts to control firm behaviour are likely to lead to responses involving socially wasteful expenditures (Tullock, 1967; Posner, 1975). Thus if the merger is important to the firms involved,[15] and the evidence suggests this would not be for reasons of efficiency, then considerable effort will be expended in convincing the appropriate group, whether 'sponsoring department',[16] Mergers Panel or Monopolies Commission, that it is indeed in the 'public interest', this effort being in addition to the private effort involved in the market operations to secure the acquisition. Both forms of waste would be avoided by a tight ban on acquisitions. But what about the impact of a ban, or the prospect of a ban? Insofar as firms are restricted from doing what they would otherwise do, then it may be optimal for them collectively to invest in attempts to secure the removal of the ban. They would undoubtedly do this via, for example, CBI lobbying, but this is unlikely to amount to significant wasteful expenditures—the only problem then being the resilience of the state in standing up to such pressure. However, if the ban is accompanied with 'let-out' clauses then each firm with a merger in mind will invest resources in convincing the appropriate authority that their case falls under at least one of these clauses. The looser the rules the greater the social waste.

However, even if strict controls were established over future mergers, such that only a minority were allowed, this would still leave a highly concentrated industry structure, the legacy of the permissive merger policy of the past. A hard-line merger policy, although important, would still have to be seen as peripheral to the central issue of monopoly power in the economy. Recent evidence consistently suggests that there is little to be gained by increases in the size of individual corporations, but potentially much to be lost. Given this, the question of divestiture has to be raised. Under existing legislation it is clearly within the power of ministers to order such action, although such action has never been taken, nor likely even threatened. The recent Green Paper, Review of Monopolies and Mergers Policy (1978), produced by the government, argued that it was '. . . unrealistic in practice to think of breaking-up a large company. . .' This prevailing view within the civil service will have to be strongly challenged. But divestiture is only one possible response by the state to the emergence of a position of substantial economic power. There may be situations where divestiture is not desirable, in which case we have to consider controls over the behaviour of such organisations. Despite the problems raised by the sometimes wasteful responses to attempts to regulate behaviour, the social costs of unregulated behaviour may be such as to require some control. Despite the existence of institutions like the Monopolies Commission and a resurrected Price Commission there would seem to be compelling arguments for an additional institutional framework for the regulation of major centres of economic power. Justification comes from perhaps three lines of argument. First, given that major private centres of economic power exist society needs an institution to keep such organisations under continuous observation and control. The present system patently does not allow this. The Monopolies Commission can only take sporadic snap-shots of the market for particular products and make recommendations on the basis of these. There is no formal mechanism for monitoring the response by the company to recommendations by the Commission which are accepted by the government. Neither is there any way in which the public regulatory system can systematically accumulate experience concerning the multifarious activities of major monopolies. Without continuous observation and access to internal information society will never be able to effectively control the behaviour of such companies.[17]

Related to this point, the second line of argument concerns the regulation and control of the corporation as a whole. It is not sufficient to look at a specific corporation's activities in a variety of markets as if they are additive in terms of the corporation's aggregate economic power. The general case is one where interdependencies between markets are significant and the ultimate power of the giant corporation as a financial institution can be decisive in establishing positions of dominance in a variety of markets.[18] The third line of argument is a political one. Institutions like the Monopolies Commission and (the former) Price Commission make recommendations directly or indirectly to the relevant minister. In most cases, this means negotiations between the government department, currently the Department of Prices and Consumer-Protection, and the corporation(s) in question. This has generally led to considerable delay, and in many cases, a watering down of the proposals. Since, as will be argued later, there is a basic assymetry in the representation of conflicting interests within Whitehall, it would appear to be in the public interest to bring more of the evidence and discussion into the public arena.

The appropriate response to these three strands of argument would seem to be parliamentary committees allocated to each major sector of the economy. Such committees would provide continuous surveillance of the major private centres of economic power and would allow for the growth of experience and expertise in the affairs of such corporations by both parliamentarians and their staff.[19] Most of their activities could and should be open and public and they would provide an effective countervailing power to the pressures put on government departments. They would, of course, be subject to pressures themselves, but operating in the public eye and with parliamentary responsibilities may provide at least a partially effective antidote. Thus the policy proposals consist of a strictly interpreted ban on mergers, a clear willingness to undertake divestiture proceedings, and parliamentary committees for the monitoring and reporting on the activities of the major corporations and providing a focus for the harnessing of public opinion to the aim of effective control of these major monopolies, leaving the other control agencies to provide sporadic checks in specific cases of suspected monopoly behaviour and a separate commission to give general control over prices.[20]

However such policies could be undermined from within the state apparatus. The state is an arena of class conflict but the capitalist class has certain inbuilt advantages which guarantee unequal access and influence. The notion of 'sponsoring department' is a case in point. It is one of the specific functions of departments of state like Industry, Agriculture and Transport, to represent the interests of their associated firms and industries within the state. The permissiveness of past and current merger policies and the unwillingness to contemplate more effective institutions to monitor and control monopoly behaviour may be partially explained by the existence of 'sponsoring departments'. It would seem important to challenge this institution. 'Industry's' case should be made openly as written or oral submission to the Mergers Panel or to the Monopolies Commission so that everyone can see clearly where the view of vested interests is being put. If the bureaucracy is to act for specific vested interests, then advocacy must be seen to be balanced and equitable. Patently this is not the case. Although 'industry' is in contact with its 'sponsors' the same cannot be said for consumers. Some might argue that the Office of Fair Trading takes on the role of consumers' advocate, but this was not the view taken by the former Director (Mr Methven) who made it quite clear that he did not regard himself as taking such a role, but rather that of a referee, trying to balance out the interests of 'industry' and the consumer. Not only does this result in a basic asymmetry, it would also seem an inappropriate stance for such a department. But even if the present Director (Mr Borrie) were to regard himself as the consumers' advocate, there would remain a basic asymmetry given the fact that final consumers, individual households, are obviously not organised or represented in as efficient a manner as is 'industry'.[21] This becomes more and more the case as industry becomes more and more concentrated. The bigger firms become, the more dominant they are within individual industries, the more incentive they have to represent 'industry's' view, in aggregate or as a specific industry. The benefits from lobbying activities accrue more completely, and more directly, to the firm in question the bigger or more dominant is that particular firm. Given this it becomes more and more crucial to develop new methods of democratic control of the operations of the state as concentration increases. The achievement of an effective monopolies and mergers policy will be crucially dependent on opening up the state to such control.

NOTES

1. For the theoretical derivation of this link see e.g. Cowling (1981a). Ignoring potential entry, the other determinants of the degree of monopoly would be the degree of collusion and the industry price elasticity of demand, but these in turn are likely to be influenced by the level of concentration.
2. Assuming constant marginal costs, and ignoring materials costs, the degree of monopoly will equal the ratio of profits plus overhead costs to value-added

$(\pi + F)/Y$, and wage share W/Y will equal $1 - (\pi + F)/Y$.

3. More recently it could be argued that union pressure has had an indirect impact on profit share by provoking state intervention to deflate the economy, and thereby reducing the degree of capacity utilisation, whilst leaving the degree of monopoly $(p - mc)/p$ unaffected.

4. The estimate available from the Office of Fair Trading relates only to large acquisitions.

5. It is easy to show that in a closed economy with no state sector and no saving by workers, aggregate gross profits will be equal to investment plus capitalist consumption, see Kalecki (1971b). This led Kalecki to the remark that capitalists earn what they spend while workers spend what they earn.

6. These various issues are analysed in some detail in Cowling (1981b).

7. The same would be true of advertising in creating wants if these wants were subsequently not capable of being met.

8. The paper does not address the problems posed by attempts by unions to secure direct control over the employment, pricing and investment decisions of corporations, although this could form a potentially important element of any anti-monopoly strategy.

9. This is perhaps not the place to go into detail about the issues raised in the regulated firm literature. Suffice it to say that attempts to regulate behaviour will generate responses by firms which may not be socially optimal. If an assumption of stockholder wealth maximisation is plausible, then regulated profit rates will generally lead to over-investment; under managerialism the firm will react by raising expenditure on those items for which managers have a positive preference. The tighter the control, the bigger the distortions.

10. This does not, of course, imply that social ownership of the means of production is not desirable, it simply means that the potential problem of monopoly remains in such a world.

11. I am obviously not talking about an attempt to maintain a more-or-less competitive economy. Rather, I am talking about trying to curtail processes which could lead to the virtual monopolisation of large sectors of the economy.

12. Following Tullock, 1967 and Posner, 1975, it could be argued that all the gains implicit in merger will be exhausted by the competitive process for the acquisition of these gains and therefore there is no trade-off, in which case mergers involving the acquisition of economic power could be regarded as unambiguously bad. However, the competitive process involved is, in itself, likely to be very imperfect and thus the most likely case might involve only a partial exhaustion of the possible gains.

13. Apparently, and depressingly, the economics profession at the time were convinced by efficiency arguments. Stigler remarks: 'Economists as wise as Taussig, as incisive as Fisher, as fond of competition as Clark and Fetter, insisted upon discussing the (merger) movement largely or exclusively in terms of industrial evolution and the economies of scale.'

14. The remaining doubt would be that managers may be translating efficiency gains into managerial income, in the broadest sense. As far as stockholders are concerned, this could not be considered an efficiency gain (unless stockholders are also managers) but as far as society is concerned, and in so far as these effects are concentrated in overheads, the question resolves into a distributional one. Output is being produced with fewer resources but a particular group, not necessarily profit recipients, are getting the goodies. This of course, reveals a major objection to studies of profitability. Efficiency is being measured by reference to the income of a particular group rather than by reference to output or incomes of people in general.

15. Stigler, 1950, conjectures that a significant motivational force behind merger

waves is the 'merger promotions industry', given that its income is conditional on the intensity of merger activity. The emergence and dominance of the Slater-Walkers on the British financial scene of the sixties give some credence to such a conjecture.

16. Each industry has a 'sponsoring department' within the existing government apparatus.

17. This has probably now been belatedly recognised in the case of the oil industry where BNOC is to some extent filling this role and making the running on the government side over the scandal of taxation, or the lack of it, of North Sea Oil.

18. Interestingly the Green Paper examines proposals for company investigations by the Monopolies Commission but decides against them, apparently because such inquiries could not lead to effective remedial action! In other words they prefer not to know about problems given that they are unwilling to *recommend* remedial action. Note that the authors of the Green Paper, as previously mentioned, rule out divestiture, despite the fact that it is clearly available to ministers.

19. This would not be a substitute for the social ownership of these companies but neither would the need for such regulatory bodies disappear after public takeover. Control over the bureaucratic competition for monopoly rents would remain a desirable objective.

20. It should be reiterated that a Price Commission would not be sufficient to achieve adequate control since such regulation (i) induces socially inefficient responses, as mentioned earlier; (ii) will generally be difficult to operate with transnational corporations with access to alternative transfer pricing strategies; and (iii) will tend to be subverted without the harnessing of public opinion via open parliamentary committee proceedings.

21. Obviously many consumers are organised, but as workers not as consumers. Clearly also they have a direct interest in merger and monopoly policy and a certain kind of representation within the state on these issues. The problem remains that the interests represented are sectional and therefore this form of representation is insufficient for the task at hand.

REFERENCES

Aaronovitch, S. and Sawyer, M., 1975, *Big Business: Theoretical and Empirical Aspects of Concentration and Mergers in the UK,* London.

Cosh, A., Hughes, A. and Singh, A., 1980, 'The Causes and Effects of Takeovers in the UK', in Mueller, D. ed., *The Determinants and Effects of Mergers,* Cambridge, Mass.

Cowling, K., 1978, 'Monopoly, Welfare and Distribution' in Artis, M. and Nobay, R. eds. *Contemporary Economic Analysis,* London.

Cowling, K., 1981a, 'Oligopoly, Distribution and the Rate of Profit', *European Economic Review* 15, pp. 195–224.

Cowling, K., 1981b, *Monopoly Capitalism,* London.

Cowling, K., Stoneman, P., Cubbin, J., Cable, J., Hall, G., Domberger, S. and Dutton, P., 1980, *Mergers and Economic Performance,* Cambridge.

Cowling, K. and Molho, I., 1980, 'Wage Share, Concentration and Unionism', paper given at Conference of European Association for Research in Industrial Economics, Milan, September.

Hannah, L. and Kay, J., 1977, *Concentration in Modern Industry,* London.

Hines, A.J., 1964, 'Trade Unions and Wage Inflation in the UK 1893–1961', *Review of Economic Studies,* October.

Kalecki, M., 1971a, 'Class Struggle and the Distribution of Income', *Kyklos*, 24.

Kalecki, M., 1971b, *Dynamics of the Capitalist Economy*, Cambridge.

Levinson, H.M., 1954, 'Collective Bargaining and Income Distribution', *American Economic Review*, May.

Mueller, D., 1977, 'The Effects of Conglomerate Mergers', *Journal of Banking and Finance*, pp. 315–347.

Murfin, A. and Cowling, K., 1981, 'Price Formation and Import Penetration in UK Manufacturing Industry', paper given at Conference of European Association for Research in Industrial Economics, Basle, September.

Posner, R., 1975, 'The Social Costs of Monopoly and Regulation', *Journal of Political Economy*, August, pp. 807–827.

Prais, S., 1976, *The Evolution of Giant Firms in Britain*, Cambridge.

Rothschild, K., 1942, 'A Note on Advertising', *Economics Journal*, April.

Singh, A., 1971, *Takeovers*, Cambridge.

Stigler, G., 1950, 'Monopoly and Oligopoly by Merger', *American Economic Review*, May.

Tullock, G., 1967, 'The Welfare Costs of Tariffs, Monopolies and Theft', *Western Economics Journal*, June.

Utton, G., 1974, 'On Measuring the Effects of Industrial Mergers', *Scottish Journal of Political Economy*.

Walshe, G., 1974, *Monopoly in British Industry*, Cambridge.

DISCUSSION

Alan Hughes

Despite the obvious connection between competition policy and industrial policy there has been relatively little attention paid to the former in the current debate over alternative economic strategies for the UK economy. Keith Cowling's paper is therefore to be welcomed as opening up this area for discussion. Cowling's argument is that in the UK the merger wave has produced an increase in the political dominance of large corporations and an attendant increase in the degree of monopoly power exercised by them in the markets in which they operate. He argues that this has also introduced stagnationist tendencies in the UK at the macroeconomic level and that in thinking about competition policy, macroeconomic as well as microeconomic perspectives are required. His paper then offers an exploration of various institutional arrangements necessary to ensure a rigorous anti-merger and anti-monopoly stance. Apart from recommending the more forceful use of existing powers, for example, of divestiture and the reintroduction of some form of Price Commission, Cowling makes two basic proposals. First the introduction of tight structural bans on · mergers involving companies meeting specific size or market share criteria. Second, the introduction of parliamentary select committees to provide continuous monitoring of individual corporations in order to bring discussion of their activities more fully into the public arena. I have reservations about both the analysis of monopoly power and the policy proposals made.

I remain completely unconvinced that UK companies have in general experienced substantial gains in monopoly power in recent decades, and in particular during or after the merger wave of the late 1960s and early 1970s. Consequently I doubt that the neutral profitability effects of merger must in general necessarily imply microeconomic 'efficiency' losses, as Cowling alleges, or that mergers have led to reductions in investment. There is no evidence to suggest that in the UK (or the other advanced economies) measured rates of return or shares of profit in value added have risen to reflect rising monopoly power. In fact since the 1960s at least, the reverse appears to have been the case and this remains true when account is taken of charges in capacity utilisation (Hill, 1979; Bank of England, 1977). Nor, in so far as the argument that wasteful expenditures have depressed reported profits is concerned, have I seen any evidence to suggest that they could, or actually have increased sufficiently to make an appreciable impact on these measured returns. For example, advertising

191

expenditure as a percentage of GDP has remained fairly constant in both the UK and the US over the two decades since the mid-1950s (Hughes, Mueller and Singh, 1980). It may be that a convincing case for the monopoly power, wasteful expenditures and excess capacity arguments can be made but I don't think it has been yet. Indeed it is equally if not more plausible to argue that competition has increased in recent decades, due to declining restrictive practices, increased countervailing power of larger retailers and other distributors and in particular to the enormous increase in direct investment and world trade in the long boom of the post-war years up to the early 1970s (Hughes and Singh, 1980; Pillay, 1981). Cowling rightly argues that careful consideration has to be given to the way in which that trade is controlled, and how competitive it actually is (something which seems to me to require a farily detailed case by case approach). On the face of it, however, it is difficult to resist the conclusion that the UK has come out of this process less dominant than before. Throughout the post-war period, and especially since the 1960s, the UK has suffered declining market shares of manufactures both at home and abroad and our largest companies have persistently lost out in terms of representation and ranking amongst the world's largest firms (Hughes, 1976; Dunning and Pearce, 1981). Finally as far as stagnation and low investment are concerned there is not much evidence to support the view that merging firms are any less dynamic than non-merging firms. In fact firms growing intensively by merger tend also to be relatively fast growing in terms of the acquisition of new fixed assets, and firms involved in mergers tend if anything to have higher joint shares of industry investment after than before merger (Meeks, 1977; Kumar, 1981; Aaronovitch and Sawyer, 1975).[1]

As far as policy recommendations are concerned I can see little basis in the evidence on the impact of merger for the introduction of structural criteria. Compared to the United States, the evidence for the United Kingdom, that structure in general systematically affects performance, is very weak (Hughes, 1978; Harf and Clarke, 1980). As far as mergers are concerned there is little to suggest that performance is affected by the scale of the companies involved (Meeks, 1977; Kumar, 1981). It seems to me that rigid structural criteria are in any case undesirable if competition policy is to be considered as part of overall economic strategy. Planning proposals for rationalisation or capacity expansion might well involve mergers or sales of subsidiaries between firms which fall foul of rigid structural bans. The result would inevitably be the associated introduction of exemption procedures as with the restrictive practices legislation of the UK (Hughes, 1978; HMSO, 1979). (Thus the wasteful pressures claimed by Cowling to characterise companies' attitudes to present competition policy would still remain.) Cowling's argument here as elsewhere would be clearer if an outline were presented of what other measures would accompany the competition policy proposals he is making. This is particularly the case with macroeconomic policy regulation and planning, where the paper is rather elusive. Some consideration at least must be given for example to the argument that some aspects of planning and control are made easier by high levels of market concentration.

To argue against rigid bans as I have done, and to cast doubt on the micro-efficiency arguments used against merger is not to argue for non-intervention, or laisser faire policies towards large firms. Instead it is to argue for a competition policy which is compatible with overall economic strategy and which has a notion of efficiency embodied in it which recognises the impact of macroeconomic disequilibrium upon the evaluation, for example, of merger outcomes. This is different from, and in my view more reasonable, than an approach wedded to structural features of markets because they are deemed capable of producing 'efficient' welfare outcomes on the basis of an essentially neo-classical conception of the notion of competition. It would be easy though I am sure incorrect, to deduce from Keith Cowling's paper that he is advocating a return to atomistic deconcentrated markets which by itself, by lowering the degree of monopoly, will be of net benefit for the economy as a whole. An explicit analysis of the supplementary policies envisaged and the reference point for the monopoly welfare loss comparisons would help dispel this impression, and make the grounds for debate clearer. In the meantime it seems worth pointing out that potentially present competition policy is quite powerful, in particular over powers of divestiture and powers to monitor behaviour and investigate 'uncompetitive' practices (see for instance the provisions of the Fair Trading Act of 1973 and the Competition Act 1980). This issue is at least as much one of implementation as of the extent of potential powers.

Two issues remain: first, the question of considering companies as a whole, rather than particular product markets, as targets for competition policy; and second, the role of select committees. Apart perhaps from the exercise of political influence which may in any case be difficult to discern, I would have expected the exercise of corporate dominance to show up in particular product markets, and therefore to be investigable under current legislation in a succession of references (despite corporate objections to the interference involved). Moreover, without specific criteria different from those at present used for monitoring performance, or proposing investigations, it is difficult to see what the select committee process would achieve except the greater 'openness' of proceedings. It would in any event be desirable, before recommending their introduction, to assess the past effectiveness of such institutions and their advantages compared, for instance, with either the adoption of a more open exemption procedure by the Mergers Panel (Hughes, 1978; HMSO, 1980) or the use of state owned companies in particular sectors, or the integration of large firms into a planning system such as that envisaged in past proposals over planning agreements. An examination of these issues would be a useful way of extending the analysis in the paper and broadening the discussion.

Competition policy *by itself* has in my view a relatively small contribution to make to the industrial recovery of the UK economy. It is important however that conflicts with other policy weapons are at least minimised, and preferably that competition policy be properly integrated into an overall strategy. This highlights the need to evaluate proposals for the reform of competition policy against the overall economic and policy background in which they are proposed (Hughes and Singh, 1979). Hopefully Keith Cowling's paper marks the beginning of a fuller discussion of these issues in the context of alternative economic strategies to solve the current crisis of the British economy.

NOTE

1. This evidence of course only bears indirectly on the issue of whether *overall* investment is higher or lower as a result of merger (see Kumar, 1981). Whilst Meeks' results contain possible upward bias due to the incorporation of an acquired firms investment flows into the merging firms' accounts, Kumar's results are not affected by this problem.

REFERENCES

Aaronovitch, S. and Sawyer, M.C., 1975, 'Mergers Growth and Concentration', *Oxford Economic Papers*, March.

Bank of England, 1977, 'Industrial and Commercial Companies: Profitability and the Cost of Capital', *Bank of England Quarterly Bulletin*, June.

Dunning, J.H. and Pearce, R.D., 1981, *The Worlds Largest Industrial Enterprises*, Gower Press, London.

Hart, P.E. and Clarke, R., 1980, *Concentration in British Industry 1935-75*, Cambridge University Press, Cambridge.

HMSO, 1978, *A Review of Monopolies and Mergers Policy*, Cmnd 7198, London.

HMSO, 1979, *A Review of Restrictive Trade Practices Policy*, Cmnd 7512, London.

Hill, T.P., 1979, *Profits and Rates of Return*, OECD Paris.

Hughes, A., 1979, 'Company Concentration, Size of Plant, and Merger Activity' in M. Panic, (ed.) *The UK and W. German Manufacturing Industry 1954-72*, NEDO London.

Hughes, A., 1978, 'Competition Policy and Economic Performance in the UK' in *Competition Policy* NEDO, London.

Hughes, A. and Singh, A., 1980, 'Mergers, Concentration and Competition in Advanced Capitalist Economies: An International Perspective' in Mueller, D.C. (ed.), *The Determinants and Effects of Mergers*, O.G. and H. Cambridge Massachusetts.

Hughes, A., and Singh, A., 1979, 'Takeovers Economic Efficiency and a Disequilibrium Economy'. Paper read at the EARIE Conference Nuremberg 1979 D.A.E. Cambridge mimeo.

Hughes, A., Mueller, D.C. and Singh, A., 1980, 'Competition Policy in the 1980s:

The Implication of the International Merger Wave' in D.C. Mueller *op. cit.*

Kumar, M.S., 1981, 'Do Mergers reduce corporate investment? Evidence from United Kingdom Experience', *Cambridge Journal of Economics*, March.

Meeks, G., 1977, *Disappointing Marriage: A study of the Gains from Merger*, Cambridge University Press, Cambridge.

Pillay, V., 1981, 'The International Economic Crisis' in Currie, D. and Smith, R.P. (eds.), *Socialist Economic Review 1981*, Merlin Press, London.

DOES MANUFACTURING DESERVE SPECIAL STATUS?[1]

Henry Neuburger

It has become a commonplace on the left to be concerned about the decline of manufacturing industry. The concern spreads over a very wide political spectrum. In this brief paper I want to argue that much of the thinking behind this concern is muddled.

There is, of course, every reason to be concerned about the current decline of the economy, but for any given level of unemployment there seems to be no particular problem if employment is more or less concentrated in manufacturing. There is of course an appropriate balance of employment in the economy for producing the variety of goods and services needed. What I wish to challenge is the idea that the more of the economy is devoted to manufacturing, the better. The effect of this belief is that the focus of attention has been on the one third of the economy which manufacturing represents at the expense of the rest, and more generally that thinking about industrial policy has taken place at a rather abstract level.

This affects both the labour movement's own tactics and the policies it supports. A particular example is the support of protection for industries like textiles or clothing. To prevent decline in this sector, the labour movement appears to be prepared to countenance discrimination against third world and centrally planned economies, to resort to arguments of the crudest chauvinism and to ally with the employers in these industries against almost everyone else. Money is given to British Leyland and British Steel on a scale which would keep many more people in jobs in hospitals or railways. All this is done in the name of preserving the manufacturing base. In terms of tactics, the faith in manufacturing has led some sections of the trade-union movement to attack the public services on the grounds that they do not create 'real wealth'. What we need are comprehensive policies to restore general full employment, not divisive sectional struggles to preserve particular jobs. The issues are not therefore academic. I therefore make only limited apology for the polemical style of my argument. My aim is to stir thought where too much has been taken for granted for too long.

In this paper I shall argue that manufacturing is inferior both in terms of efficiency and humanity. While this does not mean that I wish to see it destroyed, it suggests that we need to re-examine the criteria for industrial policy. Section I will seek to isolate some of the strands in the argument

197

in favour of manufacturing. Section II will present some statistical material about manufacturing while the conclusions will try to draw out some of the implications of the arguments in favour of manufacturing and their rejection.

Before we look at the arguments in detail it is worth pointing out that concern with the structure of the capitalist economy has little to do with socialism. There are certain arguments which relate to strategy in the class war, but otherwise nearly all are concerned with a more efficient or possibly more humane capitalism. There is nothing wrong with such an aim, of course, but the limitation of what can be achieved in such a direction must not be ignored. The writings of the left on manufacturing and de-industrialisation are fairly scattered, and I make no claim to have read comprehensively. The list of arguments tries to impose some sort of structure on what I have read or remembered.

I. Why Do People Favour Manufacturing?

Manufacturing has been praised as:

    (a) an engine of growth

    (b) an essential element of trade

    (c) the essential core of the economy

    (d) real work producing real things

    (e) a centre of trade-union organisation

It has also been defended:

    (f) as all economic activity is defended—to avoid unemployment

    (g) as something monetarists want to destroy

There are, in addition, strategic and military reasons which I cannot believe form a major part in left thinking.

    (a) *Engine of growth.* It has been argued by many economists, some of them not of the left, that manufacturing industry is the source of economic growth. It is argued that technical innovation enhances production largely in manufacturing, and that substantial technical economies of scale make growth in manufacturing self-sustaining. Insofar as this is true, contraction will be particularly painful and damaging in manufacturing. It is, however, unclear that technical innovation is confined to manufacturing production, even if it was true at some stage in capitalist development. One has only to look at such industries as telecommunications, public transport, health care, banking and retail distribution to see that technical economies of scale or innovation are by no means confined to manufacturing. It is difficult to know how the proposition could be vindicated or refuted. At the level of international cross-sectional analysis there is an association between rapid growth of productivity and manufacturing growth. This does not establish causation. This argument cannot be regarded as resolved one way or the other.

A somewhat different argument is that non-manufacturing industry is largely ancillary to manufacturing either by serving the manufacturing process or the workers in that process. There is a certain amount of truth in this claim. An econometric analysis of output trends in the UK suggests that part of private sector non-manufacturing output are heavily dependent on developments in manufacturing output. Obvious cases are energy and transport. In other words, it suggests that manufacturing and some non-manufacturing activities are all part of the same process. Nonetheless, there is a great deal of non-manufacturing output which is not directly related to manufacturing. Manufacturing may still be one of the cylinders of growth but it is not the whole engine. One special variation of this argument is that manufacturing is essential for investment. An inspection of the 1974 input/output tables undermines this view. In practice manufacturing only provides a quarter of the net output content of investment while non-manufacturing provides over 50 per cent.

(b) *Essential element of trade.* This argument tends to begin with an assertion that Britain is a trading nation highly dependent on imports for vital food and raw materials. It must therefore export or die. This argument needs to be examined for its accuracy and its implications. I am not sure whether it is also applied to other countries, although it would only apply with similar force to a few other countries, such as Japan, Germany, Hong Kong. It is important to look at why the UK imports so much of its basic requirements. Partly it is because its agriculture is naturally less effective than many other countries, and partly an imperial legacy of exotic tastes (tea, sugar, chocolate etc.). Much of it, however, is because the UK has a large manufacturing sector. There is something unsatisfactory about an argument that says we must export steel in order to pay for our imports of iron ore.

The figures in Table 5 do not support the view that imports are to any large extent of 'vital food and raw materials'. Only 33 per cent of UK imports fall into SITC 0-4 in 1979 (compared with 82 per cent in 1950 and 54 per cent in 1970). Of these SITC 3—fuel—is not relevant because it is the balance on fuel which is important not the total flows of imports and exports. SITC 0—food, drink and tobacco—itself contains a certain amount of manufactured food.

On the other hand SITC 5—semi-manufactures—(20 per cent of imports in 1979) contains a large amount which would have been imported as basic materials if it had not been imported in slightly processed form. We do not therefore need to export to prevent starvation. Most of our imports are things which could be produced in this country.

The next set of arguments suggest that manufacturing is vital for the balance of payments. We argue that this is not obviously true, nor is it relevant. For the sake of argument we take as given that the balance of trade in goods and services must be made to balance. We shall also take as given that this implies achieving a high level of exports. The question which still needs to be asked is, what does this imply for manufacturing? If we take a situation where sterling is very strong, this means that imports are relatively cheap and we do not need to export a large volume of goods to buy the required imports. The decline in output induced by the strength of sterling is a bad thing for other reasons but it has no bearing on the trade argument as such.

Alternatively, let us consider the more general argument that achieving a healthy balance of payments is a *sine qua non* for sustained economic growth. The UK needs to improve the demand for its produce relative to other countries in order to grow. Obviously not all countries can do this simultaneously. Supposing we accept this parochial aim, is support for the manufacturing sector the best way to achieve it? The fact that manufacturing may make a certain contribution to exports or possibly even net trade and has done so in the past is no argument in itself. This is one of the main arguments advanced for example by Singh (Cambridge Journal of Economics, June 1977). He looks at the trends in trade in goods and in services. He concedes that the UK's relative performance in services has actually been better than its performance in goods. He argues that this is not, however, an argument for concentrating on services rather than manufacturing because our net trade in most services is close to zero and in financial services the total scale is not large. Given that the balance of payments is small in relation to the gross flows of imports and exports, there need only be a small change to achieve our balance of payments objectives. More importantly the argument confuses the importance of manufactured goods in the balance of payments with the importance of manufacturing industry in the process of creating exports.

Table 4 illustrates the well-known proposition that exports of manufactures (SITC basis) are three times as big as exports of services. It also shows that exports of services have grown faster than exports of goods. This larger share does not mean however that manufacturing is essential to exporting. Manufacturing uses services provided by the rest of the economy in order to produce exports.

Many of these services like warehousing or transport could not be exported without being incorporated in some physical form. But it is equally true that goods could not be exported without the transport to take them abroad. Manufacturing and services are both essential parts of the exporting process. Neither is more basic than the other. For most products packing is necessary for exporting, but no-one suggests that we should preserve or enhance our packing industries. Also there are of course many services like shipping and tourism which can be exported.

What is relevant is the cost per unit of producing and delivering exports. The appropriate sectors for improvement are those where action will achieve advances in productivity. A first rough guide to this is the contribution in terms of net output made by different sectors to the process of exporting.

We can get a picture of this by looking at the input/output tables. These show that in 1974, manufacturing net output contributed 33 per cent of exports of goods and services, the same as the rest of the economy (the other third coming from imports). It is clear therefore that manufacturing is no more important to the balance of payments than non-manufacturing. Transport for example is much more important relatively to exports than is manufacturing. It is likely that the relative importance of manufacturing in exports will have declined since 1975 if for no other reason than that exports of services and oil have become relatively more important. In addition the rise in the propensity to import intermediate manufactures has meant that the domestic content of UK exports of manufactures will have declined.

(c) *Essential core of the economy.* There is an argument which relates to the issue of the effects of North Sea oil in particular but has been used more generally. This is a view that if the UK allows manufacturing capacity to disappear it will miss it when the oil is gone, and will be unable to recreate it. This is consistent with arguments about economies of scale and preserving productive organisations which preserve and develop skills. Plants will only be viable if kept running at high capacity— but this is not consistent with the idea of manufacturing as a major channel of technical innovation. It is difficult to believe that much of the manufacturing capacity available now will still be a great deal of use in twenty years time. Twenty years ago, little of the country's present steel-making capacity was in existence; while major plants open then, such as shipyards, have gone.

More important, these arguments apply with equal if not greater force outside manufacturing. Really long-lived capital exists mainly in industries like transport, housing and mining. The loss of docks, railway lines or hospitals is as serious as the closure of manufacturing plant. Similar arguments seem to apply to the preservation of skills. We can have little idea what skills are going to be in short supply in thirty years time; preserving the present structure of industry is unlikely to make a major contribution to the problem. Sometimes this argument means little more than that much of UK industry is manufacturing and more used to be. Insofar as this is true it hardly constitutes an independent argument.

(d) *Real work and real things.* This is a title used for a clutch of heterogeneous but widespread arguments. Their common theme is a concern with the status of manufacturing product or manufacturing labour. The phrase 'the candy-floss economy' used of private non-manufacturing, notions of real work, real men's work (as opposed to women's work) of productive and unproductive labour combine with even more antique notions which contrast 'free' industrial workers with feudal servants. Service trades have never completely escaped the feudal stigma. There is even sometimes an aesthetic disdain for such products as betting shops or TV programmes. There seems to be little that a socialist can find congenial in these arguments and much to abhor. They are nonetheless powerful, all the more for being vaguely expressed. More sympathetic are arguments deriving from pride in one's work. Steel workers find it difficult to believe that there isn't a perfectly good use for as much steel as could be produced. So, quite frequently do ordnance workers and soldiers and so did ostlers, handloom weavers etc. This is an argument why anyone might want their own industry preserved. There is nothing special about manufacturing in this context. A good candy-floss turner has his pride.

(e) *Centre of trade-union organisations.* Manufacturing is often defended as a centre of working-class organisation. We examine the rather limited facts in this area in Section II. The only measure used in trade-union density. A more appropriate measure would include such factors as shop floor organisation, political organisation etc. Trade-union density may tend to understate the case. Even here, where the argument is potentially quite strong, there is a danger of being misled by the category of manufacturing. The clothing and textile industries for example are very poorly organised while the docks or the mines are traditional centres of workers power. The concept of manufacturing is too broad for this kind of analysis.

(f) *No jobs should be lost.* The argument against losing any jobs must be overwhelming in current circumstances. It applies, however, with equal force to all jobs, if other things are equal. In fact they are not equal. Jobs in manufacturing are less flexible (in terms of availability of part-time work), more dangerous, involve more hours than jobs in service industries and provide less employment for women.

(g) *The monetarists and the City want to destroy manufacturing so it must be a good thing.* The issue has recently been confused by the arguments of Forsyth and Kay. They argue that the rise in North Sea oil production necessarily entails a decline in the rest of the economy. The mechanism by which this is brought about, they assert, is through the high level of the exchange rate. This makes British goods uncompetitive in both the UK and world markets. This in turn causes the collapse of manufacturing, and given that total output is fixed, non-manufacturing output (other than oil) expands to fill its place.

The argument is shot through with fallacies, only a few of which will concern us here. The main difficulty is that some of the left have felt the need to combat the argument on its own terms. If the monetarists want to get rid of manufacturing, then it must be a good thing. Clearly we can all agree that what Thatcher is currently doing to the economy has nothing to do with the adjustment of the economy to a desirable new structure. (It has a great deal, of course, to do with a capitalist restructuring of the economy with its associated attack on the working class and destruction of some elements of capital.) The left appears however to be making the opposite error of supposing that the decline of the economy can only be reversed by reviving manufacturing industry.

The argument of Forsyth and Kay is wrong in many ways. Their fundamental belief, that services will expand naturally to fill the gap caused by a decline in manufacturing, is a close relation of the idea that restricting the public sector will cause the private sector to grow. They both rely on the fallacious idea that capitalism is self-stabilising. In particular, the econometric analysis referred to above shows that some non-manufacturing activity (energy and transport are obvious examples) are ancillary to manufacturing and will decline with them.

Nor is there any reason to suppose that the rest of non-manufacturing should be stimulated by the decline of manufacturing. As employment in manufacturing and its immediate ancillaries declines, this will cut consumption which will drag down the rest of the economy. These multiplier consequences would of course follow from the decline of any sector of the economy and are not specific to manufacturing industry.

II. The Facts

This section presents some of the factors relevant to the arguments discussed above. It might be useful to start with some classifications. I have divided the economy into five sectors: manufacturing, nationalised industries, other industry, private services and public services. The nationalised industry sector is a term which is not strictly accurate. It seems a useful term to cover a group which comprises mining, energy and transport. Manufacturing covers those activities which use industrial processes to produce physical output from physical inputs. The term industry is used to cover a range of activity which also includes extractive industries, energy industries and construction.

While different classifications are useful for different purposes, I shall assume that when people want to preserve manufacturing, they are referring to those activities strictly by that definition. It is on this definition that most statistics refer. If people see from the deductions made from such an assumption that this is not what they really meant—then so much the better; my case will be making progress.

This section presents the facts which ought to be relevant to the issues raised above. It is perhaps worth starting with a section on definitions since there is surprising nomenclature. Terry Barker (randomly selected) in his opening sentence says: 'The most straight-forward meaning of de-industrialisation is a protracted decline in the share of manufacturing in employment or output,' (Conference Paper, Mexico, September 1980). The notions of industry and manufacturing are thus conflated, leaving such industries as construction, energy and agriculture in limbo. This lack of clarity does, I believe, lead to genuine confusion. The arguments on trade-union power for example apply most powerfully to sections of industry outside manufacturing while the trade arguments are usually taken to apply strictly to manufacturing. In the discussions here we shall be talking about manufacturing so defined i.e. SIC orders III–XIX.

(a) *Is manufacturing nice?* The rise of manufacturing was intimately connected with the industrial revolution. As such, it has been associated with all its most unpleasant aspects. No-one has ever had a good word to say for working in factories. Only coal-mining has a worse reputation. While wages may have been lower in agriculture and security of employment was worse in the docks, these defects may be in some sense regarded as contingent on particular economic circumstances; the unpleasantness of factory work seems somehow endemic. Average plant size is three times as large as it is for the economy as a whole. Over 60 per cent of workers in manufacturing work in establishments employing over 200 people; the proportion for the rest of the economy is one third. (If one excludes hospitals and educational establishments the proportion falls to one sixth.) This larger size is likely to lead to a more rigid and disciplined working environment (see Table 1).

Manufacturing is not the most dangerous sector of industry. Mining and construction are both worse for all kinds of accidents and agriculture and fishing for fatal accidents. Nonetheless workers in manufacturing are two-and-a-half times more likely to have an accident than other workers. (The likelihood of a fatality is about the same.) If one compares workers in manufacturing with service workers (i.e. those outside production) the ratio rises to five times for all accidents while fatalities are twice as likely in manufacturing as they are in services.

Hours of work are longer in manufacturing industry. In April 1979 full-time workers over 18 worked an average 43 hour week in manufacturing while the average for the whole economy was 41.5 hours. This difference largely reflects the higher proportion of manual workers in manufacturing industry—the average working week for manual workers was slightly higher in manufacturing than in non-manufacturing·industry. The similarity is largely due to the very long hours worked in transport.

The proportion of women working in manufacturing is lower than the proportion in the economy as a whole. There are certain branches of manufacturing like clothing and textiles where the proportion of women is relatively high but there are some like steel and shipbuilding where the number of women workers is negligible. While in many ways the current recession has hit women very hard, the concentration of the fall of employment in manufacturing has actually hit men harder. (See the paper by Rubery and Tarling in this volume for more detail.)

Manufacturing also provides less part-time employment even in industries where there is a large proportion of women.

1980	Proportion of women in total employment	Proportion of part-time workers
Manufacturing	28.3	7.8
Non-manufacturing	47.4	25.9
Steel	8.9	3.0
Shipbuilding	7.8	2.1
Clothing and Footwear	45.8	15.6
Textiles	75.5	10.8

Source: *New Earnings Survey* 1980

Pay differences between men and women are also greater in manufacturing industry:

Ratio of women's to men's pay

	Manual	Non-manual	All workers
Manufacturing	60.3	53.2	58.6
Whole economy	60.8	58.5	63.3

(b) *Is manufacturing useful?* In many stories about economic growth it has been argued that manufacturing is the engine of growth. Nonetheless, statistical analysis does not seem to support this position. Between 1951 and 1971 UK private sector output grew by 71 per cent. Of this manufacturing contributed 27 per cent, i.e. a little over a third. During that period productivity growth was much the same in manufacturing and in the rest of the private sector (74 per cent as against 71 per cent). In terms of output per person, manufacturing was one third less productive than the rest of the private sector in 1951 and 1971. Capital/output ratios are about one third lower in manufacturing than in the rest of the economy. This masks very wide differences between 'nationalised industries' and the rest. Table 3 shows that once nationalised industries are removed, capital/output ratio in the private services sector was about half that in manufacturing. The low productivity of manufacturing cannot be accounted for by low capital intensity. The sharply rising capital/ output ratio may however account for its relatively faster growth of productivity. In the 1950s, in particular, the sectors with the lowest productivity growth were nationalised industries and private services which also had stagnant or falling capital/ratios.

The fact that manufacturing is less productive than services means that if we adopt an industrial policy which succeeds in shifting resources (i.e. labour or investment) from services to manufacturing, there will be two factors at work. The factor usually indicated is that rapid growth will do more to stimulate the growth of productivity if it occurs in manufacturing than in non-manufacturing industry. I have not directly analysed this proposition. As against this, resources will be shifted from a high productivity to a low productivity industry. I am sceptical that the former effect can outweigh the latter. (This result, I believe, underlies the thinking of Chatterji and Wickens, see references.) This is an important and surprising result shown in Table 2. It is probably therefore worth describing its derivation. The National Income Blue Book breaks down net output into industries (in Table 3.1). For any given year, it is possible to compare this output with the number of workers involved. This is done in the lower half of the table. In the top half this is done not in prices of the year in question. Output is measured in 1975 prices so that comparisons can be made over time. It can be seen that the conclusion that manufacturing is less productive is sustainable whatever the measure used, but is stronger if the calculation is performed in 1975 prices.[2]

We have already dealt in Section I with the trade argument.

(c) *Trade-union density.* There is a belief that manufacturing is particularly heavily unionised. There are no official figures on this. Bain has estimates for 1960. An estimate can be made for 1978 by guessing at the industrial composition of trade-union membership. The difficult allocations are the TGWU, GMWU and ASTMS. It is likely however that in these cases the bulk will be in the sector outside manufacturing. Between them, these three unions have a membership of 3½ million. It seems unlikely that more than three quarters of a million of these will be in manufacturing. In 1960 manufacturing seems to have been about as unionised as the rest of the economy, rather less than the public service sector. By 1978 it seems to 'have fallen behind both the public sector and the rest of the private sector. Within these are sectors like private services which are very poorly unionised and others like nationalised industries where unionisation is very strong.

(d) *Concentration.* One way of looking at concentration is an analysis of 'The Times 1000 Companies'. This illustrates a greater concentration of manufacturing companies. In 1978 the top 50 manufacturing companies employed 2½ million workers and had a turnover of about £60 billion. The corresponding figures for the top 50 non-manufacturing companies is about ½ million and £70 billion, but of that turnover more than half is represented by Shell and BP. (Where UK activities in 1978 were as much manufacturing as not.)

Aaronovitch and Sawyer (*Big Business,* 1975) look at the evidence on concentration of some non-manufacturing industries and conclude that there is no strong general indication that concentration is greater in non-manufacturing than in manufacturing. There are certainly some sectors of service industries like banking which are highly concentrated but others like construction and agriculture and construction which are, at least by some measures, less so. The available evidence certainly does not suggest that manufacturing is more competitive than the rest of the private sector.

Conclusions

The present concern for manufacturing industry has long antecedents. Confining ourselves to recent history, we can see the burning up of socialism in the 'white heat of the technological revolution' in 1964 and the abandonment of industrial strategy in 1977–9 as examples of manufacture worship.

In its earlier phase, it took the form of trying to give companies stable profits so that they would invest in manufacturing. We can see now that manufacturing was a highly profligate user of resources. Productivity of the whole economy could be improved by reducing the share of manufacturing in it. Nor is it clear that in relative terms manufacturing investment did raise productivity. Finally, there is no evidence that high profits actually give rise to more investment. All the evidence suggests that what brings about high levels of investment is high levels of output.

The currently fashionable cure for manufacturing decline is an improvement in competitiveness. While this is important as a general policy, it may not necessarily achieve any selective preservation of manufacturing industry. Another popular policy which similarly is seen as preserving manufacturing is import controls. These, of course, need not be confined to manufacturing. Exchange controls, for example, were in some forms, effectively import controls on holidays. In practice they are likely to favour manufacturing in the first instance. The same argument about the long-run effects applies here as with depreciation. The services ancillary to manufacturing and tradeable services will also be affected by such policies. So again, they are a policy for saving the whole economy, not just manufacturing.

The final range of policies is straight or complicated subsidies and investment grants. SET, TES and VAT all changed the balance in favour of manufacturing. Of these only SET has any claim to have achieved even its short-term objectives of restoring the relative level, at least of manufacturing employment. It is however, unclear what further good that did.

The engine of growth argument—the only one we have found with any serious claim to validity—has rather specialised implications. It implies that we should achieve the maximum possible growth in manufacturing output. With this I would certainly agree. What is not implied is any sacrifice of any other sector. It may have done so when we were near full employment. When labour is so abundant, there can be no question of holding back growth in any other sector, or transferring resources out of one sector. The obstacles to growth in manufacturing are more likely to lie in its own capacity and organisation.

In practice the slogan of preserving manufacturing has rarely been relevant or effective. It has often been the cover for something else. The left has been so used to thinking in terms of manufacturing that there are serious problems about thinking about the rest of the economy. The notion of economic planning has usually been thought of in terms of physical production of goods. The notion of trade policy, as we noted above, has similar connotations. The concepts of input/output analysis, the notions of bottlenecks in production and of technological advance are all based on physical analogies.

It is the conclusions of this paper that if there is anything special about manufacturing, it is especially bad. It is no longer the progressive wing of capitalism; it is relatively unproductive, unpleasant, monopolistic etc. We have not even started to consider such aspects as environmental pollution, content of work or the nature of the product (raw candy floss). This clearly does not mean that we do not want it to grow from its presently depressed level. What is argued here is that we should stop seeking policies which specially favour manufacturing industries unless there is some reason other than pure industrial policy for doing so.

NOTES

1. I am grateful to colleagues who have commented on earlier drafts of this paper. The London CSE Group provided the original stimulus for the paper, as well as much valuable comment and discussion. The paper also benefited from the comments made at the SER conference itself. Some of the points made by Alan Hughes have been taken on board, and Bernard Stafford also made some important interventions which are only partly reflected in my revisions. This failure and other errors are, of course, my own fault.

2. Strictly speaking this argument is not conclusive as it stands. The argument is valid only if marginal productivities bear the same relationship to each other as average productivities. As far as I know there is no strong evidence one way or the other on this point, but it would require very considerably greater scale economies in manufacturing than non-manufacturing to upset the initial conclusion. I am grateful to Bernard Stafford for pointing out this gap in the argument. The debate over the evidence has taken up many papers in the literature. A good summary can be found in Stafford (*The End of Economic Growth*, 1981) who concludes that the engine of growth argument in its Kaldor form is more likely than not to be true.

REFERENCES

Aaronovitch, S. and Sawyer, M., 1975, *Big Business.*
Barker, T., 1980, 'De-industrialisation, North Sea Oil and Investment Strategy for the UK', Conference Paper, Oxaca, Mexico, September.
Chatterji and Wickens, 'Verdoorn's Law, the Externalities by and Economic Growth in the UK'.
Forsyth and Kay, 'Economic Implications of North Sea Oil Revenues', *Fiscal Studies,* 1979.
Singh, A., 1977, 'UK Industry and the World Economy: A Case of De-industrialisation', *Cambridge Journal of Economics*, June.
Stafford, G.B., 1981, *The End of Economic Growth,* Oxford.

Table 1
Plant Size 1976

Size of Plants	1–10	11–50	50–200	200–1000	1000+	Average Size
Whole economy						
Percentage of plants	72.5	20.9	6.1	1.3	0.2	21
Percentage of workers	49.7	31.4	13.1	4.8	0.8	
Manufacturing						
Percentage of plants	13.1	21.5	22.5	24.7	18.2	59
Percentage of workers	3.7	12.3	21.6	33.6	28.8	

Source: Census of Employment: *DE Gazette*, January 1978

Table 2
Productivity in the Private Sector

	Output per head in 1975 prices			
	Manufacturing	NIs	Other IOP	Private Services
1951	1872	2654	2872	2875
1961	2777	3189	4477	3362
1971	3550	5003	6267	4285
1975	3563	5728	5634	4084
1978	3845	6209	6296	4188

	Output per head at current prices			
	Manufacturing	NIs	Other IOP	Private Services
1951	630	622	712	751
1961	1123	1172	1171	1264
1971	1992	2446	2953	2584
1975	3563	5894	5544	4797
1979	6479	9928	8708	8555

Source: Employment *DE Gazette*—various, NIBB 1975 figures from Table 3.1 1979 Output from Table 2.3

Table 3
Capital Stock

	1951	1961	£ billion 1971	1975	1978
Manufacturing					
Capital Stock	38.7	58.7	84.5	94.1	101.1
K/O ratio	2.65	3.02	3.30	3.58	3.70
NIs					
Capital Stock	56.2	64.6	88.5	93.3	96.5
K/O ratio	7.30	7.31	7.67	7.44	7.29
Other IOP					
Capital Stock	5.6	7.9	12.9	15.3	16.5
K/O ratio	1.95	1.93	2.06	2.71	2.62
Private Services					
Capital Stock	14.7	22.8	44.1	55.8	64.6
K/O ratio	1.11	.68	.98	1.21	1.30

Source: *NIBB* 1979 for Capital Stock Table 11.12

Table 4
Exports

	£m in 1975 prices Services excluding shipping	Manufactured goods
1965	2304	9800
1970	3728	12800
Growth rate ('65–'70)	8%	5%
1975	5046	16625
Growth rate ('70–'75)	6%	5%
1979	6364	19900
Growth rate ('75–'79)	5%	4%

Table 5
Exports and Imports of Goods by Production Group OTS BASIS

	1950	1955	1960	1965	1970	1975	1978	1979
Percentage of exports in each group								
Food, beverages and tobacco	39	37	33	30	22	18	15	13
Basic materials	35	29	23	19	15	9	8	8
Fuels	8	11	10	11	10	18	12	12
Semi-manufactures	14	18	22	24	27	25	28	29
Finished manufactures	4	5	11	15	24	28	35	36
Miscellaneous	–	–	1	1	1	2	1	2
TOTAL	100	100	100	100	100	100	100	100
Percentage of imports in each group								
Food, beverages and tobacco	7	6	6	7	6	7	8	7
Basic materials	6	6	5	3	3	3	3	3
Fuels	3	5	4	3	3	4	6	10
Semi-manufactures	40	38	35	35	34	32	34	34
Finished manufactures	41	42	47	49	50	51	47	44
Miscellaneous	2	3	3	4	3	4	3	3
TOTAL	100	100	100	100	100	100	100	100

Source: *Economic Trends*, October 1980

DISCUSSION

Alan Hughes

Since the early 1950s the impact of the UK's long run industrial decline has become increasingly apparent in the progressive weakening of this country's balance of trade in manufactures. By the 1970s imports of manufactures had become a substantial part of the total import bill and the tendency for them to grow faster than manufacturing exports produced an ever declining surplus on the full employment manufacturing balance. This has had disastrous consequences for the ability of the economy as a whole to maintain persistent growth without running into ever worsening non-oil deficits, and has gone hand in hand with a relatively rapid decline in the proportion of resources and output accounted for by manufacturing compared to other industrial countries. It is not surprising therefore to find fairly widespread support for the introduction of policies to regenerate manufacturing industry as part of any strategy designed to lead the economy back towards something like a full employment growth path (Cripps, 1981; Sheriff, 1980; Aaronovitch, 1981; Singh, 1979). Neuburger's paper wishes to challenge this view. Manufacturing he argues should not be given any particular priority in industrial policy. It is, he maintains, 'no longer the progressive wing of capitalism'. In support of his position Neuburger considers a number of unattributed arguments to the effect that manufacturing has claims to special status, and provides a critique of each. Of the arguments he looks at, the claims that manufacturing is an 'engine of growth', an 'essential element of trade' and the 'essential core of the economy' (which turns out to be the argument that we shall need something else when the oil runs out) are the central issues and I will concentrate my comments on those.

Although I can recognise the views listed, Neuburger does not present them at all adequately. Nor has he considered properly the empirical issues bearing on them. This is largely because the paper does not provide any conceptual framework for analysing the 'efficient' or 'optimal' size for any particular sector or for setting out the basis for measurement in terms of either inputs or outputs. Neuburger implies that a very wide range of issues should be considered in assessing 'optimality' including pollution, accident rates, male/female employment ratios etc. Apart from the fact that current levels of these may not be a permanent feature of manufacturing in the future and may be susceptible to policy measures, it seems to me helpful to be more specific and narrow especially in relation to the questions of the dynamic role of manufacturing industry and its

213

trade potential. An analysis of these should at least clear the ground for a discussion of the others.

One way of considering the attributes of a socially efficient manufacturing sector in an open economy such as the UK is to follow the approach of Singh (1977), where to be 'efficient' manufacturing in the UK should, given the normal levels of other components of the balance of payments, not only be capable of satisfying domestic demand but also be able to sell sufficient abroad to help meet the nations import requirements (subject to the important proviso that this be at socially acceptable levels of output, inflation and the exchange rate). Looked at in this way it is worth noting first, that it is consistent with this definition for an efficient sector to have either a declining or increasing share of input resources depending upon its productivity and international competitiveness, and second that the significance to be attached to manufacturing depends upon developments in the structure of other components of the balance of payments, and the weight that must be placed upon it therefore in meeting import requirements. The view that a regeneration of manufacturing industry in the UK is essential in terms of output, and will require both extra resources and productivity improvements, stems from an analysis of the behaviour of the trade of the UK over time, the role of manufacturing in overall growth and the view that structurally manufacturing is the only sector capable of enabling a recovery to 'full employment' balance of payments equilibrium with, or without, import controls. The paper doesn't get to grips either with the conceptual or empirical issues involved in providing an effective critique of this position.

Thus on the question of whether other sectors are capable of replacing manufacturing's traditional trading role Neuburger hints that services might, but then devotes most of his analysis to a separate (though interesting) issue of the extent to which manufacturing productivity growth depends upon developments elsewhere in the economy. On the basis of the existing literature (not adequately reviewed by Neuburger) emphasising the relative scale of trade and production in manufacturing and non-manufacturing, and trends in our international competitiveness in both, it seems to me that the case for pursuing 'dynamic comparative advantage' outside manufacturing industry is weak if not non-existent. First, the service surplus on trade is small compared to that of manufacturing and has risen proportionately largely because of the decline of the latter. Second, despite this increasing contribution to the balance of payments, the UK's share of world service exports has declined as fast if not faster than that of manufactured exports, whilst the overall rate of growth of world service exports has been slower than that of manufacturers. Moreover the UK's service exports share is already a large slice of a relatively small market. In the mid-1970s to compensate for a one per cent decline of manufacturing net exports would have required over a 30 per cent increase in the UK's already declining share of world service exports (see for instance Sargent, 1979; Singh, 1977).

As far as the analysis of manufacturing as an 'engine of growth' is concerned two comments seem worth making. First that Neuburger does admit an important link in this argument, namely that progress and expansion in, for example, transport and energy may depend on a successful manufacturing sector. More generally no serious critique is offered of the wide body of literature surrounding 'Verdoorn's Law' which attributes a key role to manufacturing in the determinants of relative rates of growth of output and productivity across countries (e.g. Kaldor, 1976; Cripps and Tarling, 1973; United Nations, 1977). Second, the notion that manufacturing is in some sense a profligate user of resources, compared to services, is based on a very misleading way of looking at the data, whilst the conclusion that transferring resources to manufacturing from other services must lower overall productivity levels is based on a static arithmetical exercise rather than a dynamic assessment of the interrelationships between sectors. Even in its own terms Neuburger's analysis may be considered misleading. GDP per head in manufacturing is roughly the same as for services as a whole and greater than in Distribution, Professional and Scientific Services and Miscellaneous Services, which between them account for two-thirds of services employment (see for instance for the mid-1970s Brown and Sheriff, 1979).

Industrial expansion as a basis for economic recovery in the UK will impose demands upon, and will be influenced by the non-industrial sectors of the economy. The latter if only via the effects of health and education upon the quality of the labour force, the pace of indigenous scientific advances and technical skills. It is a mistake to proceed from this however to the view that the non-industrial sector may be *independently* the source of economic recovery, as this paper is inclined to do, or that an industrial policy must be a zero sum game in which resources (especially investment) gained by one sector must be lost by another.

REFERENCES

Aaronovitch, S., 1981, *The Road from Thatcherism,* Lawrence and Wishart, London.

Blake, D. and Ormerod, P., 1980, *The Economics of Prosperity,* Grant MacIntyre, London.

Brown, C.F.J. and Sheriff, T.D., 1979, 'Deindustrialization: A Background paper' in F. Blackaby (ed.), *Deindustrialization,* Heinemann, London.

Cripps, T.F., 1981, 'Government planning as a means to economic recovery in the UK', *Cambridge Journal of Economics,* Vol 5 No. 1, March, pp. 95–106.

Cripps, T.F. and Tarling, R.J., 1973, *Growth in Advanced Capitalist Economics,* Cambridge University Press, Cambridge.

Kaldor, N., 1967, *Strategic Factors in Economic Development,* Cornell University Press, Ithaca, New York.

Sargent, J.R., 1979, 'UK Performance in Services' in F. Blackaby (ed.) *Deindustrialisa-*

tion, Heinemann, London.

Sheriff, T.D., 1980, 'Trade, Industry and Employment' in Blake, D. and Ormerod, P. *The Economics of Prosperity,* Grant MacIntyre, London.

Singh, A., 1977, 'UK industry and the World Economy: a case of deindustrialization?' Vol 1 No. 2, June, pp. 113–136.

Singh, A., 1979, 'North Sea Oil and the Reconstruction of UK Industry', in F. Blackaby (ed.) *Deindustrialization,* Heinemann, London.

United Nations, 1977, *Structure and Change in European Industry,* United Nations, New York.

EVALUATING THE ROLE OF THE FINANCIAL SYSTEM

Jerry Coakley and Laurence Harris

It is widely recognised that the financial system has a pivotal role in the British economy. Conflicts over economic policies have involved exchange rates, interest rates and the direction and conditions of credit as often as wages and the labour process. Such financial variables are important because of their effects on the 'real' economy. The financial system's significance lies in its impact on these variables but its influence also works through other channels. We argue that to understand the effect of financial processes on the 'real' economy one needs to consider the workings of the financial system itself, and in particular, the differences that exist within it.

Financial 'processes' is a rather abstract term; it is easier to think in terms of the institutions in which the processes are at work. Thus, what we are really looking at is how the banks, insurance companies, pension funds and other financial institutions, ('the City' for convenience) have operated with respect to industrial and commercial capital in the UK.

The significance of the City lies in the specific nature of the power exercised by its institutions; it is a power which has several dimensions and political discussion sometimes concentrates on one dimension rather than another. In the present monetarist episode, as in earlier periods, the power of the City to force the government to adopt deflation and unemployment as a strategy has been at the fore. This, itself, can arise either from the direct political activities of the City or from its power to influence exchange rates and interest rates—key variables which act as constraints on governments' ability to plan and expand state expenditure. The power to influence exchange and interest rates illustrates the specificity of financial institutions as compared with other firms and bodies: for whereas any firm importing or exporting, or even any worker holidaying in Benidorm, may have an indirect influence on the demand/supply balance for foreign exchange, the financial institutions' position and role in the economic structure is to concentrate financial balances in their hands and thereby dominate the exchange market and credit markets. It is they, rather than industrial firms or other agents that act in the wholesale money and foreign exchange markets where interest and exchange rates are set. Some discussions of the City's power are concerned with another of its dimensions—its pivotal role in determining the adequacy, price and direction of finance for industry; questions about this power often ask whether the City has been instrumental in channelling capital abroad and thereby starving productive capital operating in the UK of funds.[1] Finally, the potential for influencing the supply of finance to industry gives rise to the possibility of another dimension of financial institutions' power, the ability to influence industry or control it in some circumstances. This is the aspect of the City's power on which this paper focuses.

The workings of the financial system have recently been examined by the Wilson Committee, the latest in a line of official reports on the City. Its report[2] carried the general message that all is well with the City and no significant changes are necessary or desirable. Although some members signed a note of dissent supporting the TUC proposal for a new investment facility, such a fund would hardly affect the City's operation; since the need for it was thought to arise from a gap in the funds supplied by the City, it would not even compete with the existing financial institutions. In the present paper, we reach a different conclusion on the need for government intervention in the City. We also employ a different theoretical approach from Wilson's. The Wilson Committee assumes that financial institutions are decision-making individual economic agents much like any other firm and that their decisions have the same status as those of any firm or household. We start from the assumption that the financial system as a whole is a distinct bloc (rather than a summation of its individual institutions), its operations and effects are quite specific and its position in the economy embodies specific forms of power over the other agents.

The Wilson Committee's view that all economic agents are equally significant and financial institutions have no special power implies that those institutions are essentially passive conduits[3] : their principle function is seen as merely channelling funds from one sector of the economy to another and making only technical decisions on the disposition of funds. By contrast we think it is significant that City institutions have specific objectives—the specific aim of strengthening their own competitive position.

This drive has an important implication for Wilson's central problem of financing industry. It has been at the root of particular conflicts between the interests of the City and of industry in Britain in spite of their common long-term interest in profitable accumulation. Strengthening the City's own competitive position has meant improving it as an *international* financial centre vis-a-vis those of New York, Frankfurt and others. At crucial conjunctures this has required policies to maintain a relatively high exchange rate (although that is not a permanent policy) and to ensure high interest rates irrespective of their effects upon industrial profits and accumulation.[4] This strategy, which has been predicated on a policy of allowing London's international financial business to develop relatively unhampered by controls, has succeeded in making London the strongest international centre of money and credit markets.

The City's international competition for financial business is one aspect of its specific power and dynamic that distinguishes it from other sectors of the economy. But it would be wrong to see the City as a monolith, whether as a unified conduit for funds to industry or as an entity in international competition. Distinct elements within the City have distinct roles and in the following paragraphs we examine the specific power exercised by different elements in financing industry.

Below we examine the UK's two main types of financial markets and then return to their common characteristic—their short-term perspective.

I. The Role and Nature of Financial Markets

The Wilson Committee's individualist perspective, with its assumption that all decision makers are equally significant, obscures the specificity of the power of the City as a whole. It also clouds the distinctions between the different parts of the financial system itself. We shall consider these distinctions by concentrating on the division of labour which has emerged between two types of 'financial markets', the money and credit markets on one hand and the securities or capital markets on the other. The differences between them are such that there is an ever present potential for conflict between the institutions engaged in each type of market. The markets for money and credit are dominated by banks engaged in obtaining and making short- and medium-term loans; broadly speaking the loans do not give any legal rights of ownership (although they confer some real power on the lender to affect the borrower's actions). The capital market, whose institutional framework is centred on the stock market and the bodies which operate within and around it (insurance companies, pension funds, brokers, jobbers and trusts) trades in securities which are created as a means of raising long-term capital for enterprises and which in the case of shares (but not, generally speaking, bonds) confer some legal ownership rights. A third important type of market is the wholesale foreign exchange market. Although it does overlap and interweave with the money and credit markets because of the dominant role played by London banks in Eurocurrency transactions, we do not explicitly discuss it in this paper. Instead, it is considered in the chapter by David Currie.

The possibility of conflicts between the institutions engaged in each type of market becomes especially important at times of economic crisis. In the past year financial institutions, under the informal leadership of the Bank of England, have negotiated rescue packages for several major enterprises. In these deals the differences between banks with existing loans at risk and institutions holding equity capital have been at the fore. Moreover, at times of high interest rates the benefits accruing to banks because a high proportion of their deposits are obtained at low or zero interest (the endowment effect) bring no direct benefits to pension funds, insurance companies and others in the capital market. Thus, the degree of support for high interest rate policies differs, and this difference is fostered by the fact that high interest rates (and the expectation that they will eventually fall) causes industry to favour raising loans by borrowing from banks instead of the capital (bond) market.

(a) *The securities markets.* The securities markets refer to the series of markets in which share capital and various bonds are floated *and* traded. The securities market can be further subdivided into the corporate stock market which is concerned with share capital, company loan stock and debentures, and the gilt-edged market for the issue and trading of government bonds. In this section we are concerned mainly with the stock market and particularly share capital although much of what we have to say about institutional domination may also apply to the gilt-edged market. At the outset it should be pointed out that the Wilson Report did point to some of the salient features of the stock market[5] but in that context it failed to analyse them or relate them to the ongoing debate on the ownership and control issue (a debate which is central to any evaluation of how changes in the financial system can affect industry).

The stock market really comprises two interrelated markets corresponding to its two basic functions. The first is the new issues market which raises money capital for the joint stock companies issuing new or additional shares. In the UK context the first thing to be noted about new issues is the dramatic decline in their relative contribution to industrial and commercial companies' external finance[6] from an average of over 30 per cent in the 1963–70 period to an average of only 12 per cent in the 1971–79 period. This is all the more striking because the decline occurred during a period of unprecedented growth in institutional cash flow. The second feature of the new issues market is that rights issues by larger companies (often for takeover purposes) have raised most of the money capital. A rights issue involves a company offering its existing shareholders the right to subscribe at a discount for further shares in proportion to their shareholdings. To sum up: the stock market's contribution to companies' external finance has been relatively minor during the 1970s but one cannot conclude that it has exercised no influence over industry.

Of far greater quantitative importance than the new issues market is the secondary market where *existing* shares and bonds can be bought and sold. This corresponds to the second basic function of the stock market which is to facilitate the conversion of investors' existing shares into money and which forms the basis for investors short-term outlook. The secondary market is where the increasing institutional domination of the stock market is proceeding. Basically this is a transfer or distributional shift in the ownership of shares, typically from the personal sector to financial institutions, for example pension funds and insurance companies. It does not itself involve raising any additional money capital for the companies whose shares are changing hands. But their role on the secondary market gives institutions a strong role in the new issues market too, since the principle type of new issue is the 'rights issue' where existing shareholders are the main suppliers of new funds. Now, ordinary share capital represents the risk-bearing capital of a company and confers certain ownership rights on the shareholders. In normal circumstances these rights include dividend payments and a *vote* per share on the appointment or removal of directors, and in the event of insolvency, a residual claim on the company's assets after *all creditors* have been fully repaid. It is important to bear in mind these ownership rights for they have frequently been misunderstood or exaggerated in the context of the ownership and control debate—a topic which the Wilson Report does not even mention although it implicitly discusses some related issues.

The ownership and control debate arose as a criticism of the neo-classical theory of the owner/entrepreneur profit-maximising firm. The most popular alternative (the managerial theory of the firm) to the neo-classical theory saw the modern firm as characterised by a separation between its ownership and its control or management. The joint stock form of enterprise has seen the replacement of the owner/entrepreneur by a range of shareholders all holding relatively small stakes in the enterprise. In the absence of any large shareholders, claims the theory, management stepped into the power vacuum and began running companies on a different basis. Instead of maximising profits, management was seen as pursuing growth as an objective usually subject to some financial constraint such as a minimum level of dividends or a stock market value constraint.[7] Failure to comply with the financial constraint implied a threat of takeover and the possible replacement of management.

If the managerial theory of the firm were valid it would have important implications for the Alternative Economic Strategy for it would decrease the significance of taking enterprises into public *ownership.* Has the increased institutional domination of the stock market, the concentration of shareholdings in the hands of big financial blocs, weakened the basis of the theory? Prais (1976) thinks not on the grounds that institutions spread their holdings across a range of companies (in order to reduce risk) so that no individual institution holds controlling interests in individual companies. Managers remain autonomous. Wilson similarly emphasises the dispersion of shareholdings. However, the power that institutional shareholders can exert as owners over managers is not obliterated by superficial dispersal, because shareholdings can be aggregated into financial groups to exert pressure. A common device used by the institutions to this end is the 'Investment Protection Committee' (IPC).

In the insurance companies' IPC for example, an average of ten to twenty cases per year in the 1970s have dealt with a management problem whilst a somewhat larger number have involved questions of shareholders' voting rights and the rights of consultation on major changes in company structure.[8] Moreover, since some two-thirds of pension fund assets are externally managed by merchant banks as Minns has shown,[9] the concentration of such assets in the hands of a small number of merchant banks confers the possibility of effective control on them. At the end of 1976 the merchant banks had some £7½b. funds under management on behalf of other institutions and individuals. However, the Wilson Report failed to see this concentration of funds as a source of control. The managerial theories also underestimate the constraints on companies from outside the stock market, particularly from the bank credit market. This raises the possibility of conflict between shareholders and banks not only in the more obvious cases of bank-imposed dividend restrictions and residual claims on liquidated companies' assets but also over the range of a company's major decisions. We explore this more fully in the context of the money/credit markets.

(b) *The money/credit markets.* The money/credit markets refer to those markets where banks provide short- and medium-term credit facilities and other specialist services such as trade financing. Until the late 1970s the City's sophisticated money/credit markets have been unique in their failure to supply medium-term bank credit on a more general level. This is not to deny the significance of bank credit in the financing of industry and trade at the aggregate level. As the Bank of England indicates:

> The banks increased their share of industrial and commercial companies' external finance in the 1970s. In the 1960s. . . they had provided rather less than half of the total, while the 1970s they contributed about 60% of it, often more.[10]

At least part of the increased importance of bank credit can be explained by the decline of the industrial bond market and the increased willingness of American banks in particular to supply term facilities. Now whilst it is difficult to quibble with the report's conclusion that no *general* shortage of funds for industry exists in the UK at present, it is arguable whether this has been the case for different types of bank credit until the late 1970s. There is a distinction between bank credit to finance circulating capital and that to finance fixed capital. Broadly, until the latter half of the 1970s, this led to a distinction between the lending practices of British clearing banks and American commercial banks in London and different implications for the relationship between the financial and productive sectors.

Historically, the UK clearing banks have developed a tradition of overdraft financing which still survives today. For example, overdraft facilities in 1980 accounted for some 70 per cent of the portfolio of the leading clearing bank[11] and are estimated to be at least 80 per cent of two other clearers' portfolios. Although the Radcliffe Report in 1959 recommended the development of term facilities by the clearers, the latter

have responded rather reluctantly.[12] This contrasts with the view expressed by the Wilson Committee that the British banks have moved
substantially toward medium-term lending in their credit to British
industry. And the fact that overseas banks have captured more than
30 per cent of the UK corporate lending market seems to suggest that the
clearers' adherence to overdraft financing cannot be explained by the lack
of demand for term facilities.

The nature of clearing bank finance, the fact that it has not been well
designed as a means of funding long-term planning for the development of
productive capital is indicated not only by its short-term nature. Equally
significant is the type of security that is required against the credit; until
the late 1970s the preponderant situation was one where banks required
a security which could protect the bank if the firm became unprofitable
instead of one which considered the firm as a going concern. But even the
latter type of approach has caused problems. Let us explore this further.

For all but the largest companies overdraft and medium-term credit
facilities are secured against a company's assets to protect the clearers'
interests in cases of insolvency. Security normally limits a company's
power to dispose of any of its fixed assets and, in the case of a floating
charge (simply a legal claim on a company's floating assets such as stocks
and debtors), confers on the bank the power to appoint a receiver. The
latter power becomes quite crucial at times of crisis and indeed the number
of receiverships has increased sharply in recent years.[13] Since security
requirements are normally calculated on the assumption of the liquidation
of the company concerned and the forced sale of its assets, the clearing
banks' approach to credit analysis has been characterised as the 'liquidation' or 'gone concern' approach. Clearly this approach, involving short
term facilities and a focus on a company's balance sheet, is not the most
appropriate for financing industry's fixed capital formation. Also since
all secured borrowing ranks ahead of unsecured borrowing, and as shown
in insolvencies, the banks' power to appoint a receiver is critical and
constitutes a potential source of conflict between banks and shareholders.

Since the early 1970s American commercial banks have promoted
medium-term bank credit normally on an unsecured basis to finance
fixed capital. The approach of the American banks to credit analysis
has been described as the 'going concern' approach in that it focuses on
company cash flow and profitability as a viable and not a liquidated
concern. In this form of credit security requirements are replaced by
detailed loan agreements. Fixed capital finance has several important
features. It is available over a fixed term subject to compliance with the
conditions specified in the loan agreement. For our purposes it is possible
to distinguish four broad types of loan agreement conditions which
circumscribe a company's operations during the term of its facility.[14]

The first is financial covenants such as dividends or gearing restrictions.

Banks can stipulate both capital gearing and income gearing (interest cover) ratios/limits for all but prime quality borrowers. In a regime of sustained high interest rates the income gearing ratio assumes critical importance. Note however, that this ratio is expressed in terms of the *amount* of interest payments (reflecting capital gearing and interest rates); by contrast the Wilson Report emphasises interest rates as (the major component of) the cost of capital. The Bank of England's (1980A) estimate that the income gearing of UK industrial and commercial companies rose from 17 per cent in 1978 to 24 per cent in 1979 at a time when capital gearing fell from 19 per cent to 18 per cent, illustrates the restrictive effects of this covenant. The second type of condition is standard for all unsecured borrowing and is designed to protect the bank against the possibility of future creditors taking security and so ranking ahead of it in the event of insolvency. The most common form of this type of condition is the negative pledge which prohibits further secured borrowing by enterprises. The third and perhaps most sensitive condition is that which specifies events of default. As well as failure to pay interest and principal where due or breach of financial covenants, events of default can include catch-all clauses such as the 'no material adverse change' clause which is normally determined at the discretion of the bank. Finally, a cross default clause is now standard in all loan agreements. In the case of a multi-banked company, cross default clauses imply that an event of default under *any* agreement automatically triggers default in *all* agreements. The engineering firm, Stone-Platt, is a good example of a UK company which recently fell victim to a cross default clause. The importance of cross default clauses lies in the fact that in the event of financial problems a company is not confronted by individual banks acting separately but by a group of banks representing the interests of bank capital against any other possible interests in the company. They are a symptom of the competition and conflicts of interest that can exist between different financial institutions.

The significance of the loan agreements used by American banks is that they define a new basis for relations between the banks and industry. These agreements require the creditor banks regularly to review or monitor not only their outstanding facilities but more significantly the financial performance of enterprises in respect of the loan agreement conditions. In normal circumstances this monitoring implies access to enterprises' published accounts and regular contact between bank and enterprise management. Should an enterprise be in default of any condition with any bank the cross default clause places the enterprise's banks in a powerful position to accelerate their debt which forces the enterprise into drastic short-term measures such as disposal of assets or rationalisation.

The bias of bank finance in the UK toward short-term lending is thought to have been instrumental in causing industry to take a short-term view of its investment plans, emphasising quick returns rather than long-term development. It may be asked, however, whether the existence of the capital market counteracts this influence: noting particularly the rise of the institutional shareholder may it not be the case that the stock market provides a source of funds which permit firms to take a long-term perspective? Apart from the fact that industry relied to only a small extent upon finance from the capital market, it is doubtful whether institutional investors can be characterised as taking the long view. There is some evidence that the institutions which manage pension fund assets aim for short-term profits[15] and, indeed, such a policy would be consistent with the high turnover of shares and high price volatility during the 1970s that Wilson noted. Certainly, fund managers have readily disposed of shares for short-term gains during the recent spate of 'dawn-raid' takeovers. The importance of the short-term bias of bank lending could also be qualified by noting the dependence of industry upon internal finance (retained profits and reserves) as a source of funds for accumulation. Surely managers can take a long-term view of investment and use the internal funds under their own control to finance it? Here is a specific test of the managerialist theory of the firm. The British experience suggests that the low profitability and associated low dividends that would in the short run result from that policy leaves firms vulnerable to a takeover because the price of their shares on the stock market, the secondary capital market, is driven down. Thus, even though the capital market is not often used to raise new finance, it constrains the use that is made of other finance, and it reinforces the short-term bias of bank lending.

In a general sense then UK financial markets with their short-term outlook have not been favourably disposed towards fixed capital accumulation by British industry and so may have contributed to deindustrialisation—but this theme cannot be pursued here. Instead we turn to one of the conditions which underly London's role as an international finance and trading centre—namely the relative absence of state controls—and discuss the case for, and some of the problems associated with, such controls in respect of the financing of industry.

II. Control and Nationalisation of the City

The issue of whether the major financial institutions should be controlled or nationalised has to be seen in the light of the way they have operated. But, first, the issue itself has to be stated clearly since the words 'control' and 'nationalisation' are too general and, in consequence, the programmes of left-wing parties and right-wing populists (or even fascist parties) can appear to coincide on the need to control the financiers. Socialists have no prerogative over a distrust of money.

It is important to be clear about why one should argue for the control or nationalisation of the City. The choice of argument is itself a political judgment. On the one hand, you can argue for control of the City on the basis of the view about relatively unfettered institutions are not working well enough for capitalism, while on the other hand, you can argue for control because you think they work too well for capitalism. The Wilson Committee employed only the first criterion: are the financial institutions meeting the needs of small business? Is the growth of the institutional shareholder weakening the efficiency of the stock market? Socialists should be concerned with the second criterion and base their argument on the institutions' ability to strengthen monopoly capital and inhibit socialist policies.

We employ the second criterion here but the choice is not so stark and we will qualify it in due course. A related problem is the meaning of those terms themselves, for the financial institutions of all capitalist countries are already controlled and, in some cases, nationalised to a greater or lesser extent (in the UK to a comparatively low extent) without in any way impairing their function as capital. Control takes the minimum form of 'prudential regulation' such as governments requiring banks to hold a proportion of their assets in non-interest-bearing cash to meet depositors' withdrawals. Such controls are not our main concern but conflicts do arise when banks shy away from high ratios—they have recently forced the Bank of England to abandon its initial suggestions for new prudential ratios. Our subject is the question of control over all aspects of the banks' and other institutions' disposition of assets: over the purposes for which they can buy and sell foreign exchange (see the chapter by David Currie), over the types of loans they can make and over their commitment to financing government expenditure. Similarly, with regard to nationalisation, we do not deal with the creation of state-owned profit-maximising institutions. Instead, our concern is whether financial institutions should be nationalised as a condition for planned economic growth and social improvement regardless of the institutions' own profitability except when it furthers these aims.

Consider first, the question of controls. Since the Second World War, British governments have maintained various controls over the banks and some other financial institutions (such as hire purchase companies), but have consistently pursued a policy of attempting to dismantle controls. The Heath and Thatcher governments, in particular, have taken quite determined steps. In 1971 the Heath government brought in a policy, 'Competition and Credit Control' which attempted to simplify controls over the institutions in order to permit greater competition between them; in October 1979 the Thatcher government took a step as dramatic and important as its monetarist deflation when it abolished, for the first time for half a century, all controls over the export and import of money. We say 'since the Second World War' to highlight the fact that during the war the City was subject to comprehensive controls from which lessons can be learned for today.[16]

Controls were of two types: first, capital issues control and control over bank advances which were designed to restrict and direct the ability of firms and other enterprises to borrow money on the capital and money markets; and second, foreign exchange controls which were directed towards conserving foreign exchange and ensuring it was used for the war effort. The statutory capital issues control over the sale of new securities and related bond market operations was exercised by a Treasury Committee. Non-statutory control over bank advances was loosely practised by the Treasury through the (then still private) Bank of England so that borrowing from the banks could not be used to thwart any restriction of funds through capital issues control. These controls worked, but that does not mean they are appropriate in the Alternative Economic Strategy. First, they were implemented with the support of the City at a time when government controls were legitimated by patriotism—the Alternative Economic Strategy's background will be one of intense conflict over national aims. Second, the controls did not really succeed in directing the activities of enterprises by controlling their ability to borrow; firms were more effectively constrained by shortages of labour and materials and by physical controls. However, the capital issues control was very important in affecting the terms on which money could be raised and in controlling the capital market so that the government itself could raise money in the amounts and on the terms needed to finance its expenditure. Foreign exchange controls were imposed only gradually as the war progressed; they were resisted at first by the Treasury and the City for fear of the City losing its international role forever. Nevertheless, a complex system of controls over foreign exchange was instituted in the summer of 1940. It proved broadly effective and, although there were disagreements over the particulars, it was not the subject of strong conflict between the City and the state.

Controls over foreign exchange, capital issues and other forms of lending are an essential part of any strategy to build a planned economy. However, it is important to consider whether controls over the operation of the capitalist financial institutions are alone adequate for the task, or whether nationalisation is a prerequisite. We shall not discuss exchange controls here since they are the subject of another paper. Controls over capital issues and other forms of lending are directed towards influencing the quantity and terms of credit given to enterprises and the state. During the war the terms of credit proved to be the most important aspect. Since the war the flexibility of the financial system has proved to be such that controls alone are inadequate for directing and financing enterprises. The system has shown that as soon as controls are imposed upon one type of lending operation, new institutions and techniques develop to provide uncontrolled financing. This phenomenon was remarked on by the Radcliffe Committee at the end of the 1950s and has subsequently been manifested in the growth of unstable fringe banks (free of the controls that affected the commercial banks in the 1960s and early 1970s) which channelled funds into the property market. In addition, the flexibility in the development of international financial markets raises problems which we will return to. The banks themselves sought directives on their advances during the war and the system of exchange controls in the post-war years was operated by the banks willing to act as agents of the state. In a situation of conflict, however, the personnel and structural position of the private financial institutions cannot be relied on to ensure that controls are operated in accordance with planning priorities.

Nationalisation of the financial institutions could contribute to overcoming these problems, but there are various types of nationalisation. Nationalising the major banks, insurance companies and pension funds—a version of the strategy of controlling only the 'commanding heights'—may be a popular policy and relatively easy to implement, but it is not wholly adequate. A few major institutions have a dominant effect on interest (and exchange) rates on the wholesale money market thus affecting the state's ability to control the interest rates at which it borrows to finance its expenditure (assuming that exchange control prevents overseas institutions from dominating London's credit markets). However, if the takeover is limited to the major institutions then it is not possible to control the direction of credit granted to firms. The flexibility of the financial system will ensure that new institutions and techniques develop to fill unfulfilled needs. The only type of nationalisation that can overcome that problem is the establishment of a legal monopoly for the state in the provision of credit.

There are, nevertheless, severe limits to the control of industrial finance that can be obtained by either controlling or nationalising the financial system. The first is that industrial capital in Britain is not very dependent on external finance; firms have historically relied on internally controlled funds (retained profits and depreciation funds) to finance their growth.

The second limit is that the growth of multinational corporations concomitantly with the expansion and increased sophistication of international ('Euro') credit and capital markets over the past two decades means that some of the most significant decisions on investment and production are in the hands of firms whose external finance is derived from international sources. These limits highlight the fact that control of financing alone will not be adequate to ensure that firms' activities accord with the state's priorities; control and nationalisation of financial institutions is only viable if it is part of a policy to nationalise industrial firms themselves and thereby control their activities directly.

That perspective, however, presents the matter very much as an all-or-nothing question, a problem of how to build a planned economy once secure state power has been gained. The Alternative Economy Strategy has to be considered also as a strategy for immediate policies to improve the economy's growth (without which the position of the working class cannot be improved under capitalism) while increasing control over market forces. Under that heading two particular measures are presently on the agenda. The first is the creation of local enterprise boards, such as the West Midlands Enterprise Board and the Greater London Enterprise Board. These Boards have the potential for using locally raised money and the pension funds controlled by local authorities to finance, gain strategic control, and enforce planning agreements with local industry.[17] There is no simple mechanism for these boards to change the way in which the industries they finance operate: for one thing they will not have a mono- poly of finance in the firms they fund, and for another the control of finance does not ensure control over production, investment and the firms' operations as a whole. Nevertheless, the boards are structures which can divert some pension fund money towards more socially controlled uses and thereby protect to some extent local industries and employment. The second measure is intervention to prevent the collapse of banks involved in international lending. The growth of international lending during the last decade (the recycling of the surpluses achieved by some oil exporting countries) has placed some banks in positions where their ratio of debt to capital is higher than many would consider prudent. Moreover, these international credits are concentrated on a few countries (such as Brazil and Poland) which, because of their high borrowing, can face difficulties in repayment. The danger of a bank's crash resulting from these circum- stances and causing a general financial crash is a real one. If it were to occur, it would bring an intensified crisis with increased costs to the working class. There is, therefore, a case for demanding that a Labour government intervene to enforce high capital ratios and other prudential regulations upon London banks operating in the international markets. Such a policy would reduce the attraction of London as an international banking centre, it would also be part of a policy, backed by exchange controls and taxation, to dismantle the City of London's role as a centre for international banking. The ending of that role can only have a positive effect upon the freedom of a popular left-wing government to direct the economy.

NOTES

1. See, for example, Aaronovitch et al., 1981, Chapter 14, and Aaronovitch, 1981.
2. Committee to Review the Functioning of Financial Institutions, 1981, *Report* (hereafter the Wilson Report).
3. A similar failure to recognise the specificity of financial capital is contained in Cutler et al., 1978, where the authors characterise financial institutions as

merely as a set of accounts.
4. The relation between finance capital's policies on the exchange rate and industrial and commercial capital's profits is discussed in its theoretical and empirical aspects in Coakley and Harris, 1981.
5. Wilson Report, op. cit., Chapter 13.
6. See Bank of England, 1980A.
7. See Marris, 1964. For an alternative view of size of firm as a defence against takeover see Singh, 1971.
8. See the Wilson Report, op. cit., pp. 252–253.
9. See Minns, 1980. For further evidence on the concentration of shareholdings see Minns, 1981.
10. Bank of England, 1980A, loc. cit., p. 322.
11. See *Financial Times*, 13.4.81.
12. Committee on the Working of the Monetary System, 1959: *Report*. The view that the clearing banks have in general switched away from short term lending to only a small extent appears to be supported by a survey being conducted under the Open University research project 'The Interrelationship between financial, industrial and commercial capital in the UK'.
13. See Bank of England, 1980B.
14. The changing nature of loan agreements is examined in Kurz, 1981.
15. See Lex, *Financial Times*, 25 June 1981.
16. A full examination of wartime financial controls is to be found in Sayers, 1956.
17. Minns, 1981, discusses the case for local enterprise boards.

REFERENCES

Aaronovitch, S., 1981, *The Road from Thatcherism*, Lawrence and Wishart, London.
Aaronovitch, S., Smith, R., Gardiner, J., Moore, R., 1981, *The Political Economy of British Capitalism*, McGraw Hill, London.
Bank of England, 1980A, 'Financing British Industry', *Bank of England Quarterly Bulletin*, Vol. 20, No. 3, pp. 319–323.
Bank of England, 1980B, 'Corporate Insolvency', *Bank of England Quarterly Bulletin*, Vol. 20, No. 4, pp. 430–436.
Coakley, J., Harris, L., 1982, 'Industry, The City and the Foreign Exchanges: Theory and Evidence', *British Review of Economic Issues*, forthcoming.
Committee on the Working of the Monetary System, 1959, *Report*, Cmnd 827, HMSO, London.
Committee to Review the Functioning of Financial Institutions, 1980, *Report and Appendices*, Cmnd 7939, HMSO, London.
Cutler, A., Hindess, B., Hirst, P., Hussain, A., 1978, *Marx's Capital and Capitalism Today, Volume Two*, Routledge and Kegan Paul, London.
Kurz, W., 1981, 'New Form in the Loan Agreement', *Euromoney*, February, pp. 47–59.
Marris, R., 1963, *The Economic Theory of Managerial Capitalism*, Macmillan, London.
Minns, R., 1980, *Pension Funds and British Capitalism*, Heinemann, London.
Minns, R., 1981, 'Challenging the Bankers', *New Statesman*, 21 August, pp. 6–10.
Prais, S., 1976, *Evolution of Giant Firms in Britain: A Study of the Growth of Concentration in Manufacturing Industry in Britain 1909-70*, Cambridge University Press, London.
Sayers, R.S., 1956, *Financial Policy 1939-45*, HMSO, and Longmans Green, London.
Singh, A., 1971, *Takeovers: Their Relevance to the Stock Market and the Theory of the Firm*, Cambridge University Press, London.

THE VOLATILE POUND AND EXCHANGE RATE POLICY

David Currie

Over recent years, the pound, together with other major currencies, has performed wild gyrations in foreign exchange markets. The degree of volatility of nominal exchange rates has been much greater than in any earlier period, whether this volatility is measured in terms of day-to-day, month-to-month or year-to-year movements. Moreover, the monetarist claim that greater stability in exchange rate movements would be obtained by adherence to a stable growth path for the money supply does not seem particularly consistent with experience.[1] Indeed, over the past decade of floating, short-run variability in money supply growth has tended to be inversely associated with short-run variability in exchange rates.[2]

Over a three to five year horizon, goods prices and wages seem broadly to adapt to sustained changes in the nominal exchange rate, so that there is rather little impact on international competitiveness whether measured in terms of relative prices or relative unit labour costs.[3] But, in the shorter run, movements in competitiveness will largely follow short-run fluctuations in the nominal exchange rate, so that the traded goods sector experiences marked volatility in demand conditions, with resulting fluctuations in employment conditions in this sector and elsewhere in the economy. And this added uncertainty may well act as a deterrent to innovation and investment, impairing the longer run capacity to compete in terms of product quality and other factors. Thus exchange rate volatility raises critical questions for macroeconomic policy that need careful consideration.

The purpose of this paper is to consider this issue and other associated questions concerning exchange rate policy within the context of the left's Alternative Economic Strategy (AES).[4] There are four main questions that I want to take up. Thus, we need to consider:

(1) What should be the left's response to the volatile pound? This issue has been posed in the past two years or more in terms of the appropriate response to the high pound, and there has been much confusion within the labour movement on this question. But it is important to appreciate that the issue is one of volatility, and that the low pound might become the pressing issue in the future.

(2) What type of exchange rate policy does the left envisage in the AES? This question is clearly less immediate, but needs serious attention, particularly in the light of the major destabilising role that the foreign exchanges can, and have, played when left, or even social democrat,

231

governments have come to power in various parts of the world. The question is directly linked to the issue of policy towards financial institutions and multinational companies within the AES. But the formulation of the AES on this issue is rather underdeveloped and requires more thought.

Relating to both these issues are two further questions:

(3) Do we take the view that there is an appropriate level of the pound? If so, how is this to be arrived at? Should it apply to all international transactions or just to a limited class by means of a split exchange rate system?

(4) What mechanisms of control are envisaged to enforce whatever policies are aimed at? How is evasion of these controls (by, for example, multinational companies) to be avoided?

These questions range broadly; and cannot be dealt with fully in a paper of this kind, though I hope that I tackle the main issues. I take for granted, without repetition, the main planks of the AES.

The Immediate Issues—The Volatile Pound

Over the past five years or more, exchange rates have exhibited a very high degree of volatility. In this, the pound has been no exception. Falling to its low point of $1.56 in 1976, it appreciated to around $2.30–2.40 by the end of 1980, despite the fact that UK inflation was above average world inflation in the intervening period. In consequence, price competitiveness declined by 31 per cent from 1976, and competitiveness in terms of relative unit labour costs has declined still more by 44 per cent. To put this in perspective, this decline in price competitiveness was more than four times that caused by Churchill's return to gold in 1925, which pushed the UK into severe and prolonged slump five years before other major capitalist countries. From about Easter 1981, the pound has fallen sharply against the dollar, reaching about $1.90 in the mid-year. But the fall against European currencies has been rather slight, so that the traded weighted effective exchange rate has declined by only about 10 per cent from its peak.

Using the low point of $1.56 exaggerates the loss of competitiveness, since it was itself a position of rather high competitiveness. But a more normal base point (e.g. 1975) still reveals a major change: a 27 per cent loss of price competitiveness and a 34 per cent rise in relative unit labour costs. Against this background, two immediate questions spring to mind. First, why has the pound, along with other currencies, exhibited such marked volatility? Second, is the unprecedented movement in real price competitiveness simply a reflection of this volatility in the nominal exchange rate, so that it will eventually return to its usual long-run level; or has real price competitiveness itself undergone a trend shift?

In answer to the first question, there are sound theoretical reasons for thinking that the exchange rate will be a rather volatile, jumpy variable so long as the authorities, either domestically or abroad, pursue monetary targets and disregard movements in the exchange rate in formulating domestic policy.[5] This is because wages and goods prices adjust only sluggishly, while the foreign exchange market adjusts very rapidly, to disturbances to the system. Consider, for example, an increase in money demand which is not accommodated. The resulting rise in domestic interest rates will cause the exchange rate to appreciate as operators in the foreign exchange market react to the scope for profitable arbitrage or speculation. With very mobile capital and an absence of risk aversion, the exchange rate will rise to the point where the expected future rate of depreciation just offsets the increased interest differential in favour of sterling. And, since the future level of sterling will depend, in turn, on future expected interest rate differentials, we can see that the size of the initial exchange rate appreciation will depend on how long higher UK interest rates are expected to persist. If the source of disturbance is correctly perceived, the expected duration of the disturbance to money demand will be critical.

This argument applies similarly to any type of disturbance that impinges, directly or indirectly, on domestic interest rates, or to the expectation of that disturbance. Pursuit of monetary targets precludes the impact of disturbances on interest rates being offset by monetary targets. Monetary targets, therefore, make the exchange rate a very volatile, noisy variable. Since goods prices adjust only slowly, the real exchange rate (or price competitiveness) will itself be very volatile, making the market conditions facing firms in the traded goods sector very uncertain.

The generally high level of the pound over the past two years may be explained in these terms. The adoption of tight monetary policy, embodied in the Medium Term Financial Strategy, led to the expectation of generally high UK interest rates over a lengthy period of time. The consequence was a marked appreciation of the exchange rate to a level where it was expected subsequently to fall.[6] The subsequent decline can be understood as a realisation of this expectation, combined with a market appreciation of the dollar as a similar strategy was adopted by Reagan in the USA.

On this view of exchange rate movements, the problem is one of volatility. Although the exchange rate has generally been high over the past two years or so, there is no reason to rule out the possibility that the problem may be transformed into a over-depreciated level of sterling. The weakness of sterling in the period August/September, 1981 may be a portent in this respect, though UK price competitiveness still shows a drastic deterioration from its long-run trend.

The alternative view of the behaviour of sterling over the past few years emphasises the importance of North Sea oil and the recent hikes in the international price of oil, attributing to these factors the shift in trend real price competitiveness. The status of the pound as a petro-currency is argued to require an appreciation of the currency as the real price of oil rises. This is linked to the Forsyth and Kay (1980) argument that the same factors require a decline of UK manufacturing. The increased income from North Sea oil is spent in significant part on non-tradeable goods, and, therefore, only in part on tradeables, while North Sea oil is necessarily an increase in the supply of tradeable goods. The immediate effect, therefore, is an excess demand for non-tradeables and an excess supply of tradeables. The rise in the real terms of trade (i.e. the loss of competitiveness) is required to correct this imbalance by lowering the price of tradeables relative to non-tradeables. The conse-quence is a loss of competitiveness and a major squeeze on the non-oil tradeables sector, notably manufacturing. Far from being seen as disastrous, Kay sees this as an advantage: 'It will be impossible to enjoy the fruits of North Sea oil without allowing a strong exchange rate to reduce the size of our manufacturing sector.'[7]

Forsyth and Kay estimate the oil premium on sterling to be around 20 per cent. It should be noted, however, that realistic assumptions about the trade elasticities that underly this calculation can halve this estimate to 10 per cent.[8] Moreover, under conditions of monopolistic or oligo-polistic production with increasing returns to scale, any premium will be still lower. Thus this view can account only very partially for the past behaviour of sterling.

It should also be noted in passing that the advent of North Sea oil need not require an absolute, as against a relative, decline of the manu-facturing sector. On the view, espoused for example by the Cambridge Economic Policy Group, that the balance of payments has constrained domestic output, the advent of North Sea oil relieves this constraint and permits an economic expansion within which the manufacturing sector and the rest of the non-oil tradeables sector will expand, albeit relatively more slowly than non-tradeables. And, if a major re-equipping of industry occurs by means of imported capital goods, any premium on sterling will be reduced significantly, or may disappear altogether. In essence, the advent of North Sea oil, or a change in the international price of oil, should represent a signal for a reconsideration of the stance of monetary and fiscal policy.

In a very real sense, therefore, any oil premium on sterling is under-written by the macroeconomic commitment to monetary targets and domestic contraction by the UK government. In the absence of domestic expansion associated with the coming-on stream of North Sea oil, the balance of payments has moved into substantial surplus, causing the pound to appreciate, undermining the markets for UK products both domestically and overseas. The benefits of North Sea oil have been taken in enforced unemployment.

It is not surprising that this is attractive to the foreign exchange market. But there is nothing inevitable about it. A rational response to the increasing value of North Sea oil reserves would be to boost investment, public spending or consumption domestically, thereby maintaining the demand for the output of UK industry; or in the longer run to alter depletion rates to conserve reserves. A combination of these policies, as envisaged by the AES, could be used to bring down the pound, and avoid squandering North Sea oil in a flood of imports and unemployment. In a real sense, therefore, it is the unwillingness to expand demand to enjoy the benefits of North Sea oil, rather than the oil revenues themselves, which is responsible for the high pound.

Given all of this, should the left have been arguing for a lower level of the pound over the past two years? My answer is an unequivocal yes, for the following reasons:

(a) The high exchange rate is the key weapon in the present government's attack on the trade unions and the labour movement. It is via the high pound that tight monetary policy is operating on wages by intensifying foreign competition and eroding domestic profit margins, so that the threat of redundancy forces acceptance of lower wage settlements. Employers are seizing the opportunity wherever possible to weaken trade-union organisation and control in the production process. Clearly we must oppose this, and as part of that opposition we need to be arguing for a lower exchange rate.

(b) Import controls, which we advocate to help domestic industries threatened by overseas competition, cannot help those industries dependent on overseas markets. Clearly the high pound is a major threat to large sections of the UK exporting industry. It is wrong to be misled by the relative strength of exports even in volume terms during 1980 (though the last quarter of 1980 and early 1981 saw a significant decline). The buoyancy of exports is despite an unprecedented squeeze on export profitability, with many companies exporting at a loss. The explanation is that companies are clinging onto markets in the hope that the pound will come down soon—they know that, once abandoned, overseas markets are hard to recover. If the loss of international competitiveness is sustained, the effect on exports will be very severe, with major consequence for future UK economic performance.

(c) A lower pound is a necessary part of the programme of expansion envisaged by the AES. This is partly because (as noted in (b)) an expansion without a fall in the pound would be curiously lopsided and ill-founded, leaving out the major export sector. But more important, just as Thatcher's contractionary policy has driven the pound up, so expansion would bring it down. (This raises the issue, which I take up later, of whether a major expansion of the UK economy would not create the need for measures to stop the pound falling too far.) To argue for a lower pound now, as part of a package to reverse the decline of UK industry, is, therefore, wholly consistent with our overall economic strategy.

Against these points, there seem to be two main arguments:

(d) A fall in the exchange rate is inflationary. All the empirical evidence seems to agree that domestic prices eventually adjust to reflect fully the sterling equivalent of foreign prices. A fall in the exchange rate is, therefore, likely to result in an equal rise in domestic prices, though after some considerable and uncertain delay. However, this argument requires some qualification. For much of the period 1979–1981, prices and wages had not fully adjusted to the high level of the pound. (This was a major reason for the substantial boost to real wages in 1979–80.) The high pound was bringing down the rate of inflation quite sharply. Some reduction in the effective exchange rate, perhaps of the order of 5–10 per cent, would have been possible without raising the rate of inflation (though, of course, the resulting rate of inflation would have been higher than it otherwise would have been). In any event, the policy of the Thatcher government is to sacrifice jobs and large sections of industry in favour of a savagely anti-inflationary policy. If we are honest about the issue, an alternative which reverses this attack on industry may well be relatively more inflationary (unless specific anti-inflation measures can be brought to bear).

(e) Because of its inflationary impact, a fall in the exchange rate will cut into real wages, and is, therefore, to be opposed by the labour movement. This view tended to influence the attitude of the left towards devaluation in the past, and it may seem inconsistent to reverse that judgment now. But no real inconsistency is involved, for circumstances have changed. In the past, there was some presumption that policy would maintain the level of aggregate demand and employment, whereas Thatcher's government disingenuously disclaims responsibility for the level of real demand and employment. While the appreciation of the pound gave short-run benefits to real wages during 1979–80, by holding down prices relative to wages, the long-run adverse effects of the high pound on real wages are now being felt via unemployment and the threat of redundancies. While we might welcome a high exchange rate with a high level of employment (if this unlikely combination could even be brought about), we must surely argue against the high pound at the current time, for it is the principal weapon in the attack on working people. The high pound is cutting into real wages (as well as into real profits). Even if this were not so, opposition to the resulting rapidly rising unemployment should lead us to oppose the high pound.

The upshot of all of this is, therefore, that we should be arguing for a lower level of the pound, both as an immediate response to the current crisis of UK industry, but also as part of the overall strategy of expansion envisaged by the AES. An obvious question that then arises is what level of the pound is appropriate. Clearly, it is not easy to give a precise figure in response to this, but some answer is required if only to dispel the illusion that no answer is possible.

My own view is that we should be thinking in terms of a level of the pound which eliminates a substantial part, if not the whole, of the loss of international competitiveness experienced over the past two or three years. This would suggest bringing the effective exchange rate down towards about 80, as compared with its level of around 90 in the third quarter of 1981. (Even with the exchange rate at this level, relative unit labour costs might still be around 10–15 per cent out of line with their historical trend.) The inflationary consequences of this are hard to judge, since they depend rather critically on how much prices have adjusted to recent exchange rate changes: my own guess would be that, in itself, this change would give rise to additional, but not excessive, upward inflationary pressures over the following two or three years.

In arguing for this, the left needs to avoid the appearance of lack of concern about inflation. This might best be done by arguing for relative stability in the value of the pound, so that, for example, we might need to argue at some future date for avoiding a slide of the pound. Indeed, our earlier argument about exchange rate volatility suggests that this possibility is very likely. We should be absolutely clear that there is no contradiction in arguing for a lower pound now and later arguing that the pound must not be allowed to fall. A degree of *stability* in real exchange rates is called for so that a volatile exchange rate is not allowed to play games with the real economy. Indeed, it is this that enables us to answer question (3) above: one might think in terms of aiming in a flexible way (depending on the method of control of the exchange rate—see below) at a possibly changing, level of the exchange rate, movements which reflect differences between the appropriate inflation rate domestically and world inflation rates.[9] Such a policy would avoid the foreign exchanges having a major disruptive effect on domestic industry and trade. But we can only sensibly think about such policies in the context of specific methods of control over the exchange rate, to which I now turn.

Control of the Exchange Rate
It is clear from what I have said so far that it is a myth that the level of the nominal exchange rate cannot be controlled. There is considerable scope for the authorities to influence the nominal exchange rate (through a variety of instruments which we consider in a moment) both in the short and long run. If such controls are used to eliminate the marked volatility in the nominal exchange rate that has been observed over the past five years, they would also reduce the associated variation in real competitiveness that has resulted from these nominal movements. There is, therefore, scope for exerting a short- to medium-term influence on the real exchange

rate. But the scope for using the instruments considered below to influence the long-run real exchange rate is probably quite limited. I consider in turn the feasibility of each means of influencing the exchange rate.

(i) *Direct intervention in the foreign exchange market.* In the past, we have often thought of the monetary authorities intervening directly in the foreign exchange market to determine the exchange rate by buying or selling sterling. This was feasible when the intervention that the authorities could make was significant in relation to total transactions in the market. But the growth of international financial capital means that this is no longer possible. What flowed across the exchanges in a quarter in the late 1960s flowed across the exchanges in a day in the early 1970s, and in an hour nowadays. Feasible scales of intervention cannot have a significant and lasting impact on the level of the exchange rate unless enforced by other measures (such as (ii)–(vi) below). It therefore makes little sense to talk in isolation of the authorities devaluing the exchange rate; instead we should think of the authorities changing the exchange rate by measures such as (ii)–(vi). (However, direct intervention does have a subsidiary, short-term role when used in conjunction with these measures, since it may be used to smooth out temporary fluctuations in the exchange rate.)

(ii) *Changes in monetary and fiscal policy.* The most straightforward way to alter the exchange rate is by changes in domestic demand policy. The main instrument here is monetary policy—a relaxation of monetary policy generating a fall in the exchange rate. Fiscal policy would be a rather blunt instrument to use here, but the need to avoid monetary and fiscal policy pulling in different directions may require some subsidiary adjustment of fiscal policy. Thus, at the current time, the most sensible package to induce a fall in the pound would be a combination of expansionary monetary and fiscal policy.

By expansionary monetary policy, I mean here a clear signal from the authorities that they intend to allow the money supply to expand rather more than had been envisaged hitherto. A point that sometimes causes confusion is that, under monetary targets, a cut in interest rates may not provide this clear signal. For the foreign exchange market may take this as a sign that the monetary targets are being hit, leading to a rise, rather than a fall, in the exchange rate. In these circumstances, the clearest signal is provided by an announced relaxation of monetary targets: this would bring the pound down sharply at the current time. But, to avoid this decline becoming precipitate and disorderly, it may be necessary to announce a specific target or range for the exchange rate to be defended by monetary and other measures.

More expansionary policy is, of course, consistent with the AES, it is equally consistent with 'wet monetarism'. (Thus, a German central banker was recently arguing before the Select Committee on the Treasury that monetary policy should be relaxed in the UK.) From our perspective, the disadvantage of this approach is that, while it reduces the vulnerability of the exchange rate to speculative changes and other disturbances, it does so by transmitting these disturbances to the domestic economy via changes in demand policy. While expansionary measures are clearly needed now, we can easily think of circumstances where domestic and exchange rate objectives would conflict. Thus, a left government committed to domestic expansion is likely to find the exchange rate falling sharply, and may not be able to rely on contractionary monetary policy to check this fall without bringing domestic expansion to an abrupt halt.[10] Other, more interventionist, measures will then be required (such as (iii)–(vi) below).

(iii) *Exchange controls.* The Thatcher government abolished exchange controls in October, 1979. Such measures were inevitably limited in that they only operated on residents, and even then there were loopholes whereby the regulations could be evaded. However, exchange controls had an impact in restraining outflows of money capital, as is clear from the substantial outflow of funds since abolition. (It remains to be seen how much of this is a once-for-all response to abolition.) The fact that the dollar premium (paid on the transfer of funds for portfolio investment outside the Sterling Area) remained high until its abolition prior to EEC entry is evidence that controls worked to some degree: if they were entirely evaded, the premium would have been at, or close to, zero. Moreover, the significance of abolition is broader than that, since the technical expertise required to administer these, and other more stringent, controls (see below) has been dispersed. We should not underestimate the technical difficulties of administering controls of any kind in this area. Any restoration of controls, however limited, is, therefore, to be welcomed, if for no other reason, because it will require the rebuilding of the type of expertise that will be indispensable with more ambitious and extensive controls.

(iv) *Tax on capital flows.* A measure which could fall equally on residents and foreigners is the proposal for an interest equalisation tax. This tax, operated for a long period by the USA, would impose a variable tax on interest paid to foreigners on deposits in the UK, so that net return received is just equal to the (average) return obtained overseas. This would prevent foreigners benefiting unduly from high UK interest rates, and would also insulate the exchange rate from a significant part of speculative disturbances. This measure has received the support of a range of orthodox economists as a means of getting the pound down without relaxing monetary targets. The full logic of the scheme would require domestic holders of foreign deposits to be subsidised when overseas assets are less attractive than domestic ones; and foreign depositors in the UK to be subsidised when UK rates were lower than world levels; but it is not clear whether advocates

advocates of the scheme do propose this latter unappealing possibility.

The Bank of England is firmly opposed to such a scheme, partly because it is administratively messy (it requires renegotiation of well over 50 double taxation treaties, as well as the awkward definition of 'the' average overseas return), but also because of its profound distaste for interfering with the free operations of the international money markets. However, such distaste is not universal amongst central banks: the German central bank operated taxes on foreign deposits for long periods of time in the late 1960s and early 1970s to prevent excessive appreciation of the Deutschmark.

(v) *A split or multiple exchange rage system.* A further possibility would be to introduce a multiple exchange rate system, whereby different types of balance of payments transactions face different exchange rates. However, many different exchange rates are complicated to administer, and the simplest scheme would be for a dual exchange rate. Thus, there could be an exchange rate for trade (in both goods and services) and certain other current account transactions (it would have to be decided whether profit and interest remittances are included here), which would be maintained at a relatively stable level; and a separate, 'financial' exchange rate for all other transactions, notably capital flows, which could be allowed to find its own level.

The monetary authorities would have to intervene to control the trade exchange rate by direct intervention (and other means—see below), otherwise normal fluctuations in trade would induce wild short-term variations (which are currently largely avoided by offsetting stabilising capital flows). The separation of the large volume of capital flows from the markets for trade transactions would mean that feasible intervention of this kind would be effective in influencing the rate, in contrast to the current position (see (i) above). Capital account fluctuations would be largely reflected in the free 'financial' exchange rate.

This scheme is not without its difficulties. The principal one is that firms engaged in international trade can easily take up a speculative position through the trade account simply by the device of 'leading and lagging' (speeding up payments for imports and delaying payments for exports when a fall in the exchange rate is expected). Furthermore, the simple act of not hedging (or covering forward) the foreign exchange risk associated with future settlement of trade can involve taking up a speculative position and thereby putting pressure on the trade, or supported, exchange rate. This is possible for all companies engaged in trade, not simply MNCs. Thus, the trade exchange rate would not be free of speculative pressures: there were speculative pressures on the pound in the late 1940s and early 1950s, before there was significant freedom for capital flows, with the speculative attacks coming via the trade account and related trade credit position.

The significance of these problems depends on the manner in which the split exchange rate system is operated. Speculative pressures will undoubtedly cause a dual exchange rate system to collapse if the attempt is made to keep the trade exchange rate at quite a different level from the financial rate over a long period of time. A marked and sustained divergence between the trade and financial rates could not be allowed to persist, for it would give a great incentive to get round the regulations. In the event of such a divergence, measures would need to be taken. This might take the form of a gradual adjustment over time of the trade exchange rate (the 'crawling peg' idea) to prevent it getting obviously out of line, with domestic interest rates compensating for the rate of 'crawl', so the undue speculative pressures are avoided. Alternatively, changes in domestic demand policy, in import tariffs or quotas, or other measures might be used depending on circumstances.

Countries such as Belgium and France have used a split exchange rate for significant periods of time, and the two rates did establish themselves at different levels for periods of time, proof in itself that the scheme was not ineffective. The difficulties would be greater in the UK, if only because of the greater degree of sophistication of the financial system (though suitable controls may help here—see (vi)). But, for dealing with short-run disequilibria and speculative pressures, the scheme would be of assistance.

(vi) *Direct controls and nationalisation.* Finally there is the possibility of a major extension of controls over the financial system coupled with nationalisation of strategic parts of the financial system (including making real the present, largely nominal, nationalisation of the Bank of England by bringing the Bank under effective government control). These measures are frequently proposed as an important component of the AES, but almost always without serious and detailed discussion of what is involved. If these proposals are to be more than programmatic, analysis is needed of are the detailed and technical issues of how controls would be operated. This is still true if extensive nationalisation is proposed, since then the rules governing the operations of the nationalised sector need to be spelt out. As our experience of the present nationalised sector shows, the act of nationalisation does not in itself alter significantly the way the industry operates.

This takes us far beyond the immediate issue of this paper—the pound and exchange rate policy—though the issues are closely linked. Forms of control relevant to the control of the pound can be devised: a separation of the City's internal financial role and its international position as an entrepot centre for international finance; restrictions on the freedom of the commercial banks to take an open, speculative position with regard to the pound; controls on the overseas investment of UK based pension and insurance companies; consideration of the City's role in financing international trade; and the discouragement of the use of the pound as an international reserve currency (as, for example, in the case of the Deutschmark).

An assessment of the benefits and costs of such controls is far from easy. Thus restrictions on the ability of the banks to take an open position with respect to the pound may in certain circumstances stem unstable speculative pressures; but it may also add to instability by ruling out the stabilising speculative position that the banks have taken up on occasions in the past under floating rates. Undue restrictions on the City's activities may simply lead to a transfer of such business overseas. The consequent loss of income must be set against any gains from stability of exchange rates and wider macroeconomic variables.

The difficulty we have in assessing this type of proposal is that the left generally has tended to be dismissive of the City and the financial sector, and has, therefore, not spent much time thinking of the real problems that it poses. We have no clear view as to which activities of the financial system are inconsistent with the AES and how they might be controlled whilst maintaining the functioning of those parts vital to the economy. Unfortunately, space precludes a discussion of these issues here.

Multinational Companies

The previous discussion makes it clear that all companies engaging in international trade have scope for getting round restrictions on the export of money capital. But MNCs are particularly well placed in this regard, because of the scope of that intra-company trade across national boundaries provides for disguising the export (or import) of capital as trade by means of suitable transfer pricing. That transfer pricing is used in this way is' unquestionable, though hard evidence is, by the nature of the matter, hard to come by. That it is always used to export profits from the UK (a common presumption on the left) is more doubtful: certainly in recent years the low level of company taxation in the UK has created a strong incentive to declare profits here.[11]

These problems are not easily confronted, but once again it is a mistake to be defeatist about them, since the balance of power is not all on one side. A left government will have the authority of law on its side, and should, if it represents a real majority, carry public opinion. MNCs would have a strong interest in bringing down a left government, but a further interest in avoiding disruption to its domestic activities, integrated as they often are into their broader international business. But here the links with democratic demands in the AES are strongest: the need to 'open the books', making illicit transactions vulnerable to exposure, and increasing accountability to the workforce and the wider public would be critical here. A left government, which carried public opinion, could rely on support from a large section of an MNC's employees, making concealment and evasion difficult.

The Merits of Alternative Proposals

It is a reflex on the left to prefer administrative controls and regulations to flexible measures that make use of market mechanisms to achieve policy objectives. This reflex is rooted in a healthy, though often excessive, mistrust of the efficacy of market mechanisms and a rejection of the neo-classical vision of a self-equilibrating, well-oiled economy. But, if the result is not to be wildly unrealistic, this mistrust needs to be strongly tempered with an awareness of the practical problems of administrative controls, particularly in the area that concerns us here, that is, the foreign exchanges. It takes considerable time and expertise to set up tolerably effective controls over capital flows and other foreign exchange movements, and even then they are likely to leak fairly extensively. Even if such policies can be made to work in the longer run, a left government will need short-term measures to deal with the exchange rate in the short run. Otherwise experience suggests that a left government would face a severe crisis in the foreign exchange market, with the pound falling sharply (possibly in advance of it coming to power), disrupting foreign trade on a wide scale. An economic crisis of this kind may easily sweep a government off course or lead to an undermining of its political base.

From this perspective, the proposals reviewed above may be regarded as complements, not substitutes. Tight monetary policy to sustain the exchange rate may be the only possibility in the short run (as in France, where interest rates were raised sharply by the incoming Mitterand administration). A move towards a dual exchange rate may be attractive in the somewhat longer perspective, once the necessary administrative machinery can be set up. A split exchange rate could be used to separate, as far as possible, the crisis of capital flight from trading activities. The attempt to export funds via the financial account would then be self-defeating, since it would drive down the financial exchange rate. Firms and individuals may well attempt to evade the system, which at its inception could not be watertight. But the threat of a subsequent 'opening of the books', backed by legal sanctions, might be made a sufficient deterrent. Even if nationalisation were in prospect, the threat of less favourable terms could be used unless compensation is entirely ruled out.

In the long run, there may be a move towards much greater direction of foreign exchange flows by direct controls. I am bound to say, however, that I see that as a rather remote possibility, and that the case for the efficacy of such controls needs to be made much more firmly than hitherto before such a move is worth taking. A left government will, anyway, be heavily involved in complex administration in a whole number of social and economic areas, and the feasibility of a multiplication of these functions must be in doubt.

Immediate Issues

I have travelled a long way from immediate issues concerning the pound to strategic proposals for dealing with the foreign exchanges and the City. Clearly, the latter, as with other parts of the AES, have no prospect of being implemented in current political circumstances. But, what I hope my discussion makes clear is that there is a spectrum of meausres, ranging from those which are immediately possible through to those that require dramatic political changes for them to be implemented. The relevance of the more modest proposals for control is that they help to establish the basis (in the form of experience and expertise) for further extensions of control to be feasible and effective.

This is important at the current time, since there is a widespread concern, not confined to the left, with the way the financial sector is being given free range to play games with the industrial base of the UK economy. There is, therefore, the possibility of gaining, over the next few years, a return to forms of direct control over financial capital. This would represent only a small advance, but nonetheless important: partly because it will help UK industry, employment and wages, but more important, perhaps, because if the left does advance to power it will need all the instruments of control over the financial sphere at its disposal. The question of the volatile and disruptive pound needs to be linked to the issues of the dominant role of the City and financial capital.

NOTES

1. For this position, see, for example, Laidler, 1981.
2. See Artis and Currie, 1982, for some empirical and theoretical observations on this point.
3. See Brown, Enoch and Mortimer-Lee, 1980. Longer run relative unit labour costs may be influenced indirectly by the effects on productivity noted below.
4. For an account of the AES, see Aaronovitch, 1981, and the London CSE Group, 1980. See also the contributions to the *Socialst Economic Review*, 1981.
5. See, for example, Dornbusch, 1976; Niehans, 1981.
6. It is consistent with this account that holders of UK securities made substantial returns in the period of appreciation. Thus, foreign investors in UK Treasury Bills in 1979 obtained a *real* return of nearly 14 per cent over the subsequent period.
7. See J. Kay, *Guardian,* July 14th, 1980.
8. See M. Miller, *Guardian,* August 18th, 1980; and Niehans, 1981.
9. For further discussion, see Artis and Currie, 1981, 1982.
10. Though the example of the incoming Mitterand government in France in defending the franc by a sharp rise in domestic interest rates may be instructive in this regard, subsequent events have highlighted the limitations of such action.
11. See Kay and King, 1978.

REFERENCES

Aaronovitch, S., 1981, *The Road from Thatcherism*, Lawrence and Wishart.

Artis, M.J. and Currie, D.A., 1981, 'Monetary Targets and the Exchange Rate: A Case for Conditional Targets', *Oxford Economic Papers*, Vol 33, supplement, pp. 176-200.

Artis, M.J. and Currie, D.A., 1982, 'Monetary and Exchange Rate Targets', in Courakis, A.S. and Harrington, R.L. (eds.), *Monetarism: Traditions, Debates and Policy*, Macmillan.

Brown, R.N., Enoch, C.A. and Mortimer-Lee, P.D., 1980, 'The Interrelationships between costs and prices in the UK', Bank of England Discussion Paper No. 8.

Dornbusch, R., 1976, 'Exchange Rate Dynamics', *Journal of Political Economy*, Vol. 84, pp. 1161-1176.

Dornbusch, R., 1980, 'Exchange Rate Economics: Where Do We Stand?', *Brookings Papers on Economic Activity*, pp. 143-205.

Forsyth, P.J. and Kay, J.A., 1980, 'The Economic Implications of North Sea Oil Revenues', *Fiscal Studies*, Vol. 1, pp. 1-28.

Kay, J.A. and King, M.A., 1978, *The British Tax System*, OUP.

London CSE Group, 1980, *The Alternative Economic Strategy: A Response by the Labour Movement to the Economic Crisis*, Labour Coordinating Committee.

Niehans, J., 1981, 'The Appreciation of Sterling—Causes, Effects, Policies', SSRC Money Study Group Discussion Paper.

DISCUSSION

Grahame Thompson

In this discussion I shall focus first on Coakley and Harris's paper and then make some comments on Currie's paper. With respect to Jerry Coakley and Lawrence Harris's paper three general issues will be addressed. These concern the role of the Wilson Committee, the discussion of nationalisation and the relationship between financial policy and corporate policy.

It probably surprised no one on the left that the Wilson Committee came out against changing radically the practices of the financial system or altering the legal status of the financial institutions. But how far were these conclusions of Wilson an effect of the left's own practice with respect to the Committee? Wilson was important because the question of nationalisation was written into its terms of reference which could have given the left a real opportunity to press its case. But it did not. In fact it more or less ignored the Committee. Of the 356 pieces of evidence submitted only about eight came from anything approaching leftish sources. Very few left academics or trade unions bothered to give any evidence. Given this lack of input is it any wonder that the nationalisation issue was virtually ignored by the Committee and only tacked on as a chapter to the back of the report? All the arguments were held by the right and were between the right.

The reasons why the left ignored the Wilson Committee are difficult to assess though a first attempt at this can be found in CSE Money Group (1981). The implication however is for the left to work hard at developing realistic and sound analysis and arguments about the financial system which are not simply distrustful or hostile to 'money', something which the papers under discussion begin to open up.

With respect to nationalisation itself, there is a certain 'romance' on the left with this though it is difficult to see how any change simply in legal ownership of financial institutions will affect the financing of industry and trade. Perhaps also it is worth exploring alternatives to direct nationalisation. For instance, there is already a publicly owned banking system in existence in the UK—the NGB and the NSB. Wilson rejected the combination and expansion of these, but with a stronger leftish input to the Committee this might not have been so easy as it turned out. What was needed was ammunition for any sympathetic members of the Committee to argue an alternative case, but this was missing. Second there are ways open to governments, for instance, to bypass the financial system if they wish to raise money. The now available to all 'granny-bond' is a case in point which has the advantage of being non-marketable and hence not open to speculative activity by financial intermediaries.

There is also of course policy with respect to the Bank of England itself. This already has elaborate and wide ranging powers of regulation and supervision of the financial system which should be seriously scrutinised by the left. With determination 'dis-intermediation' might be prevented. The general point is, however, that these different approaches are much more likely to gain political support than calls for outright nationalisation.

One problem with the paper is its exclusive focus on financing industry and trade. It is clear that we cannot look at this without at the same time looking at any institutions not directly involved with financing industry, like the Building Societies, or at the conditions of financing the state itself. After all, the state probably controls something like 30 per cent–40 per cent of productive capacity of the economy through the public corporations and the like. In addition the more general point here is that it is impossible to look at the financial system independently of looking at the company sector and corporate policy at the same time. Companies themselves are heavily involved as agents in the money and credit markets, as well as in the capital markets, as *lenders* as well as borrowers. Without attending to this only a partial picture is gained. The financial system *includes* manufacturing companies in a number of respects.

David Currie's paper sets up the problem of the volatility of the exchange rate and the way this might be controlled. As far as I can make out a central thread of the argument is that restrictive monetary policy had been the main reason why the sterling exchange rate was relatively high until mid-1981 and that this could be brought down by loosening monetary policy and expanding demand. But then, in September 1981, it fell rapidly without there seeming to be such a change in policy on the part of the government. How does he account for this? Whilst I accept that there is some 'overhang' here, it strikes me that all this is not independent of changes elsewhere in the international economy—namely the USA in this instance. This relates to his discussion of the options and instruments outlined at the end of the paper for coping with the volatile exchange rate. It is surprising that these are developed only with respect to the UK in isolation. If an AES were attempted would these really be sufficient to stabilise the exchange rate within fairly acceptable broad limits in the face of the inevitable massive speculation against sterling? The British economy, in one sense, is rather like a large bank. It borrows short, holds minimal reserves and lends long, but this makes it particularly vulnerable without a 'lender of last resort' facility. Clearly the left has good reasons to be suspicious of the IMF. But what other alternatives are there? The UK economy is not in the same strong position as was the

French economy which increased interest rates to cope with something of a similar situation in 1981. Perhaps specific bilateral arrangements would need to be made. What about the EMS or the EMF to develop a co-ordinated *European* policy against international speculation and for an orderly withdrawal of sterling as an international reserve currency (Fishman, 1980)? Will what is euphemistically called a 'currency reform' have to be resorted to? Clearly there are no easy answers to this problem.

Finally there is a feeling from the paper that it would be possible to bring down the exchange rate and improve competitiveness, and to put at least some of the AES into operation without a reduction in living standards of those still employed. Is this realistic? Given the international and internal constraints on the British economy, will not any attempted expansion of demand plus reasonable financial safeguards for those un-employed mean a reduction in real wages of those employed, in the short run (and even medium run)? If so how is this to be confronted and organised? This is an extremely pressing problem in my view.

REFERENCES

CSE Money Group, 1981, 'The Wilson Committee and Financial Institutions', *Politics and Power No. 4*, RKP, London.
Fishman, D., 1980, 'A Radical View of the European Monetary System', *Politics and Power No. 1*, RKP, London.

THE CAMBRIDGE ECONOMIC POLICY GROUP AND PROFITS

Andrew Glyn

The work of the Cambridge Economic Policy Group has attracted much attention recently. (See the interview with Wynne Godley in *Marxism Today* for an excellent discussion.) It may be regarded as a revision of Keynesianism to take account of both the class and competitive nature of the capitalist system. Their model reflects the class struggle in the attempt by workers to secure a 'target' real wage which is the decisive factor behind inflation. The struggle by national capitals for shares of the world market determines the growth of output and therefore employment. Indeed, the CEPG's picture of the decline of British capitalism seems to be based on the twin pressures of wage militancy and international competition. Such accounts (see, for example, Glyn and Sutcliffe) usually focus on profit—failure of the capitalist class to impose a high enough rate of exploitation leading to insufficient investment, lack of competitiveness, loss of markets and inability to maintain employment. This indeed is precisely the logic of the CEPG's own model. Yet their analysis and prescriptions contain ambiguous and contradictory attitudes to profitability.

Trade, Investment and Profits
A major theme in the CEPG's analysis is that the pattern of shares of world trade has been dominated by 'strong long-run trends' (Fetherston, Moore and Rhodes, p. 66) based on the dynamism of the manufacturing sector concerned. A sluggish manufacturing sector, such as Britain's, has slow productivity growth and low investment. This low investment is at the heart of the problem, since it implies 'a relatively slow rate of adaptation by industry to technical progress, particularly in growth industries, to changing demand and innovation in product ranges and to the need for modernising whole production and marketing processes' (Moore and Rhodes, p. 40). Cripps (p. 95) emphasises that for 100 years 'the techniques used and the productivity achieved has continued to lag behind newer, more efficient industries elsewhere', and he links improved productivity and investment (p. 99).

But what determines the level of investment? In the verbal descriptions of their model CEPG are not explicit. Total private expenditure (that is, corporate investment *plus* consumers' expenditure *plus* personal sector investment-dwellings and incorporated enterprise investment) is determined by current and lagged private sector disposable income (post-tax

251

retained profits *plus* personal disposable income) see CEPR 1980, p. 41. But within total private spending, nothing is said about the determination of corporate (or, more broadly, business) investment. A normal Keynesian assumption might be that investment depends on demand. But this is quite inconsistent with the relationship they specify for total private spending. For example, a shift in the distribution of income from post-tax profits to post-tax wages would leave total private disposable income constant. On their model this would also leave demand unaffected. And if demand determines investment then investment would be unchanged. So, with a constant level of private spending, consumption must be constant too. Thus, all the increase in real wages would have to be saved and lent to companies to finance investment. This is completely implausible. The only coherent interpretation of their function is that corporate investment is determined by post-tax profits and personal consumption (and investment) by personal disposable income.[1]

However un-Keynesian, the idea that investment is determined solely by post-tax profits immediately implies that inadequate UK profitability is the fundamental factor behind inadequate UK investment. As an explanation of the low level of UK investment in the post-war period as a whole low profitability can only be part of the story (see Glyn and Harrison, Ch. 1, for some international comparisons of profit and accumulation rates). Indeed, it is probably unfair to interpret a medium-term model like the CEPG's as implying a simple explanation of such a complex and historically determined phenomenon as low investment. But their model *is* used for medium-term policy projections, and one of its implications is that a massive improvement in profitability would be a sufficient condition for British capital achieving a competitive rate of capital accumulation. To restore the pre-tax rate of profit to that of the early 1960s would require that company output was increased by 25 per cent *and all of that should go to profits*.[2] Even to restore the post-tax rate of profit, which has fallen less, requires an extra 15 per cent of company output to be diverted to post-tax profits—so over half of the output that Godley estimates could come from expansion (Godley 1981) would have to be diverted to profits. And even returning the profits to the level of the early 1960s would (on the CEPG's reasoning) only push UK's investment level back to that of the same period. This was inadequate by international standards then. Whilst the slow-down in investment elsewhere means that such a rate would probably prevent the further erosion of British capital's position, it would hardly begin to reverse it.

Profits and Expansion

The CEPG rightly stresses the important effect capacity utilisation has on profitability via the spreading of overhead costs (see Godley 1981).

The 1979 review (EPR, 1979, p. 43) says: 'The share of property income would hold up under the import controls strategy because of much improved capacity utilisation.'

A return to 'full employment', whilst obviously improving profits, would not, *per se*, restore them to the level of the 1960s. First, there has been the well-known downward trend in the share of profits—even discounting the effects of increasingly underutilised capacity. The CEPG believes that capitalists set their prices in relation to historic costs so that profits, inclusive of stock appreciation, retain a certain fraction of the value of sales (see Coutts). Even this model yields a significant negative time trend for the profit share before 1973; it appears that this trend may have accelerated in the mid-1970s because their model can only explain about half the decline in the profit share, between 1973 and 1976, by the pre-1973 downward trend and decreased capacity utilisation (Table 6.1).[3] Moreover, since that part of nominal profits due to stock appreciation is available only to finance increased money values of stocks, it is obvious that only 'real' profits (that is, after stock appreciation) can finance real capital accumulation. CEPG projections typically yield quite high inflation rates (e.g. 20 per cent in 1985 in their 1980 projections with tariffs and devaluation in 1981, see CEPR, 1980, p. 53). This must imply correspondingly high levels of stock appreciation and low levels of 'real' profits (always assuming, of course, that the capitalists never catch on to what is happening and price on the basis of replacement costs). What this adds up to is that even a return to 'high' employment levels would *not* restore the real profit share to the 1960s' levels.

Furthermore, if the level of investment is determined by the level of profits then the growth rate of the capital stock will be determined by the *rate* of profit (profits in relation to the existing capital stock).

The profit rate has shown a sharper downward trend than the profit share as the capital/output ratio rose persistently from the mid-1960s. In fact, in the period from 1960 to 1973 about one-half of the decline in the profit rate of the sector comprising companies and public corporations was due to increased capital/output ratio (ratio of net fixed capital stock plus stocks at current prices to net value added). A part of this rise in the capital/output ratio may well have reflected accelerated scrapping due to increases in the real cost of employing labour, which left fixed capital still included in the capital stock statistics but not being used. Really this *should* have been shown as higher capital consumption and thus a lower profit share. It is also not clear how strongly any underlying trend towards higher capital/output ratio has continued in the years of stagnation since 1973. But in any case it is highly unlikely that a return to high employment of itself would bring the capital/output ratio back down to the level of the 1960s. So the profit rate, and thus the accumulation rate, would be lower on that account as well.

The logic of the CEPG's model leads to the conclusions that a return to full capacity utilisation of itself would not generate a high enough rate of profit even to restore the rate of business accumulation to the level of the 1960s. Whilst the rate of profit and rate of business capital accumulation is not shown explicitly in their projections they give some confirmation of this conclusion.

The CEPG's 1979 version based on a policy of import controls shows private gross fixed investment at 11.3 per cent of GDP at market prices in 1985, as compared with 10.5 per cent in 1965. But this would seem to imply a lower, and perhaps substantially lower, rate of business capital accumulation in 1985 than 1965, bearing in mind that:

(i) a lower share of real profits in 1985 should imply a lower proportion of private capital accumulation contributed by business (and correspondingly more housebuilding); and (ii) the higher capital/output ratio means that a given share of business investment implies a lower rate of capital accumulation.

So our analysis of the logic of the CEPG's model appears to be confirmed by their projections: that even the successful implementation of the CEPG's strategy would hardly return the rate of capital accumulation to that of the 1960s. However much an improvement on present performance this hardly constitutes a recipe for British capitalism to ensure real competitiveness.

Expansion and Real Wages
So a policy of expansion would only show limited gains for capital without a radical increase in profitability at the expense of real wages. But could the expansion even be achieved without real wages being held back tightly? The CEPG is determined that increased real wages (or more correctly, increased real cost of employing labour—that is, wages gross of tax and deflated by the price index for value added) have played no role in explaining unemployment. Moore, Rhodes, Tarling and Wilkinson say that since the fall of employment is accurately explained by the behaviour of (lagged) output, and if the validity of the relationship is accepted, it is impossible to sustain the view that 'the recent increase in unemployment has been caused by real wages being too high' (footnote, p. 26). But this is a *non-sequitur*. An increase in real wages may provide the explanation for low output, and thus employment, as it forces scrapping of old plant.

True, this might affect the relationship of output to employment. In 1973–5 when the real cost of employing labour rose very sharply, they show (Table 3.3) employment falling more than would be predicted on the basis of the relationship to output. This seems consistent with far more rapid scrapping and concentration of production in the more efficient plants, than in 'normal' downswings. But so many other factors are involved (like worker militancy, levels of investment, government job-saving measures, etc.) that it would be rash to draw firm conclusions without much more detailed work. The rising real cost of employing labour is the other side of the profits-squeeze coin. The CEPG seems to admit that the profits squeeze since the mid 1960s has been more than can be simply explained by cyclically low productivity. It would be strange indeed had it not played a role in decreasing employment. Indeed the stress laid in the 1980 review (CEPR, 1980, p. 11) on the adverse effects of sterling appreciation imply that the increased cost of employing labour (in relation especially to prices in export markets) at least partly explains the present slump. This is why the review includes devaluation as a condition for a successful protectionist strategy, and so 'the devaluation would, we assume, require a short-term incomes policy to reduce its inflationary aftermath' (p. 15)—that is, enforce the reduction in real wages.

Even if the CEPG were correct in arguing that until comparatively recently a cut in real wages was not necessary for a return to full employment, seen in a longer term context, their model does imply that the excessive cost of employing labour has caused rising unemployment. Since in their view output has been constrained by poor trade performance, which reflects low investment which in turn reflects low profits, we are led inescapably back to the conclusion that the 'problem' has been precisely excessive real wages. The CEPG seems to be reluctant to draw this conclusion, perhaps feeling understandably though wrongly, that this would be to 'blame' the workers for the crisis.

The CEPG's Solution—Protectionism, etc.

Much of the debate about the CEPG's suggestion for wide-ranging control of imports has centred round the probability of retaliation. Leaving aside this crucial, but exhaustively discussed issue, here is succinct summary of why they prefer protectionism to devaluation:

> In our view the devaluation strategy necessarily requires that prices initially increase relative to money earnings and that the implied cut in real earnings must be tolerated for some years if the policy is to succeed. . . On the other hand the protection strategy can in the short term yield higher output and better terms of trade than devaluation with no shift to profit other than normally generated in the cyclical upswing. Therefore protection need at no stage lead to an increase in prices relative to money incomes; all the impulses are positive from the start. . . (CEPR, 1980, p. 36).

Now what is striking in this view is that devaluation is condemned for doing precisely what the CEPG's model implies is *necessary* for any long-term improvement—that is, it increases the share of profits. If devaluation simply led to worsened terms of trade, with no effect on the distribution of income, its disadvantages would be clear. But the CEPG believes, with good reason, that the effect of devaluation on the terms of trade is very limited as exporters take much of the benefit of devaluation in the form of higher export prices and profits. *This is exactly what is required to increase investment.*

Now the CEPG believes that, although required, a redistribution to profits cannot be achieved because of workers' pressure to maintain take-home pay. This is a perfectly defensible point of view but CEPG should be more open about it. In principle, devaluation would be preferable to protectionism because it goes some way to meet the *real* problem of too low profitability and investment. 'Unfortunately' it cannot be successfully carried out because of the impasse between capital and labour. The only (grudging) admission of this *central* point I can find is the following:

> A devaluation policy if successful will, corresponding to a given level of domestic output and the balance of payments, generate a higher level of both imports and exports and also profits and investment than a successful protectionist strategy. This *could* [our emphasis] ultimately lead to a better long-term trend of productivity.
>
> Godley and May, p. 39

Ironically support for import controls on the grounds that they do not lead to a redistribution from wages to profits[4] indicates their weakness from the point of view of the capitalist class. This represents an admission, not only that they must opt out of the competitive capitalist world economy but also, *or rather because* they must concede stalemate in the domestic class struggle.

Alternative Strategies

The main point of this paper has been to argue that the CEPG's strategy represents, at best, a holding operation for British capital. Nothing is solved. All you can do is retreat behind tariff barriers and hope to reach accommodation with the working class based on dreams of going 'back to the 1960s' with steady, if modest, improvements all round.

It is interesting, though, that a strategy of public spending cuts is quite consistent with the CEPG model. If public spending could be cut radically then there could be a corresponding increase in post-tax profits, and therefore, investment. This could be achieved, most crudely, by just channelling the public spending cuts straight to capital through higher tax concessions and investment grants. More subtly, and perhaps better for trade performance, the public spending cuts could be balanced by tax cuts for workers and devaluation. The tax cuts would ensure that workers did not react to higher import prices with money wage increases. The public spending cuts themselves are assumed to provoke no wage response. So the increase in profits flowing from the devaluation would not be threatened by money wage increases.

Provided the combination of import controls and devaluation led to an equality between exports and 'full employment imports' there would be no problem of effective demand. The exports and government spending provide the injections which, with the private sector spending any additions to its income, guarantees full employment. Perhaps the CEPG was kicking around such ideas when the 1978 Review mentioned increasing manufacturing investment by an additional £3 billion a year 'supposing that some means were found of bringing it about' (Cripps, Fetherston and Ward, p. 15). The CEPG never seems to take a clear position on whether such a strategy, which seems quite consistent with their model and which would go much further to restore the competitiveness of industry than their own prescriptions, is actually viable (even if objectionable).

It is clear that there is nothing in the CEPG's analysis which could qualify it as a socialist alternative strategy. All the CEPG and the labour movement's Alternative Economic Strategy (see, e.g. CSE) share is the demand for import controls. Even the agreement on expansionism is illusory. For whereas the AES demands substantial public spending increases to reflate the economy, CEPG would hold this to be unnecessary (providing a big enough cut in the share of imports could be achieved) and in any case inflationary (if tax increases were required to balance the budget these would provoke wage claims). The last projection they made showing the effects of their policy of tariffs (CEPR, 1980, Table A9) aims at an unemployment rate just below 2 millions in 1985; but public spending is actually shown as growing much less than total output (16 per cent as against 26 per cent) and the public sector deficit does not rise at all. So the public sector does not play a dynamic role even in the Keynesian sense of providing demand.

Only in one article (Moore and Rhodes) is the case for much more government intervention to secure additional investment discussed. Direct public investment and planning agreements backed up by selective financial assistance (typical AES policies) are mentioned, but only as possible alternatives to 'relying on improving the working of the price mechanism' (i.e. fiscal incentives). Francis Cripps, an advisor to Tony Benn and obviously part of the left wing of the CEPG, calls for a system of planning agreements. These are seen as a framework for selectively channelling 'subsidies and other forms of aid to ensure that options which accord with government objectives are reasonably profitable' (p. 103). He does say that managers should have 'reduced freedom to cut back production, to refrain from investment' (p. 104). He quotes the case of the Industrial Development Certificates used to *prevent* expansion in full-employment areas and calls for a system of 'employment licences'. But the analogy seems a false one—how are licences to prevent firms from *not* employing or *not* investing? No mention is made of nationalising profitable firms as a basis for planning industry. What seems to be involved is a beefing up of the regional policies of the 1960s in the context of an overall restoration of profitability. There is little awareness even in Cripps' paper, and in the CEPG's work as a whole, of the need to transform radically the functioning of the British economy.

Monetarism represents an attempt to do this in the interests of capital by using mass unemployment to weaken the labour movement. This is not just so as to permit the redistribution to capital implied by a Bacon and Eltis strategy of cutting public spending, but more important to allow capital to force through much higher productivity levels on the shop floor. The AES (at least in its radical versions) is an attempt to transcend the profit system, through using the power of the labour movement to force capitalists to expand, invest and so forth, regardless of profitability. Whatever the weaknesses of this strategy (see Glyn and Harrison, ch. 5 for an argument that a much more thoroughgoing socialist programme is necessary to achieve the same ends) it does intend a decisive shift in the functioning of the economy. The real battles in the 1980s will be between these strategies. There will no doubt be intervals in which a return to the 1950s and 1960s will be attempted. The Social Democrats, and their fellow thinkers on the right of the Labour Party, are relying on the attraction of that period in the context of Thatcher's attempt to recreate the 1930s. But the 1950s and 1960s were the period of British capital's decline, masked by the world boom. The relation of class forces both internally and internationally makes it impossible to recreate those conditions. This is the central weakness of the CEPG.

NOTES

1.   In a situation where money incomes are growing, some part of private sector incomes is used to accumulate financial assets (see CEPR, 1981, p. 7). Even when incomes are not growing, so that total private spending equals private disposable income, corporate investment does not have to equal post-tax profits —there could, for example, be some regular level of borrowing by companies from the personal sector. But still the only way to achieve an increase in investment would be to increase post-tax profits (unless some means could be found to increase lending by the personal sector to companies, rather than its own consumption and investment, a possibility CEPG apparently never discusses). This is the sense in which within their model, post-tax corporate profits determine corporate investment. Paul Hare (1980) has pointed out that the detailed specification of the CEPG's model includes an equation for private investment as a function of current and lagged incomes (mainly profits) and interest rates. The point being made here is that the dependence of investment on post-tax profits is *necessarily* imposed by their broad private expenditure function which is one of the key characteristics of their model.

2.   The pre-tax rate of profit of industrial and commercial companies (excluding North Sea oil) was estimated by the Bank of England (1981, June, p. 228, September, p. 318) at around 2 per cent as compared with 11½ per cent in the early 1960s. With a ratio of fixed capital plus stocks to output of nearly 2.8 (CSO 1981 tables 1.10, 11.11, 12.4) to earn an extra 9½ per cent on capital employed requires an addition to profits representing slightly more than 25 per

cent of output. Since the post-tax rate of profit fell from around 7½ per cent to about 2 per cent, the profits required to restore the post-tax rate are about 15 per cent of output.

3. The normal cost pricing model reported for manufacturing only (CEPR, 1980, pp. 37–8) shows the persistent failure of prices to rise as fast as lagged normal costs until 1973, but since 1973 prices have risen rather faster reversing some part of the downward trend in the profit share *before* deduction of stock appreciation. The immediate explanation which springs to mind is that the acceleration of inflation forced something of a move towards replacement cost pricing, as a reaction to the devastating effect of stock appreciation on real profits. Even if it could be argued that there is no longer a downward underlying trend in the profit share gross of stock appreciation, rapid inflation and consequent high levels of stock appreciation mean low levels of real profit, as argued in the text.

4. This is itself a highly contentious issue. Obviously everything hangs on producers of import substitutes not taking advantage of tariffs to restore profit margins. CEPG claims that 'price movements since 1973 are completely inconsistent with the idea that profit margins on home sales by domestic producers are on aggregate influenced by the prices of competing imports' (CEPR, 1980, p. 37/39). But while year-to-year movements may be unrelated, it is not clear that there is a better explanation for the declining trend of the profit share than international competition. Turner has shown that amongst concentrated industries, those subject to heavy and increasing import competition have low profits. Of course the mechanism *could* be simply that import competition leads to low utilisation of capacity and thus low profits due to the spreading of fixed costs, and not a fall in the price relative to 'normal' costs. But it is hard to imagine that the kind of tariffs envisaged, rising to 70 per cent on imported finished manufactures in 1990 (CEPR, 1980, p. 15), would have no effect on prices of domestically produced substitutes. Would Leyland really keep the price of Metros constant if the price of Renault 5s went up by 70 per cent?

REFERENCES

Bank of England Quarterly Bulletin, June 1981, September 1981.

Cambridge Economic Policy Review, (CEPR) Vol. 6, No. 1, 1980, Vol. 7, No. 1, 1981.

Conference of Socialist Economists (CSE), 1980, *The Alternative Economic Strategy*, London.

Coutts, K., 1978, 'Short-run Variations in Company Profits', EPR.

Cripps, F., 1981, 'Government Planning as a Means to Economic Recovery in the UK', *Cambridge Journal of Economics*, March.

CSO, 1981 Edition, *National Income and Expenditure*.

Economic Policy Review (EPR), 1975–79, Annual.

Fetherston, M., Moore, B., Rhodes, J., 1977, 'Manufacturing Export Shares and Cost Competitiveness of Advanced Industrial Countries', *EPR*.

Glyn, A. and Sutcliffe, R., 1972, *British Capitalism, Workers and the Profit Squeeze*, Penguin.

Glyn, A. and Harrison, J., 1980, *The British Economic Disaster*, Pluto.

Godley, W. and May, R., 1977, 'The Macro-economic Implications of Devaluation and Import Restrictions', *EPR*.

Godley, W., 1981, Interview in *Marxism Today*, July.

Hare, P. June 1980, 'Import Controls and the CEPG's Model of the UK Economy', *Scottish Journal of Political Economy*.

Moore, B., and Rhodes, J., 1976, 'The Relative Decline of the UK Manufacturing Sector', *EPR*.

Moore, B., Rhodes, J., Tarling, R. and Wilkinson, F., 1978, 'A Return to Full Employment', *EPR*.

Turner, P., December 1980, 'Import Competition and Profitability of United Kingdom Manufacturing', *Journal of Industrial Economics*.